ARE WE NOT MEN?

ARE WE NOT MEN?

Masculine Anxiety
and the Problem of
African-American Identity

PHILLIP BRIAN HARPER

New York   Oxford
OXFORD UNIVERSITY PRESS
1996

Oxford University Press

Oxford   New York
Athens   Auckland   Bangkok   Bogotá   Bombay
Buenos Aires   Calcutta   Cape Town   Dar es Salaam
Delhi   Florence   Hong Kong   Istanbul   Karachi
Kuala Lumpur   Madras   Madrid   Melbourne
Mexico City   Nairobi   Paris   Singapore
Taipei   Tokyo   Toronto

and associated companies in
Berlin   Ibadan

Copyright © 1996 by Phillip Brian Harper

Published by Oxford University Press, Inc.
198 Madison Avenue, New York, New York 10016

Oxford is a registered trademark of Oxford University Press

Library of Congress Cataloging–in–Publication Data
Harper, Phillip Brian.
Are we not men? : masculine anxiety and the problem of
African-American identity / by Phillip Brian Harper.
p.   cm.
Includes bibliographical references and index.
ISBN 0–19–509274–0
1. Afro-American men—Attitudes.   2. Afro-Americans—
Race identity.   3. Afro-Americans and mass media.   I. Title.
E185.86.H33   1996
305.38'896073—dc20   95–26485

1 3 5 7 9 8 6 4 2

Printed in the United States of America
on acid-free paper

The author is grateful for the opportunity to reprint the following materials:

"SOS," by Imamu Amiri Baraka (LeRoi Jones), from *Black Magic: Poetry, 1961–1976;* "Poem for Half White College Students," and "CIVIL RIGHTS POEM," by Imamu Amiri Baraka (LeRoi Jones), from *Selected Poetry of Amiri Baraka/LeRoi Jones.* Copyright ©1969 by Amiri Baraka. Reprinted by permission of Sterling Lord Literistic, Inc.

"blk/rhetoric" and "a chant for young / brothas & sistuhs." *From We a BaddDDD People.* Copyright ©1970 by Sonia Sanchez. Reprinted by permission of the author.

"The True Import of Present Dialogue: Black vs. Negro," by Nikki Giovanni. From *Black Feeling, Black Talk/Black Judgment.* Copyright ©1968, 1970 by Nikki Giovanni. Reprinted by permission of William Morrow and Company, Inc.

"Move Un-Noticed to Be Noticed: A Nationhood Poem," by Don L. Lee (Haki Madhubuti). From *We Walk the Way of the New World.* Copyright ©1970 by Don L. Lee (Haki Madhubuti). Reprinted by permission of Broadside Press.

"Okay 'Negroes,'" by June Jordan. From *Some Changes.* Copyright ©1970 by June Jordan. Reprinted by permission of the author.

Lyrics from "Language Is a Virus from Outer Space," by Laurie Anderson and Richard Coe. Copyright ©1985 Difficult Music. Reprinted by permission.

Lyrics from "In and Out of Love," by Brian Holland/Lamont Dozier/Eddie Holland. Copyright ©1967 Jobete Music Co., Inc. Reprinted by permission.

Lyrics from "Without the One You Love," by Brian Holland/Lamont Dozier/Eddie Holland. Copyright ©1964 Jobete Music Co., Inc. Reprinted by permission.

Lyrics from "A Natural Man," by Bobby Hebb and Sandy Baron. Copyright ©1970 Beresofsky/Hebb, Ltd. Reprinted by permission.

Lyrics from "Natural High," by Charles McCormick. Copyright ©1972 Crystal Jukebox, Inc. Reprinted by permission.

Parts of Chapter 1, from *Writing AIDS,* edited by Timothy F. Murphy and Suzanne Poirier. Copyright ©1993 by Columbia University Press. Reprinted by permission of the publisher.

Parts of Chapter 2, from *Critical Inquiry* 19.2 (Winter 1993). Copyright ©1993 by the University of Chicago. Reprinted by permission.

Parts of Chapter 7, from *The Black Columbiad,* edited by Werner Sollors and Maria Diedrich. Copyright ©1994 by the President and Fellows of Harvard College. Reprinted by permission.

For Thom;

for my sister, Judy;

and for my brothers, 'Rocky' and Roger

PREFACE

"I am proud to be a black American."
—Michael Jackson

What is the meaning of this statement by the self-proclaimed "King of Pop," made to Oprah Winfrey during a live television interview in February 1993? The answer perfectly emblematizes the subject of this book. For while Jackson's profession of racial pride was most obviously meant to counter judgments that his physical appearance is unacceptably "white," it also spoke to a widespread suspicion that his feminized demeanor signals a lack of self-respect, the "feminine" still strongly connoting degradation even at this late historical moment. Jackson's assertion carried this dual significance because the abiding worry over his sexual and gender identities is itself also a manifestation of concern about the status of his blackness. After all, since the dominant view holds prideful self-respect as the very essence of healthy African-American identity, it also considers such identity to be fundamentally weakened wherever masculinity appears to be compromised. While this fact is rarely articulated, its influence is nonetheless real and pervasive. Its primary effect is that all debates over and claims to "authentic" African-American identity are largely animated by a profound anxiety about the status specifically of African-American *masculinity*. This is the principal argument of *Are We Not Men?*

By interrogating the primacy of conventional masculinity to received conceptions of blackness, this book constitutes a critique of masculinism in African-American culture. At the same time, because those conceptions incorporate no lesser burden of proof than does masculinity itself, the book is also a critique of black "authenticity" and of the conformist demands that the concept implies.

Hence, it explores in particular manifestations of *difference* in African-American culture, which typically precipitate the most intense controversies about what—or who—qualifies as "black." As the specific types of difference examined here entail variations not only in class and skin color but also in gender and sexuality, *Are We Not Men?* ultimately questions the very definition of traditional masculinity, as well as its import to black identity. My object of analysis, then, is not an African-American culture distinct from the context in which it emerges, but one that derives in ongoing relation to a broader U.S. culture in which it is crucial.

That broader culture, too, conceives African-American society in terms of a perennial "crisis" of black masculinity whose imagined solution is a proper affirmation of black male authority. This line of thought was most infamously instanced in the Moynihan report of 1965, but it also has its more recent manifestations: the fall 1995 march by African-American men on Washington D.C., intended to demonstrate black men's sense of social responsibility; Louis Farrakhan's prescriptive speeches to single-gender-only audiences; book-length treatises by Lawrence Carter, J. Carroll George, Haki Madhubuti, and Earl Hutchinson on African-American men's precarious social position; mass-release fictional films like *Boyz N the Hood* and documentary features like *Hoop Dreams*, which address the condition of black "inner-city" youth; the ongoing public dialogue between scholars Cornel West and Henry Louis Gates, Jr., on the role of the African-American intellectual; and the by-now-routine journalistic assessments such as that offered by Bob Herbert in a December 1994 *New York Times Magazine*, published with the cover headline, "The Black Man Is in Terrible Trouble." These various examples represent an appeal to black manhood that, while not new in the late twentieth century, has taken on a particular significance during it. Indeed, when in 1845 escaped bondman and abolitionist Frederick Douglass pointedly characterized himself as "a slave . . . made a man" (p. 107), he was specifically contrasting his new condition with the *brutishness* he argued was the signal lot of the slave (p. 105). On the other hand, and as I indicate more fully in Chapter 3, when in 1965 Ossie Davis eulogized the slain Malcolm X by declaring that "Malcolm was our manhood, our living, black manhood!" (p. xii), he was distinguishing legitimate black masculinity against the "smallness," "puniness," and "weakness" connoted by conventional "Negro" identity (p. xi)—against, in other words, racialized stereotypes of the nonmasculine, the effeminate, the feminized, and the feminine. Because the anxious gynophobia underlying this characterization seems particularly pronounced in twentieth-century assertions of black manhood, that period constitutes the primary focus of the analysis I undertake here.

This is especially the case in the first part of the book, comprising Chapters 1 through 4: Focusing on recent challenges to black identity posed by potent intraracial differences of sexuality, gender, and class, this section posits those challenges as provoking within African-American culture a masculinist anxiety that forecloses certain possibilities for black subjectivity. In its turn, Part II—Chapters 5 and 6—works to ground this black masculine anxiety in the paranoid racial and sexual fantasies characterizing U.S. culture generally in the nineteenth and twentieth centuries. In particular, this section posits skin-color variation among U.S. blacks as a highly fraught issue within the culture as a whole, concern about which motivates attempts to regulate both African-American social formations and the boundaries of legal black identity. Discerning in those attempts a general masculinist impulse that actually works against the interests of black men, Part II broadens the implications of the book's subtitle, indicating that the masculine anxiety to which it refers is not race-specific, and that African-American identity constitutes a problem not for black people alone. Finally, Part III, which includes Chapters 7 and 8, considers some of the ways that recent African-American cultural interventions have negotiated class, gender, and sexual differences without sacrificing them to a constraining notion of uniform authentic blackness. The book thus closes by positing possible models for expansive African-American cultural practice while also recognizing, in a short epilogue, the continuing challenges that such practice must confront.

Are We Not Men? ranges across a wide array of issues relevant within contemporary African-American culture, and it does this, moreover, by examining a large assortment of cultural productions and historical events from both the nineteenth and the twentieth centuries, including court cases, medical epidemics, literary works, television programs, pop-music recordings, music videos, journalistic publications, and performance pieces. Despite this scope, the book is not a cultural history, and it does not pretend to the status of systematic historical explication. Nor is it a work of cultural theory per se, in that it does not purport comprehensively to "explain" black men, black masculinity, black masculinism, or social difference among African-Americans, as though any of these could be fully accounted for. It is, rather, a work of cultural criticism—composed as a series of interpretive readings—intended to demonstrate some significances of certain elements in the cultural contexts in question, both African-American in particular and U.S. in general. What it lacks in linearity of design, then, I trust it makes up in an evident interweaving of its analytical threads and a critical suggestiveness issuing therefrom.

Because *Are We Not Men?* is constructed as a set of analytical investigations rather than as a linear argument, and because it is concerned specifically with various types of difference within African-American culture, I may seem in this book to resist taking any identifiable cultural-political stand. On the contrary, though, I am actually striving to register my abiding belief that African-American social difference must be acknowledged, attended to, engaged, and interrogated, rather than denied or deemed inadmissible, and this belief itself constitutes both a theory of cultural-critical practice and a political position. It also entails the recognition that key social and cultural formations serve disparate functions in different contexts, thus rendering intelligible what would otherwise appear to be contradictions in the book's argumentation—the fact, for instance, that one section can function as an apology for black bourgeois culture while another constitutes a critique of bourgeois social structures; or that one chapter criticizes patriarchal practice while another demonstrates some of its socially useful effects. These incongruities are not merely accidents of the analytical method that I follow; rather, they indicate the fundamental complexity of the relation between social structure and cultural practice at all events, and its especially intricate character in the African-American context. Any such demonstration can, I think, only enhance our appreciation of African-American experience. And that, after all, is precisely my objective in the work presented here.

This book culminates a critical exploration that first began some years ago. Chapter 1, which originally took a much shorter form, was drafted in the winter and spring of 1988–1989, when I felt compelled by the death of Max Robinson to address the urgency of AIDS in African-American communities. A section of it was presented at the conference on "Nationalisms and Sexualities" at Harvard's Center for Literary and Cultural Studies in June 1989, and at the Modern Language Association Convention held in Chicago in December 1990. It was first published in *Social Text* in the fall of 1991, and thereafter in *The Lesbian and Gay Studies Reader* (ed. Abelove et al., 1993), *Fear of a Queer Planet* (ed. Warner, 1993), and *Writing AIDS* (ed. Murphy and Poirier, 1993). I am grateful to Columbia University Press for permission to reprint the essay in its expanded version here.

Chapter 2 incorporates my first conscious inquiry into the negotiation of difference in African-American culture. I wrote the initial version of it in the fall of 1990, and during the following year presented it to colleagues at Brandeis and Harvard and to an extremely helpful group of faculty and graduate students at Johns Hopkins. It was published in *Critical Inquiry* in the winter of 1993. Chapter 4 extends an early exploration in the politics of pop-music crossover that I undertook in the fall and winter of 1986–1987, and that was published in the fall/winter 1989 issue of *Social Text*.

A short preliminary version of Chapter 5 was presented at the international "Narrative" conference held in Albany in 1993, and a draft of the full chapter was delivered at the University of Chicago in January 1995. A short draft of Chapter 7 was presented in the special session on "Television and Collective Politics" held at the 1989 MLA convention in Washington, D.C., and a longer one was delivered at the conference on "Contested Boundaries in African-American Textual Analysis" at the University of California–Irvine and at the weekly colloquium of Harvard's W. E. B. Du Bois Institute, both in 1993. Versions of it appear in *The Black Columbiad* (ed. Sollors and Diedrich, 1994) and in *Living Color* (ed. Torres, 1996). Finally, Chapter 8 represents some of the earliest work in the volume, incorporating material written in 1987 and 1988 along with much more recent considerations of pop-musical form. An early version of the latter was presented at the meeting of the American Studies Association held in Boston in 1993.

The remainder of the book was written between May 1993 and August 1995, with the whole being pulled together during a period of faculty leave sponsored by Harvard University and by the National Endowment for the Humanities in 1994 and 1995. I am grateful to both institutions for their support. Additionally, some of the production costs associated with the book's publication were covered by the Rollins/Robinson funds of the Harvard University English department, which constituted an invaluable resource.

Given the wide variety of contexts in which portions of the book have been composed and presented, it is to be expected that an enormous number of people have helped in its production. Many of them, undoubtedly, no longer remember exactly how they assisted me, even if they were aware of doing so at the time. It is my pleasure to remind them here of the nature of their support, and to acknowledge all of those who have helped me bring this project to fruition. First of all, the book would not now exist were it not for the tireless efforts of three extremely talented students who served as my research assistants in 1993 and 1994; Miriam Thaggert, Jen Chertow, and Becca del Carmen spent countless hours not only locating primary materials, but determining what areas it would be useful for me to research, and they are consequently largely responsible for the final shape of the project. I extend to them my deepest gratitude. I would also like to thank a number of other people who directed me to source materials that proved helpful for my undertaking: Harold Dufour-Anderson, Julie Rioux, Maria-Christina Villaseñor, Rosemary Williams, and the late Thomas Scott Whitaker.

I am very fortunate to have a wonderful group of friends and colleagues who have contributed to my work on this book in a variety of ways—commenting on early versions of various chapters, sponsoring the publication or presentation of different sections, providing stimulating discussion of issues addressed in the text, and collectively constituting an intellectual community that I continue to find immensely congenial. I am particularly grateful for the support of a group of scholars whom I flatter myself to consider my compeers in black cultural criticism, including Elizabeth Alexander, Lindon Barrett, Jennifer Brody, Farah Jasmine Griffin, Kim Hall, Saidiya Hartman, Arthur Little, Paul Rogers, Tricia Rose, and Sasha Torres. Their very presence, not to mention the example of their intellectual practice, sustains me in my work. Additionally, conversations with Manthia Diawara helped me tremendously in conceptualizing the book with respect to definitions of "blackness," and I am thrilled to be able to draw on the combination of critical intelligence and warm collegiality that he embodies.

I would also like to thank John Ackerman, Laura Doyle, Lee Edelman, David Halperin, Joe Litvak, Paul Morrison, Timothy Murphy, Suzanne Poirier, Amy Robinson, David Scobey, and Werner Sollors, all of whom either heard or read portions of the book at different stages and provided valuable commentary and guidance. I am grateful to Mark Seltzer for suggesting in 1988 that I circulate my work among the editorial collective of *Social Text*, which has been extremely supportive from the very beginning. Andrew Ross, in particular, has been as tireless a sponsor, as careful a reader, and as good-humored a friend as anyone could want.

As my readers for Oxford University Press, Ann duCille and Patricia J. Williams discerned and appreciated what I was doing long before I did myself. Their brilliant insights into my project and generous suggestions for revision provided me with the direction and the impetus necessary to bring the work to completion. From the earliest drafts through the initial stages of production, Oxford editor Elizabeth Maguire demonstrated exemplary patience and great professional skill, as well as offering wit and warm encouragement. T. Susan Chang uniquely manifested these same attributes after taking over the project late in its development. Oxford's Elda Rotor has remained remarkably calm while negotiating the difficult logistics of bringing the book to print. Fran Bartlett expertly coordinated production work. As has long been the case now, Brian Johnson afforded me expert photographic services. Mandy Harris and June L. Reich proofread the entire book with skill and efficiency.

The institutional support extended by Harvard University would not have been forthcoming without the sponsorship provided by Anthony Appiah, Leo Damrosch, Philip Fisher, Marjorie Garber, Henry Louis Gates, and Barbara Johnson, or the assistance granted by Jodi Goldberg, Anne Sudbay Furbush, Gwen Urdang-Brown, and Joanne Kendall. I extend thanks to them all, and, for making my time there thoroughly worthwhile, to my peers in the Harvard English department from 1991 to 1995: Anne Cheng, Meredith McGill, Jeffrey Masten, Wendy Motooka, Jonah Siegel, and Lynn Wardley.

For all the divergency of our official "specialties," two classmates from graduate school remain my most valued readers. Not only do Rosemary Kegl and Jeff Nunokawa bring a phenomenal intelligence to their considerations of my work, but the spirit of friendship that marks those considerations makes me cherish them greatly, though not nearly so greatly as the friendships themselves. Similarly, my life outside the academy would be significantly less rewarding without the support of Bruce Ledbetter, which has been wonderfully consistent throughout the writing of this book.

Finally, to Thom Freedman, who not only has seen this volume take shape from start to finish, but shares in every other aspect of my life as well, I give my absolute deepest thanks for his affection, his humor, his insight, and his patience; they are fundamental to all that I do.

New York City   P. B. H.
February 1996

CONTENTS

PART I

BLACK
MASCULINE
ANXIETY

ELOQUENCE
AND EPITAPH

Aids, Homophobia,
and Problematics
of Black Masculinity

Black Men and the AIDS Epidemic

Over the ten years ending in June 1991, some 179,694 persons in the United
States were diagnosed as having Acquired Immune Deficiency Syndrome. Of that
number of total reported cases, 41,179—or roughly 23 percent—occurred in
males of African descent, although black males accounted for less than 6 percent
of the total U.S. population.[1] It is common enough knowledge that black men
constitute a disproportionate number of persons with AIDS in this country—
common in the sense that, whenever the AIDS epidemic achieves a new statistical
milestone (as it did in the winter of 1991, when the number of AIDS-related
deaths in the United States reached 100,000), the major media generally provide a
demographic breakdown of the figures. And yet, somehow the enormity of the
morbidity and mortality rates for black men (like that of the rates for gay men of
whatever racial identity) doesn't seem to register in the national consciousness as
a cause for great concern. This is no doubt largely due to a general sense that the

trajectory of the average African-American man's life must "naturally" be rather short, routinely subject to violent termination. And this sense, in turn, helps account for the magnitude of shock that was required to impress the public with the particular threat posed to black men by AIDS, well after white men's vulnerability had been dramatized by the death of Rock Hudson. Indeed, it was six years after Hudson's death (and a full decade after the beginning of the epidemic) that NBA superstar Earvin "Magic" Johnson announced his infection with the human immunodeficiency virus (or HIV, long recognized as the chief factor in the etiology of AIDS), thereby drawing attention to the implications for black men of the ongoing health crisis. This is not to say that no nationally known black male figure had yet died of AIDS-related causes by November 1991, but rather that numerous and complex cultural factors conspired—and continue to conspire— to prevent such deaths from effectively galvanizing AIDS activism in African-American communities.[2] I attempt, in this chapter, to explicate some of the most important of these factors, since it is necessary to understand them before we can begin to stem the ravages of AIDS among the African-American population. More than this, though, such explication will also usefully indicate some of the ways that black masculinity is rendered problematic in contemporary U.S. culture, thereby establishing terms of reference for the analyses that I undertake in the rest of this book, and thus serving as a fitting, if unfortunate, prolegomenon to my consideration of the condition(s) of African-American masculinity.

The Sound of Silence

In December 1988, National Public Radio (hereafter referred to as NPR) broadcast a report on the death of Max Robinson, who had been the first black news anchor on U.S. network television, staffing the Chicago desk of ABC's *World News Tonight* from 1978 to 1983. Robinson was one of 4,123 African-American men to die in 1988 of AIDS-related causes (of a nationwide total of 17,119 AIDS-related deaths),[3] but rather than focus on his death itself at this point, I want to examine two passages from the broadcast that, taken together, describe an entire problematic conditioning the significance of AIDS in many black communities in the United States. The first is a statement by a colleague of Robinson's both at ABC News and at WMAQ-TV in Chicago, where Robinson worked after leaving the network. Producer Bruce Rheins remembered being on assignment with Robinson on the streets of Chicago: "We would go out on the street a lot of times, doing a story . . . on the Southside or something . . . and I remember one time, this mother leaned down to her children, pointed, and said, 'That's Max Robinson. You learn how to speak like him.'" Immediately after this statement from Rheins, the NPR correspondent reporting the piece, Cheryl Devall, announced that "Robinson had denied the nature of his illness for months, but after he died . . . his friend Roger Wilkins said Robinson wanted his death to emphasize the need for AIDS awareness among black people" (*ATC*, 1988). These were the concluding words of the report, and as such they reproduced the epitaphic structure of Robinson's deathbed request, raising the question of to just what extent information about AIDS was reaching black communities.

That these two statements should have been juxtaposed in the radio report is striking because they testify to the power of two different phenomena that appear to be in direct contradiction. Rheins's story underscores the importance of Robinson's speech as an affirmation of black identity for the benefit of the community from which he sprang. Devall's remarks, on the other hand, implicate Robinson's denial that he had AIDS in a general silence regarding the effects of the epidemic among the African-American population. It will be useful for the purposes of this analysis to examine how speech and silence actually interrelate to produce a discursive matrix that governs the cultural significance of AIDS in black communities. Indeed, Max Robinson, news anchor, inhabited a space defined by the overlapping of at least two distinct types of discourse which, though often in conflict, intersect in a way that makes discussion of his AIDS diagnosis—and of AIDS among blacks generally—a particularly difficult activity.

As it happens, the apparent conflict between vocal affirmation and the peculiar silence effected through denial was already implicated in the very nature of Robinson's speech. There is a potential doubleness in the significance of the "speaking" that Robinson did, which the mother cited previously urged her children to emulate. It is clear, first of all, that this mother was referring to Robinson's exemplification of the articulate, authoritative presence that is ideally represented in the television news anchor—an exemplification noteworthy because of the fact that Robinson was black. Rheins's comments illustrate this particularly well:

> Max really was a symbol for a lot of people. . . . Here was a very good-looking, well-dressed, and very obviously intelligent black man giving the news in a straightforward fashion, and not on a black radio station or a black TV station or on the black segment of a news report—he was the anchorman. (*ATC*, 1988)

Rheins's statement indicates the power of Robinson's verbal performance before the camera, for it was through this performance that Robinson's "intelligence," which Rheins emphasizes, was made "obvious." Other accounts of Robinson's tenure as a television news anchor recapitulate this reference. An article in the June 1989 issue of *Vanity Fair* remembered Robinson for "[h]is steely, unadorned delivery, precise diction, and magical presence" (Boyer, 1989, p. 70). A *New York Times* obituary noted the "unforced, authoritative manner" that characterized Robinson's on-air persona, and backed its claim with testimony from current ABC news anchor and Robinson's former colleague, Peter Jennings: "In terms of sheer performance, Max was a penetrating communicator. He had a natural gift to look in the camera and talk to people" (Gerard, 1988). A 1980 *New York Times* reference asserted that Robinson was "blessed with a commanding voice and a handsome appearance" (Schwartz, "Are TV Anchormen," p. 27). A posthumous "appreciation" in the *Boston Globe* described Robinson as "[e]arnest and telegenic," noting that he "did some brilliant reporting . . . and was a consummate newscaster" (Kahn, 1988, p. 67). James Snyder, news director at WTOP-TV in Washington, D.C., where Robinson began his anchoring career, has said that Robinson "had this terrific voice, great enunciation and phrasing. He was just a born speaker" (Boyer, 1989, p. 72). Elsewhere, Snyder succinctly summarized Robinson's appeal, noting his "great presence on the air" ("Max Robinson, 49," 1988).

All of these tributes manifest allusions to Robinson's verbal facility that must be understood as praise for his ability to speak articulate Received Standard English, which linguist Geneva Smitherman (1977, p. 12) has identified as the dialect upon which "White America has insisted . . . as the price of admission into its economic and social mainstream." The emphasis that commentators have placed on Robinson's "precise diction" or on his "great enunciation and phrasing" is an index of the general surprise that was evoked by his facility with the white bourgeois idiom considered standard in "mainstream" U.S. culture, and certainly in television news. The black mother cited previously surely recognized the opportunity for social advancement inherent in this facility with standard English, and this is no doubt the benefit she had in mind for her children when she urged them to "speak like" Max Robinson.

At the same time, however, that the mother's words can be interpreted as an injunction to speak "correctly," they might alternatively be understood as a call for speech per se—as encouragement to *speak out* like Max Robinson, to stand up for one's interests as a black person as Robinson did throughout his career. In this case, the import of her command is traceable to a black cultural nationalism that has waxed and waned in the United States since the mid-nineteenth century, but which, in the context of the Black Power movement of the 1960s, underwent a revival that continues to influence black cultural life in this country.[4] Smitherman (1977, p. 11) has noted the way in which this cultural nationalism has been manifested in black language and discourse, citing the movement "among writers, artists, and black intellectuals of the 1960s, who deliberately wrote and rapped in the Black Idiom and sought to preserve its distinctiveness in the literature of the period." Obviously, Max Robinson did not participate in this nationalistic strategy in the context of his work as a network news anchor. Success in television newscasting, insofar as it depends upon one's conformity to models of behavior deemed acceptable by white bourgeois culture, largely precludes the possibility of one's exercising the "Black Idiom" and thereby manifesting a strong black consciousness in the broadcast context. We might say, then, that black people's successful participation in modes of discourse validated in mainstream culture— their facility with Received Standard English, for instance—actually implicates them in a profound *silence* regarding their African-American identity.

It is arguable, however, that Max Robinson, like all blacks who have achieved a degree of recognition in mainstream U.S. culture, actually played both sides of the behavioral dichotomy that I have described—the dichotomy between articulate verbal performance in the accepted standard dialect of the English language and vocal affirmation of conscious black identity.[5] Though on the one hand his performance before the cameras provided an impeccable image of bourgeois respectability that could easily be read as the erasure of black consciousness, Robinson was at the same time known for publicly affirming his interest in the various sociopolitical factors that affect blacks' existence in the United States, thus continually emphasizing his African-American identification. For example, in February 1981, Robinson became the center of controversy when he was reported as telling a college audience that the various network news agencies, including ABC, discriminate against their black journalists, and that the news media in general constitute "a crooked mirror" in which "white America views itself" (Schwartz, "Robinson of ABC News"; Gerard, 1988). In this instance, not only did Robinson's statement semantically manifest his consciousness of his own black identity, but the very form of the entire incident could be said to constitute an identifiably black cultural behavior. After being summoned to the offices of then-ABC News president Roone Arledge subsequent to making his allegations of network discrimination, Robinson said that "he had not meant to single out ABC for criticism" (Gerard, 1988), thus performing a type of rhetorical backstep by which his criticism, though retracted, was effectively lodged and registered both by the public and by the network. While this mode of protecting one's own interests is by no means unique to African-American culture, it does have a particular resonance within an African-American context. Specifically, Robinson's backstepping strategy can be understood as a form of what is called "loud-talking" or "louding"—a verbal device, common within many black-English-speaking communities, in which a person "says something of someone just loud enough for that person to hear, but indirectly, so he cannot properly respond," or so that, when the object of the remark *does* respond, "the speaker can reply to the effect, 'Oh, I wasn't talking to you'" (Abrahams, 1976, pp. 19, 54; see also Mitchell-Kernan, 1972). Robinson's insistence that his remarks did not refer specifically to ABC News can be interpreted as a form of the disingenuous reply characteristic of loud-talking, thus locating his rhetorical strategy within the cultural context of black communicative patterns and underscoring his African-American identification.

Roone Arledge, in taking Robinson to task after the incident, made unusually explicit the suppression of African-American identity generally effected by the networks in their news productions; such dramatic measures usually are not necessary because potential manifestations of strong black cultural identification are normally subdued by blacks' very participation in the discursive conventions of the network newscast.[6] Thus, the more audible and insistent Robinson's televised performance in Received Standard English and in the white bourgeois idiom of the network newscast, the more secure the silence imposed upon the vocal black consciousness that he always threatened to display. Robinson's articulate speech before the cameras always implied a silencing of the African-American idiom.

Concomitant with the silencing in the network-news context of black-affirmative discourse is the suppression of another aspect of black identity alluded to in the previously quoted references to Max Robinson's on-camera performance. The emphasis these commentaries place on Robinson's articulateness is coupled with their simultaneous insistence on his physical attractiveness: Bruce Rheins's remarks on Robinson's "obvious intelligence" are accompanied by a reference to his "good looks"; Tony Schwartz's inventory of Robinson's assets notes both his

Max Robinson in Chicago. Photo copyright © 1995 CAPITAL CITIES/ABC, INC.

"commanding voice" and his "handsome appearance"; Joseph Kahn's "appreciation" of Robinson cites his "brilliant reporting" as well as his "telegenic" quality. It seems that it was impossible to comment on Robinson's success as a news anchor without noting simultaneously his verbal ability and his physical appeal.

Such commentary is not at all unusual in discussions of television newscasters, whose personal charms have taken on an increasing degree of importance since the early days of the medium. Indeed, Schwartz's 1980 *New York Times* article titled "Are TV Anchormen Merely Performers?"—intended as a critique of the degree to which television news is conceived as entertainment—actually underscores the importance of a newscaster's physical attractiveness to a broadcast's success; and by the late 1980s that importance had become a truism of contemporary culture, assimilated into the popular consciousness, through the movie *Broadcast News,* for instance.[7] In the case of a black man, such as Max Robinson, however, discussions of a news anchor's "star quality" become potentially problematic and, consequently, extremely complex, because such a quality is founded upon an implicitly acknowledged "sex appeal," the concept of which has always been highly charged with respect to black men in the United States.

The black man historically has been perceived as the bearer of a bestial sexuality, as the savage "walking phallus" that poses a constant threat to an idealized white womanhood and thus to the whole U.S. social order.[8] To the extent that this is true, for white patriarchal institutions such as the mainstream media to note the physical attractiveness of any black man is for them potentially to unleash the very beast that threatens their power. Max Robinson's achievement of a professional, public position that mandates the deployment of a certain rhetoric—that of the news anchor's attractive and telegenic persona—thus also raised the problem of taming the threatening black male sexuality that that rhetoric conjures up.

This taming, I think, was once again achieved through Robinson's articulate verbal performance, references to which routinely accompanied acknowledgments of his physical attractiveness. In commentary on white newscasters, paired references to both their physical appeal and their rhetorical skill serve merely to defuse accusations that television journalism is superficial and "image-oriented." In Robinson's case, however, the acknowledgment of his articulateness also served to absorb the threat of his sexuality that was raised in references to his physical attractiveness; in the same way that Robinson's conformity to the "rules" of standard English language performance suppressed the possibility of his articulating a radical identification with African-American culture, it also, in attesting to his refinement and civility, actually *domesticated* his threatening physicality which itself *had to be* alluded to in conventional liberal accounts of his performance as a news anchor. James Snyder's reference to Robinson's "great presence" is a most stunning example of such an account, for it neatly conflates and thus simultaneously acknowledges both Robinson's *physical* person (in the tradition of commentary on network news personalities) and his virtuosity in standard *verbal* performance in such a way that the latter mitigates the threat posed by the former. Robinson's standard English speech, then, served not only to suppress black culturolinguistic forms that might have disrupted the white bourgeois aspect of network news, but also to keep in check the black male sexuality that threatens the social order that the news media represent.[9] Ironically, in this latter function white bourgeois discourse seems to share an objective with forms of black discourse, which themselves work to suppress certain threatening elements of black male sexuality, resulting in a strange reaction to Max Robinson's death in African-American communities.

Homophobia in African-American Discourse

Whether it is interpreted as a reference to Robinson's facility at Received Standard English, whereby he achieved a degree of success in the white-run world of broadcast media, or as a reference to his repeated attempts to vocalize, in the tradition of African-American discourse, blacks' grievances over their sociopolitical status in the United States, to "speak like Max Robinson" is simultaneously to silence discussion of the various possibilities of black male sexuality. We have seen how an emphasis on Robinson's facility at "white-oriented" discourse serves to defuse the "threat" of rampant black male sexuality that constitutes so much of the sexuopolitical structure of U.S. society. Indeed, some segments of the black population have colluded in this defusing of black sexuality, attempting to explode whites' stereotypes of blacks as oversexed by stifling discussion of black sexuality generally (noted in "AIDS & Blacks," *ME,* 5 April 1989). At the same time, the other tradition in which Max Robinson's speech derives meaning also functions to suppress discussion about specific aspects of black male sexuality that are threatening to the black male image.

In her book on "the language of black America," Geneva Smitherman (1977, p. 52) cites, rather non-self-consciously, examples of black discourse that illustrate this point. For instance, in a discussion of black musicians' adaptation of themes from the African-American oral tradition, Smitherman mentions the popular early-1960s recording of "Stagger Lee," based on a traditional narrative folk poem. The hero for whom the narrative is named is, as Smitherman puts it, "a fearless, mean dude," so that "it became widely fashionable [in black communities] . . . to refer to oneself as 'Stag,' as in . . . 'Don't mess wif me, cause I ain't no fag, uhm Stag.'" What is notable here is not merely the homophobia manifested in the "rap" laid down by the black "brother" imagined to be speaking this line, but also that the rap itself, the very verbal performance, as Smitherman points out, serves as the evidence that the speaker is indeed *not* a "fag"; verbal facility becomes proof of one's conventional masculinity and thus silences discussion of one's possible homosexuality, in a pattern that has been extended—to wide notice—in much contemporary rap music.[10]

If verbal facility is considered an identifying mark of masculinity in certain African-American contexts, however, this is so only when it is demonstrated specifically through use of the vernacular. Indeed, a too-evident facility in the standard white idiom can quickly identify one not as a strong black man, but rather as a white-identified Uncle Tom who must also, therefore, be weak, effeminate, and probably a "fag." To the extent that this process of homophobic identification reflects powerful cross-class hostilities, it is certainly not unique to African-American culture. Its imbrication with questions of racial identity, however, compounds its potency in the African-American context. Simply put, within some African-American communities the "professional" or "intellectual" black male inevitably endangers his status both as black and as male whenever he evidences a facility with Received Standard English—a facility upon which his very identity as a professional or an intellectual in the larger society is founded in the first place. Max Robinson was not the first black man to face this dilemma;[11] a decade or so before he emerged on network television, a particularly influential group of black writers attempted to negotiate the problem by incorporating into their work the semantics of "street" discourse, thereby establishing an intellectual practice that was both "black" enough and virile enough to bear the weight of a stridently nationalist agenda. Thus, a strong "Stagger Lee"–type identification can be found in a parenthetical passage from the poem "Don't Cry, Scream," by Haki Madhubuti (Don L. Lee) (1969, p. 29):

(swung on a faggot who politely
scratched his ass in my presence.
he smiled broken teeth stained from
his over-used tongue. fisted-face.
teeth dropped in tune with ray
charles singing "yesterday.")

Here the scornful language of the poem itself recapitulates the homophobic violence that it commemorates (or invites us to imagine as having occurred); and the two together attest to both the speaker's aversion to homosexuality and, by extension, his own unquestionable masculinity, indicating the degree to which homophobia is implicated in "Black Arts" nationalism, whose influence has long outlasted the actual aesthetic movement.[12]

Consequently, Max Robinson was put in a very difficult position with respect to talking about his AIDS diagnosis. Robinson's reputation was based on his articulate outspokenness; however, as we have seen, that very well-spokenness derived its power within two different modes of discourse that, though they are sometimes at odds, both work to suppress issues of sexuality that are implied in any discussion of AIDS.[13] The white bourgeois cultural context in which Robinson derived his status as an authoritative figure in the mainstream news media must always keep a vigilant check on black male sexuality, which is perceived to be threatening generally (and it is assisted in this task by a moralistic black bourgeoisie that seeks to explode notions of black hypersexuality). At the same time, the African-American cultural context to which Robinson appealed for his status as a paragon of black pride and self-determination embodies an ethic that precludes sympathetic discussion of black male homosexuality. However extensively the demography of AIDS in this country may have shifted since 1981 as more and more people who are not gay men have become infected with HIV, the historical and cultural conditions surrounding the development of the epidemic ensure its ongoing association with male homosexuality, so it is not surprising that the latter should emerge as a topic of discussion in any consideration of Max Robinson's death. The apparent *inevitability* of that emergence (and the degree to which the association between AIDS and male homosexuality would become threatening to Robinson's reputation and discursively problematic, given the contexts in which his public persona was created) was dramatically illustrated in the 9 January 1989 issue of *Jet* magazine, the black-oriented weekly. That issue contained an obituary of Max Robinson that was very similar to those issued by the *New York Times* and other nonblack media, noting Robinson's professional achievements and his controversial tenure at ABC News, alluding to the "tormented" nature of his life as a symbol of black success, and citing his secrecy surrounding his AIDS diagnosis and his wish that his death be used as the occasion to educate blacks about AIDS. The *Jet* obituary also noted that "[t]he main victims [*sic*] of the disease [*sic*] have been intravenous drug users and homosexuals," leaving open the question of Robinson's relation to either of these categories (*Jet*, 1989, p. 14).[14]

Following Robinson's obituary in the same issue of *Jet* was a notice of another AIDS-related death, that of the popular disco singer, Sylvester. Sylvester's obituary, however, offered an interesting contrast to that of Robinson, for it identified Sylvester, in its very first sentence, as "the flamboyant homosexual singer whose high-pitched voice and dramatic on-stage costumes propelled him to the height of stardom on the disco music scene during the late 1970s" (*Jet*, 1989, p. 15). The piece went on to indicate the openness with which Sylvester lived as a gay man, noting that he "first publicly acknowledged he had AIDS at the San Francisco Gay Pride March last June [1988], which he attended in a wheelchair

Sylvester in performance. Photo courtesy of Photofest.

with the People With AIDS group" (15), and quoting his recollection of his first sexual experience, at age 7, with an adult male evangelist: "[Y]ou see, I was a queen even back then, so it didn't bother me. I rather liked it" (18).

Obviously, a whole array of issues is raised by Sylvester's obituary and its juxtaposition with that of Max Robinson (not the least of which has to do with the complicated phenomenon of sex between adults and children). What is most pertinent for discussion here, however, is the difference between *Jet*'s treatments of Sylvester's and Robinson's sexualities, and the factors that account for that difference. It is clear, I think, that Sylvester's public persona emerged from contexts that are different from those that produced Robinson. If it is true that, as *Jet* (1989, p. 18) put it, "[t]he church was . . . the setting for Sylvester's first homosexual experience," it is also true that "Sylvester learned to sing in churches in South Los Angeles and went on to perform at gospel conventions around the state." That is to say that the church-choir context in which Sylvester was groomed for a singing career has stereotypically served as a locus in which young black men both discover and sublimate their homosexuality, and also as a conduit to a world of professional entertainment generally conceived as "tolerant," if not downright encouraging, of nonnormative sexualities. In Sylvester's case, this was particularly true, since he was able to help create a disco culture—comprising elements from both black and gay contexts—in which he and others could thrive as openly gay men. Thus the black-church milieu, though ostensibly hostile to homosexuality and gay identity, nevertheless has traditionally provided a means by which black men can achieve a sense of themselves as homosexual and even, in cases such as Sylvester's, expand that sense into gay-affirmative public personae.[15]

On the other hand, the public figure of Max Robinson, as we have seen, was cut from entirely different cloth, formed in the intersection of discursive contexts that do not allow for the expression of black male homosexuality in any recognizable form. The discursive bind constituted by Robinson's status as both a conventionally successful media personality and an exemplar of black male self-assertion and racial consciousness left him with no alternative to the manner in which he dealt with his diagnosis in the public forum—shrouding the nature of his illness in a secrecy that he was able to break only after his death, with the posthumous acknowledgment that he had AIDS. Consequently, obituarists and commentators on Robinson's death were faced with the "problem" of how to address issues relating to Robinson's sexuality—to his possible *homo*sexuality—the result being a large body of wrongminded commentary that actually hindered the educational efforts Robinson supposedly intended to endorse.

It would be a mistake to think that, because most accounts of Robinson's death do not mention the possibility of his homosexuality, it was not conceived of as a problem to be reckoned with. On the contrary, since, as I have attempted to show, the discursive contexts in which Max Robinson derived his power as a public figure function to prevent discussion of black male homosexuality, the silence regarding the topic that characterizes most of the notices of his death actually marks the degree to which the possibility of black male homosexuality is worried over and considered problematic. The instances in which the possibility of Robinson's homosexuality *does* explicitly figure actually serve as proof of the anxiety that founds the more usual silence on the subject. A look at a few commentaries on Robinson's death will illustrate this well; examining these pieces in the chronological order of their appearance in the media will especially help us to see how, over time, the need to quell anxiety about the possibility of Robinson's homosexuality became increasingly desperate, thus increasingly undermining the educational efforts that his death was supposed to occasion.

Within the two weeks following Robinson's death, there appeared in *Newsweek* magazine an obituary that, once again, included the obligatory references to Robinson's "commanding" on-air presence, to his attacks on racism in the media, and to the psychic "conflict" he suffered that led him to drink ("Max Robinson: Fighting the Demons"). In addition to rehearsing this standard litany, however, the *Newsweek* obituary also emphasized that "[e]ven [Robinson's] family . . . don't know how he contracted the disease." The reference to the general ignorance as to how Robinson became infected with HIV (as though the precise mode of infection can ever be definitively determined in most cases) leaves open the possibility that Robinson engaged in unprotected sex with a man (or with *men*), just as the *Jet* notice left unresolved the possibility that he was a homosexual or an IV drug user. Yet, the invocation in the *Newsweek* piece of Robinson's "family," with all its conventional heterosexist associations, simultaneously indicates the anxiety that the possibility of Robinson's homosexuality generally produces, and constitutes an attempt to redeem Robinson from the unsavory implications of his AIDS diagnosis.

The subtlety of the *Newsweek* strategy for dealing with the possibility of Robinson's homosexuality gave way to a more direct approach by the Rev. Jesse Jackson, in an interview broadcast on the National Public Radio series on AIDS and blacks (*ME,* 5 April 1989). Responding to charges by black AIDS activists that he missed a golden opportunity to educate blacks about AIDS by neglecting to speak out about modes of HIV transmission soon after Robinson's death, Jackson provided this statement:

> Max shared with my family and me that he had the AIDS virus [*sic*], but that it did not come from homosexuality, it came from promiscuity.... And now we know that the number one transmission [factor] for AIDS is not sexual contact, it's drugs, and so the crises of drugs and needles and AIDS are connected, as well as AIDS and promiscuity are connected. And all we can do is keep urging people to not isolate this crisis by race, or by class, or by sexual preference, but in fact to observe the precautionary measures that have been advised, on the one hand, and keep urging more money for research immediately, because it's an international health crisis and it's a killer disease.

A number of things are notable about this statement. First of all, Jackson, like the *Newsweek* writer, is careful to reincorporate the discussion of Robinson's AIDS diagnosis into the nuclear-family context, emphasizing that Robinson shared his secret with Jackson *and his family,* and thereby attempting to mitigate the effects of the association between AIDS and male homosexuality. Second, Jackson invokes the problematic and completely unhelpful concept of "promiscuity," wrongly contrasting it with homosexuality (and thus implicitly equating it with heterosexuality) in such a way that he actually appears to be endorsing it over that less legitimate option, contrary to what he must intend to convey about the dangers of unprotected sex with multiple partners; and, of course, since he does not actually mention safer sex practices, he implies that it is "promiscuity" per se that puts people at risk of contracting HIV, when it is, rather, unprotected sex with however few partners that constitutes risky behavior. Third, by identify-

ing IV drug use over risky sexual behavior as the primary means of HIV transmission, Jackson manifests a blindness to his own insight about the interrelatedness of various factors in the spread of AIDS, for unprotected sexual activity is
often part and parcel of drug cultures (especially that of crack) in which transmission of HIV thrives, as sex is commonly exchanged for access to drugs in such
contexts (noted in "AIDS & Blacks," *ATC*, 7 April 1989). Finally, Jackson's sense of
"all we can do" to prevent AIDS is woefully inadequate: to "urge people to observe
the precautionary measures that have been advised" obviously presupposes that
everyone is already aware of what those precautionary measures are, for Jackson
himself does not outline them in his statement; to demand more money for
research is crucial, but it does not go the slightest distance toward enabling people
to protect themselves from HIV in the present; and to resist conceptualizing AIDS
as endemic to one race, class, or sexual orientation is of extreme importance
(though it is equally important to recognize the relative degrees of interest that
different constituencies have in the epidemic), but in the context of Jackson's
statement this strategy for preventing various social groups from being stigma-
tized through their association with AIDS is utilized merely to protect Max
Robinson in particular from speculation that his bout with AIDS was related to
homosexual sex. Indeed, Jackson's entire statement centers on the effort to protect
Robinson from potential charges of homosexuality, and his intense focus on this
homophobic endeavor works to the detriment of his attempts to make factual
statements about the nature of HIV transmission.[16]

Jackson is implicated, as well, in the third media response to Robinson's
death—a response that, like those just discussed, represented an effort to silence
discussion of the possibility of Robinson's homosexuality. In his June 1989 *Vanity
Fair* article, Peter J. Boyer reported on the eulogy Jackson delivered at the Washington, D.C., memorial service for Max Robinson. Boyer's piece cites Jackson's
quotation of Robinson's deathbed request—"He said, 'I'm not sure and know not
where [*sic*], but even on my dying bed . . . let my predicament be a source of education to our people'"—and asserts that "[t]wo thousand people heard Jesse Jackson keep the promise he'd made to Robinson . . . : 'It was not homosexuality,'
[Jackson] told them, 'but promiscuity,'" implicitly letting people know that
Robinson "got AIDS from a woman" (p. 84). Apparently, then, the only deathbed
promise that Jackson kept was the one he made to ensure that people would not
think that Robinson was gay; no information about how HIV is transmitted or
about how such transmission can be prevented has ever escaped his lips in connection with the death of Max Robinson, though Boyer, evidently, was fooled into
believing that Jackson's speech constituted just such substantive information.
This is not surprising, since Boyer's article itself is nothing more than an anxious
effort to convince us of Max Robinson's heterosexuality, as if that were the crucial

issue. Boyer's piece mentions Robinson's three marriages (p. 74); it comments extensively on his "well-earned" reputation as an "inveterate womanizer" and emphasizes his attractiveness to women, quoting one male friend as saying, "He could walk into the room and you could just hear the panties drop," and a woman acquaintance as once telling a reporter, "Don't forget to mention he has fine thighs" (p. 74); it notes that "[n]one of Robinson's friends believe that he was a homosexual" (p. 84); and it cites Robinson's own desperate attempt "to compose a list of women whom he suspected as possible sources of his disease" (p. 84), as though to provide written corroboration of his insistence to a friend, "But I'm not gay" (p. 82).

From early claims, then, that "even Robinson's family" had no idea how he contracted HIV, there developed an authoritative scenario in which Robinson's extensive heterosexual affairs were common knowledge and that posited his contraction of HIV from a female sex partner as a near-certainty. It seems that, subsequent to Robinson's death, a whole propaganda machine was put into operation to establish a suitable account of his contraction of HIV and of his bout with AIDS, the net result of which was to preclude the effective AIDS education that Robinson reputedly wanted his death to occasion, as the point he supposedly intended to make became lost in a homophobic shuffle to "fix" his sexual orientation and to construe his death in inoffensive terms.

In order to ensure that this work not become absorbed in that project, which would deter us from the far more crucial tasks at hand, it is important for me to state flat out that I have no idea whether Max Robinson's sex partners were male or female or both. I acknowledge explicitly my ignorance on this matter because to do so, I think, is to reopen sex in all its manifestations as a primary category for consideration as we review the significance of the predominant discourse about AIDS among African Americans. Such a move is crucial because the same homophobic impulse that informed efforts to establish Max Robinson's heterosexuality is also implicated in a general reluctance to provide detailed information about sexual transmission of HIV; indeed, a deep silence regarding the details of such transmission has long characterized almost all of what passes for government-sponsored AIDS-education efforts throughout the United States.

Sins of Omission: Inadequacy in AIDS-Education Programs

Even the slickest, most visible print and television ads promoting awareness about AIDS consistently thematize a silence that has been a major obstacle to effective AIDS education in communities of color. Notices distributed around the time of

AIDS education poster from the mid-1980s. Copyright © March 1986 by the American National Red Cross.

Max Robinson's death utilized an array of celebrities—from Rubèn Blades to Patti Labelle—who encouraged people to "get the facts" regarding AIDS, but didn't offer any, merely referring readers elsewhere for substantive information on the syndrome.[17] A bitter testimony to the inefficacy of this ad campaign was offered by a thirty-one-year-old African-American woman interviewed in the NPR series on AIDS and blacks. Sandra contracted HIV through unprotected heterosexual sex; the child conceived in that encounter died at ten months of age from an AIDS-related illness. In her interview, Sandra reflected on her lack of knowledge about AIDS at the time she became pregnant:

> I don't remember hearing anything about AIDS until . . . either the year that I was pregnant, which would have been '86, or the year after I had her; but I really believe it was when I was pregnant with her because I always remember saying, "I'm going to write and get that information," because the only thing that was on TV was to write or call the 1-800 number . . . to get information, and I always wanted to call and get that pamphlet, not knowing that I was going to have first-hand information. I didn't know how it was transmitted. I didn't know that it was caused by a virus. I didn't know that [AIDS] stood for "Acquired Immune Deficiency Syndrome." I didn't know any of that. ("AIDS & Blacks," *ATC*, 4 April 1989)

By 1986, when Sandra believes she first began even to hear about AIDS, the epidemic was at least five years old.

If, even today, response to AIDS in black communities is characterized by a profound silence regarding actual sexual practices, either heterosexual or homosexual, this is largely because of the suppression of talk about sexuality generally and about male homosexuality in particular that is enacted in black communities through the discourses that constitute them. Additionally, however, this continued silence is *enabled* by the ease with which the significance of sexual transmission of HIV can be elided beneath the admittedly significant (but also, to many minds, more "acceptable") problem of IV drug–related HIV transmission that is endemic in some black communities. George Bellinger, Jr., then a "minority outreach" worker at Gay Men's Health Crisis, the New York City AIDS service organization, recounted for the NPR series the "horrible joke that used to go around [in black communities] when AIDS first started . . . : 'There's good news and bad news. The bad news is I have AIDS, the good news is I'm an IV drug user'" ("AIDS & Blacks," *ATC*, 3 April 1989); this joke indicates the degree to which IV drug use can serve as a shield against the implications of male homosexuality that are always associated with AIDS, and which thus hover as a threat over any discussion of sexual transmission of HIV. This phenomenon was at work even in the NPR series itself. For all its emphasis on the need for black communities to "recognize homosexuality and bisexuality" within them ("AIDS & Blacks," *ATC*, 9 April 1989), and despite its inclusion of articulate black lesbians and gay men in its roster of interviewees, the radio series still subordinated discussion of sexual transmission of HIV to a focus on IV drug use. One segment in particular illustrates this point.

In an interview broadcast on *Morning Edition*, 4 April 1989, Harold Jaffe, from the federal Centers for Disease Control, made a crucial point regarding gay male sexual behavior in the face of the AIDS epidemic: "The studies that have come out saying gay men have made substantial changes in their behavior are true, but they're true mainly for white, middle class, exclusively gay men." As correspondent Richard Harris reported, however, Jaffe "doesn't see that trend among black gays." Harris noted that Jaffe "has been studying syphilis rates, which are a good measure of safe sex practices." Jaffe himself proclaimed his discoveries: "We find very major decreases [in the rate of syphilis] in white gay men, and either no change or even increases in Hispanic and black gay men, suggesting that they have not really gotten the same behavioral message." Harris continued: "White gay men have changed their behavior to such an extent that experts believe the disease has essentially peaked for them, so as those numbers gradually subside, minorities will make up a growing proportion of AIDS cases." Up to this point, Harris's report focused on important differences between the rates of syphilis and HIV transmission among gay white men and among gay black and Latino men, suggesting the inadequacy of the educational resources made available to gay men of color. As his rhetoric shifted, however, to refer to the risk that *all* members of "minority" groups face, regardless of their sexual identification, the risky behaviors on which he focused also changed. After indicating the need for gay men of color to adapt their sexual behavior in the same way that gay white men have, and after a pause of a couple beats that would conventionally indicate the introduction of some narrative into the report to illustrate this point, Harris segued into a story about Rosina, a former IV drug user with AIDS, and to a claim that "about the only way to stop AIDS from spreading more in the inner city is to help addicts get off of drugs." Thus, Harris's early focus on AIDS among black and Latino gay men served, in the end, merely as a bridge to discussion of IV drug use as the primary factor in the spread of AIDS in communities of color. Moreover, the diversity of those communities was effaced through the conventional euphemistic reference to the "inner city," which, because it disregards class differences among blacks and Latinos, falsely homogenizes the concerns of people of color and glosses over the complex nature of HIV transmission among them, which, just as with whites, implicates drug use *and* unprotected sexual activity as high-risk behaviors. The ease with which middle-class blacks can construe IV drug use as a problem of communities that are completely removed from their everyday lives (and thus see it as unrelated to high-risk sexual activities in which they may engage) makes an exclusive emphasis on IV drug–related HIV transmission among blacks actually detrimental to efforts at effective AIDS education.

To the extent that Max Robinson hoped his death would occasion efforts at *comprehensive* AIDS education in black communities, we must consider programs that utilize the logic manifested in Richard Harris's NPR report as inadequate to meet the challenge that Robinson posed. The inadequacy of such efforts is rooted, as I have suggested, in a reluctance to discuss issues of black sexuality that is based simultaneously on whites' stereotyped notions (often defensively adopted by blacks themselves) about the need to suppress black (male) sexuality generally, and on the strictness with which traditional forms of black discourse preclude the possibility of the discussion of black male homosexuality specifically. Indeed, these very factors necessitated the peculiar response to his own AIDS diagnosis that Max Robinson manifested—initial denial and posthumous acknowledgment. I suggested at the beginning of this chapter that Robinson's final acknowledgment of his AIDS diagnosis—in the form of his injunction that we use his death as the occasion to increase blacks' awareness about AIDS—performs a sort of epitaphic function. As the last words of the deceased that constitute an implicit warning to others not to repeat his mistakes, Robinson's request was promulgated through the media with such a repetitive insistence that it might as well have been literally etched in stone. The repetition of the request ought itself to serve as a warning to us, however, since repetition can recapitulate the very silence that it is meant to overcome. As literary critic Debra Fried (1986, p. 620) has said, regarding the epitaph, it is both

> silent and . . . repetitious; [it] refuses to speak, and yet keeps on saying the same thing: refusal to say anything different is tantamount to a refusal to speak. Repetition thus becomes a form of silence. . . . According to the fiction of epitaphs, death imposes on its victims an endless verbal task: to repeat without deviation or difference the answer to a question that, no matter how many times it prompts the epitaph to the same silent utterance, is never satisfactorily answered.

In the case of Max Robinson's death, the pertinent question is, How can transmission of HIV and thus AIDS-related death be prevented? The onus of response at this point is not on the deceased, however, but on those of us still living; and a disproportionate share of that burden has, since the beginning of the epidemic, fallen to those whose identities and social positions have been judged to make them "natural" leaders in the education effort. Gay men have long predominated in this group, which also, however, includes HIV-infected persons who are not gay-identified. If the close association of HIV infection with male homosexuality has made it difficult for a significant number of such persons to acknowledge publicly their HIV status—as the example of Max Robinson clearly indicates that it has—so too does this association complicate the effects when one of them does decide to "come out" as HIV-infected. In the instance of basketball star Magic Johnson, the salient factors of fame and black male identity at work in Max Robinson's case are joined with Johnson's status as a celebrated professional athlete to make for a particularly complex situation. Because Johnson's story is currently continuing, it is impossible to posit a final analysis of its significance. Nevertheless, we can already see that, just as whatever projects in AIDS education Robinson's death was supposed to impel gave way to anxiety-driven efforts to protect his heterosexual identity, the later case has been dominated by attempts to affirm the heterosexuality of both Johnson and his associates, the primary result of which may well have been to constrain the effectiveness of the AIDS-education projects that he has endorsed and undertaken. That Johnson himself has proclaimed the urgency of disseminating information about AIDS and HIV among African-American youth makes it particularly important for us to consider how his own mode of embodying black masculinity might have helped to undermine this very project.

Identification and Disavowal:
The Example of Magic Johnson

As this book goes to press, Earvin Johnson—whose unprecedented virtuosity on the basketball court earned him the nickname "Magic" when he was still a high school player in Lansing, Michigan—is launching a comeback as a professional player for the Los Angeles Lakers (see Friend, 1996), thus opening a new chapter in story that had seemed to culminate in 1992. Prior to this latest sortie, Johnson enjoyed a twelve-season career that had a defining impact on professional basketball during the 1980s. Indeed, most commentators largely credit Johnson and longtime rival Larry Bird (Boston Celtics)—plus such contemporaries as Michael Jordan (Chicago Bulls) and Isiah Thomas (Detroit Pistons)—with elevating the game to a level of popularity that was unimagined before that heady decade, swelling both live and television audiences for the sport and lending it a new air of glamour and excitement.[18] Consequently, when in November 1991 Johnson announced his retirement from the Lakers, owing to his infection with HIV, media assessments that focused on his unique athletic achievement inevitably implied that his withdrawal represented a profound crisis for professional basketball.[19] This is not to say that commentators did not recognize the *personal* crisis that Johnson himself faced with the discovery of his infection, but rather that this latter crisis is, in many ways, inextricable from the former, insofar as the continued significance of the sport greatly depends on the fortunes of the individual larger-than-life personalities involved in it.

Thus, for example, among the concerns addressed in press coverage right after Johnson's retirement—and consistently followed up in later accounts—were both the fate of Johnson's own product endorsement deals with major corporations *and* the continued desirability of athletes, generally, for use in high-profile advertising campaigns.[20] Similarly, Johnson's announcement triggered speculation about whether his case might be just the tip of an HIV-infection iceberg in the NBA that could have serious impact on the future of the entire league (see Araton, "Players"). And while the primary dangers in these instances might have been framed in terms of Johnson's possible loss of public sympathy "once he is visibly sick" (to quote from marketing researcher Judith Langer's ruminations on Johnson's prospects as an endorser; see Elliott, "Magic Johnson's Ad Career") or NBA stars' easy access to female sex partners (one agent expressed particular concern about an unidentified player who, he said, "isn't able to keep his hands off women wherever he goes"; see Araton, "Players," p. S11), the very nature of these terms indicates that the fundamental crisis precipitated by Johnson's announcement derived from the questions it raised regarding his (and other players') sexual practices and, by extension, masculine identity. To put it simply, the sight of a man who is identifiably ill with HIV disease engenders, among other things, a heightened consciousness of male homosexual activity whose denial is precisely what is at stake in the insistent references to pro basketball players' uncontrollable heterosexual desire. And, given the essential link that current conventional wisdom asserts between heterosexual orientation and normative gender disposition, it is easy to locate the greater purpose of that denial in the establishment and maintenance of proper masculinity.[21]

Clearly, this mode of shoring up masculinity is not unique either to professional sports or to the media commentary attending Magic Johnson's announcement of his HIV seropositivity; rather, it is pervasive in contemporary culture, and accounts for (to name but one obviously pertinent instance) the anxious insistence on Max Robinson's heterosexuality that I have noted in the foregoing pages. At the same time, though (and paradoxically), because sports and athletic competition constitute a primary context in which masculine identity is forged—a key "arena of masculinity" as Brian Pronger (1990) has put it—the need to ensure that male athletes actually possess the heterosexual orientation supposed to found masculinity is particularly great. Consequently, while the circumstances surrounding the revelations of Max Robinson's AIDS diagnosis and Magic Johnson's HIV seropositivity differ in some very important ways—not the least of which is that Johnson publicized his own HIV status before becoming ill rather than issuing instructions for a posthumous disclosure—the general anxiety about Johnson's sexuality that was occasioned by his announcement was even more intense, allowing for the athlete's greater celebrity, than the concern about Robinson's orientation that developed after his death, and it extensively conditioned both the dissemination and the reception of the basic, crucial facts at issue in his declaration.

The facts to which I refer are of two principal orders, pertaining, first, to the ramifications of Johnson's HIV infection for his career (on what we might call the sports-news level of public concern) and, second, to the various means by which the transmission of HIV can be prevented, on the rather more pressing level of public-health education. While both these orders of information were addressed in the voluminous media response to Johnson's announcement, coverage of them was attended by a persistent focus on a third, much more dubious area, falling under the infamous industry rubric of "human interest." Specifically, an inordinate effort was expended in clarifying not the general means of HIV transmission, but rather the mode by which Johnson himself became infected, with the overall result that relatively little accurate information about preventing the spread of HIV was disseminated to the public.

As is indicated by the joke referenced in the preceding section, male homosexuality—with which HIV has always been associated in the United States—is widely perceived as much more shameful than the intravenous drug use that HIV infection also often connotes. Insofar as the very shamefulness of male homosexuality both signals and inspires a general societal fixation upon it—and given the complex relation among sexual orientation, masculine gender identity, and athletic competition that I have noted—it should not surprise us that it was the possibility that Magic Johnson contracted HIV through sex with a male partner, rather than the possibility that he injected drugs, that generated most anxiety and concern upon his disclosure of his HIV status. Indeed, it is precisely because this anxiety underlay so much of the public discussion about Johnson during the year following his announcement that whatever sports-news and, especially, public-health information was disseminated in connection with his case was deeply confused and confusing.

It effectively took Magic Johnson an entire year to retire fully—albeit temporarily—from the NBA, largely because the circumstances that he had to negotiate in making a definitive decision about his career continually changed over that time. If the instability of those circumstances appeared to derive from the supposed novelty of the medical questions his situation seemed to raise, however, those very questions—and thus the uncertainty of Johnson's position—emerged not from any real epidemiological mystery, but out of the welter of gossip that circulated in and around the NBA through the fall of 1992 and that largely constituted the human-interest reportage to which I have already alluded. This fact, and the difficulty Johnson faced in managing the complexities of his situation, indicates his ongoing engagement not only with questions regarding his physical well-being, but with the pressures of masculine identity (and of celebrity) over and above the specific medical ramifications of HIV.

It did not take long at all for those pressures to manifest themselves. Within the first day after Johnson announced his infection, many press accounts either noted that he had neglected to explain exactly how he contracted HIV (see, for instance, Kolata, "Studies") or, in a subtle acknowledgment of the potential impossibility of determining the actual means of transmission in any given instance, cited his doctor's claim that the mode of infection was unknown (see, for instance, Specter, 1991).[22] While the simple declarative mode in which these observations were generally rendered worked to suggest the supposed benign "objectivity" of responsible journalism, the fact that they were made at all indicates a widespread concern that someone of Johnson's popularity and recognized masculine accomplishment might have had a sexual relationship with a man. This concern both informs and explains certain features of the media response to Johnson's announcement, from the relatively subtle instance in which reporter Gina Kolata ("Studies") asserted the statistical rarity of sexual transmission of HIV from women to men and declared that "[t]he primary risk groups for infection are gay men and intravenous drug users" to sportswriter Ira Berkow's

("Magic Johnson's Legacy") explicit reference to "the inevitable questions that will arise about [Johnson's] sexual preferences."[23] If nothing else, the very speed with which commentators raised the issue of Johnson's possible homosexual activity indicated that the general anxiety about it was too intense to be quelled by Johnson's rather oblique assertion, during his press conference, that "sometimes we think, well, only gay people can get it—'It's not going to happen to me.' And here I am saying that it can happen to anybody, even me, Magic Johnson" (quoted in Stevenson, "Magic Johnson Ends His Career," p. B12). If Johnson's heterosexuality—and, by extension, his masculinity—was to be effectively established, a much more decisive move on his part would be necessary, a fact that he clearly realized and to which he responded with startling promptness.

Magic Johnson announced his HIV seropositivity and retired from professional basketball on 7 November 1991. The just-cited press accounts problematizing Johnson's heterosexual identity were published the following day. That evening, Johnson made a widely remarked appearance on the popular late-night talk show hosted by Arsenio Hall, during which he countered the offensive insinuations by proclaiming, "I'm far from being homosexual"—an announcement that was greeted with wild cheers and applause from the studio audience. Four days later, *Sports Illustrated* published a sort of print-media companion piece to this appearance in which Johnson wrote, "I am certain that I was infected by having unprotected sex with a woman. . . . I have never had a homosexual encounter. Never." And, as if to underscore what was really at stake in his detailing the extent of his heterosexual activity in this article, Johnson pointedly referenced his own putative bravery in publicizing his promiscuity: "I'm being a man about my past" ("I'll Deal," pp. 21, 22).[24]

Had there been a live audience for this last proclamation, it might well have cheered as loudly as did the crowd in Arsenio Hall's studio, since it is precisely Magic Johnson's manhood that was in question in the latter venue—and in the national consciousness—from the moment he announced his infection with HIV. At the same time, the fact that Johnson perceived a need to continue asserting his masculinity—specifically by publicizing his heterosexual exploits—even after he had supposedly set the record "straight" on national television indicates that masculinity, as generally conceived, is a condition whose very validity in any individual instance consists in its being experienced as under constant threat. Moreover, Johnson's continued protestations seemed to belie his early, poorly worded pledges to be "a spokesperson for the HIV virus" (Heisler, "Magic Johnson's Career Ended," p. A1) and "to help young people, and especially blacks, to understand that AIDS is more of a threat than they can even imagine" (M. Johnson, "I'll Deal," p. 25), since they suggest that he was initially most interested, not in promoting AIDS awareness, but rather in safeguarding his masculine identity against the unsavory connotations of HIV. That the media shared this interest was indicated by their insistence on verifying the specific means of Johnson's infection, as that means was understood to encompass the "truth" of his sexual orientation. Indeed, in their obsession with thus confirming Johnson's masculinity, some commentators even went so far as to posit public knowledge of how Johnson contracted HIV as the necessary condition for the success of the AIDS-education efforts he promised to undertake, thereby construing that knowledge as the paramount concern, in relation to which AIDS education was unavoidably secondary. In his 8 November 1991 "news analysis," *New York Times* reporter Michael Specter asserted vaguely that "[s]ome health experts [have] said . . . that to become an effective AIDS educator, Johnson will have to discuss how he got the virus." While these "experts"—whose ilk is ubiquitous in media discourse—are never identified by Specter, and nor is the opinion that he imputes to them ever explained in the article, both the substance of the claim and the larger context in which it was registered make clear the assumptions that underlie it.

One of the most basic of those assumptions is that Johnson, like other AIDS educators who are known to be HIV positive, will serve not only as a dispenser of information, but also as an object lesson for those whom he would educate. To the extent that this is the case, his credibility is inherent in his very status as one who has actually engaged in the activity he is warning his audience against and who has consequently suffered the fate that it dreads. The maintenance of this credibility is an extremely delicate matter, however, since—and this is precisely what Specter's analysis fails to address—the specifics of the educator's risky behavior, beyond grounding his credibility, can carry such social stigma as to cause his listeners to resist identifying with him and thus neglect to take personally the warning he sounds, however much they may recognize the "truth" of his own predicament. We can imagine, for instance, the degree to which a well-heeled professional who occasionally injects amphetamines in a private home with similarly affluent friends might demur at identifying with a speaker who acknowledges having been addicted to heroin and regularly passing the needle with strangers in a rather more public "shooting gallery." In this case the educator's revelation of the specifics of his or her risky behavior would actually militate against the listener's acceptance of the HIV-prevention message, despite the fact that the latter's behavior is no less potentially dangerous than that to which the educator has "confessed." Consequently, the educator's discussion of "how he got the virus," in order to enhance rather than undermine his object-lesson function, should comprise no more than an acknowledgment of his having shared unwashed needles while injecting drugs.

Similarly, in Magic Johnson's case, which is supposed to implicate not drug use but sexual activity, an announcement from Johnson that he likely contracted

HIV through unprotected sexual intercourse with another man (a possibility that evidently did not occur to Specter and his experts), rather than enhancing his credibility, would likely occasion a general homophobic disavowal that would undoubtedly mitigate his effectiveness as an AIDS educator among a large segment of the population to which he presumably speaks. The better tack, clearly, would be for him to announce simply that he engaged in unprotected sex, and to fend off further inquiries by invoking a desire for solidarity with other HIV-affected people that would probably be undermined were he to specify more narrowly the nature of his past sexual activity. As I have already shown, Johnson's failure to undertake this strategy in the days just following his retirement indicates that he saw the preservation of his normative masculine identity, rather than the effective dissemination of HIV-prevention information, as his most immediately pressing concern; and he was supported in this evident assessment by press commentary that, while manifesting a similar anxiety about the status of his masculinity, revealed none of the putative interest in effective AIDS education that was invoked in Michael Specter's analysis. *Los Angeles Times* media critic Larry Stewart identified as a "key question" whether "Magic [had] ever had a sexual encounter with a man." "[T]hat he hadn't," Stewart ("Up-Close") asserted by way of considering the import of Johnson's *Sports Illustrated* piece, was "[w]hat needed to be said." But, of course, as the foregoing discussion makes clear, no such thing needed to be said at all (especially if it was not true)—at least not insofar as responsible AIDS education is concerned; rather, it needed to be said only to quell a rapidly developing fear that Magic Johnson might not be such a "man" after all, which in the aftermath of his 7 November announcement clearly outweighed any perceived need for accurate reporting on the epidemiology of HIV by the "mainstream" media.

One reason for the magnitude of this fear seems to stem from a noteworthy form of identification operative in relation to star athletes in general and Magic Johnson in particular. It bears remembering that in announcing his HIV infection, Johnson emphasized that, "it can happen to anybody, even me, Magic Johnson," as if in anticipation of his audience's protestation that "only gay people can get it." To the extent that Johnson's assertion functioned as an instance of AIDS education, it depended for its effect on the audience's identification with Johnson himself, whereby implied in his "it can happen to anybody, even me" was the point, "if it can happen to me, then it can happen to you." The remarkableness of this audience identification derives from the extreme unlikelihood (not to say impossibility) that most of what has "happened" to Magic Johnson in terms of athletic achievement and financial gain will happen to anyone among his fans or even his fellow players—an unlikelihood constantly underscored by media assertions of his uniqueness and simultaneously obscured by media formulations holding up his success as an objective toward which his admirers should strive. Its speciousness on that account aside, though, such identification certainly seemed at work in reactions to Johnson's announcement of his HIV seropositivity—at least with respect to the challenge his infection apparently posed to his masculine identity—in that fellow athletes and supporting figures alike appeared to feel equally besieged by the insidious threat.

An initial sign of this sense of threat consisted in the frequency with which members of the male sports community contextualized their reactions to Johnson's announcement in relation to their own heterofamilial arrangements, much as Jesse Jackson emphasized his having learned of Max Robinson's AIDS diagnosis while nestled in the bosom of his own nuclear family. Such contextualization did not by any means obscure the depth of the emotions Johnson's compatriots displayed; it did, however, serve to indicate that those emotions were properly channeled so as not to constitute either the men's homoerotic attraction specifically to Magic Johnson or a general homosexual orientation of which they might otherwise be suspected. Thus, for instance, Johnson's business manager, Lon Rosen, marveled to the *Los Angeles Times*'s Mike Downey at the composure and compassion that Johnson manifested on the day following his announcement:

> "And, all the while, he's aware of what the day's been like for me. He knows how my telephone is ringing off the hook and how anybody who can't reach *him* is probably out there trying to reach *me*. So, before the night's over, he goes up to my wife, Laurie, and asks: 'How's he holding up?' He says she should make sure I get some rest because he's worried about me.
>
> "Because he's worried about *me*." (in Downey, "This House," p. C15)

In this account, Johnson's sensitivity toward and tender concern for Rosen, which the latter is specifically noting, are directed through Rosen's wife, who becomes the vehicle of care and nurturing attention. This classic triangulation of male homosocial affection was repeated in an account by Los Angeles sportscaster Chick Hearn, who reported in an interview that Johnson "called last Thursday night [7 November], after the press conference. . . . The first thing he did was ask how Marge and I were doing. Can you imagine? That's just so typical of him" (L. Stewart, "Up-Close").[25]

Equally typical is such men's invocation of their wives, not only as filters for their personal feelings for Johnson, but in general discussion of AIDS itself, where such references have long seemed meant to ward off those connotations of the syndrome that threaten conventional masculine identity. Indeed, when *New York*

Times columnist George Vecsey (1991), in listing people with AIDS whom he had known, mentioned "an artist my wife had worked with," his reference to his wife apparently defended as much against the effeminizing effects of art as against the emasculation threatened by AIDS itself. So standard were such references by the time of Johnson's press conference that when the *New York Times* reported the announcement by a player for the Charlotte Hornets, Rex Chapman, that "he and his wife, Bridgette," planned to donate $50,000 toward research on HIV (R. Thomas, 1991), it was easy to conceive of it as offering up Bridgette Chapman as a sort of apologia for her husband's interest in the syndrome.

However suspect such heterofamilial references may be, though, they nonetheless often indicate that Johnson and his friends from the NBA enjoyed attachments that, precisely because they are based on such depth of emotion as stereotypically characterizes family connections, usefully invite a progressive reconsideration and expansion of the definition of family tie. This is evidenced less at the surface level of the friends' comments about Johnson than in the syntax that characterizes them. For instance, in an interview published two days after Johnson's retirement, teammate Byron Scott insisted:

> "The way he handled it just shows the type of person he is, but it did-
> n't make it any easier for the people who love him, who've been with
> him for so long. It doesn't make it any easier for me. It doesn't make it
> any easier for my wife. It doesn't make it any easier for (teammates)
> James (Worthy), Coop [Michael Cooper], Kareem [Abdul-Jabbar]. To
> see how he handled it shocked a lot of people—but it's not going to
> make it any easier." (in Heisler, "Scott"; parentheses added, brackets in
> original)

At first glance this statement seems much like those by Lon Rosen and Chick Hearn previously cited: on the one hand, Scott's referential shift from "the people who love [Johnson]" to the more personal "me" sets up a powerful affective bond between Scott and Johnson that, on the other hand, is conditioned and narrowed with the introduction of Scott's wife, which serves both to broaden the friendship in quantitative terms and yet to sanitize it by disrupting its homosocial aspect. With the subsequent mention of other Lakers teammates, however, the relationship being figured here further exceeds the limits of the standard hetero-familial configuration while at the same time drawing on its connotative signifi-cance for the sense of emotional depth and commitment comprised therein. In other words, for all the anxiety about masculinity that can be discerned in state-ments by Johnson's associates, those statements nevertheless make it clear that the affection among the men was intense in ways that approximate the familial. Considering the generally conflicted quality of family relations, however, it stands to reason that the friendships between Johnson and various other members of the NBA community should have been characterized not only by love and affection, but also by the fear, anger, shame, and other distressing emotions that inevitably inform our most intimate acquaintances. Thus it follows that the identification with Johnson that many of his friends manifested should have been attended by an impulse toward disavowal that could only intensify with the publication of his HIV status. Finally, since it seems to have been specifically with other African-American players that Johnson forged his closest connections, it is not surprising that it was primarily black men who enacted the especially complicated processes of identification and disavowal that marked Johnson's association with the NBA in the year following his announcement, and that, unfortunately, worked to militate against the success of the AIDS-education effort on which he fitfully embarked in November 1991.

The interrelatedness of these processes was not particularly salient through the first two months following Johnson's historic press conference, during which he pretty much remained in the good graces of public commentators. It was his relation of the extent of his sexual activity that drew the bulk of criticism—most notably from tennis star Martina Navratilova, who astutely cited the sexist and homophobic double standard at work in the general response to Johnson's revelation (see "Navratilova's View," 1991). In January 1992, however, Johnson was elected by fans to play on the Western Conference team in the February NBA All-Star game, sparking a widespread controversy about the chances of his transmitting HIV on the court should he or other players sustain cuts during play. The debate followed close on the heels of a claim by a physician for the Australian Olympic basketball team that Johnson—who had long before been slated to compete in the Barcelona Games that summer—would pose a threat to players whom he met on the floor; the physician proposed a boycott of the Olympic competition.[26] While none of Johnson's fellow players in the NBA seemed ready to forgo the All-Star game, a number of them did call for Johnson himself to withdraw from the team. Noteworthy among these was Byron Scott, whose emotional attachment to Johnson we have already remarked, and whom the *Los Angeles Times* identified as Johnson's closest friend among the Lakers (Heisler, "Controversy," p. C6). Focusing (along with teammate A. C. Green) on the technicalities of Johnson's status in the league, Scott was reported to have asked rhetorically, "If they vote (retired Laker) Kareem [Abdul-Jabbar] in, should he play? The way I see it, he is retired, and once you are retired, you are retired" (Almond, "Magic's Decision," parenthesis added); later Scott tried to clarify the reason for his hesitation, insisting, "It's definitely my concern for [Johnson's] health" (Heisler, "Controversy," p. C6). Privately, though, players and coaches cited the risk of infection as the primary factor in their resistance to Johnson's participation in the game, and they dismissed researchers' assurances that the chances of on-court transmission were infinitesimal: "That's easy for you to say. . . . You're not in huddles with all that sweat," one anonymous player reportedly responded to health officials (Almond and Heisler, 1992, p. C9). Fans, too, were drawn into the debate, with newspaper polls tracking popular opinion on whether Johnson should play (see Almond, "Magic's Decision"), and the controversy continued unabated until after Johnson's characteristically dominating performance in the contest, for which he was voted the game's most valuable player.[27]

This success in the All-Star game apparently strengthened Johnson's interest in returning to regular play in the NBA, in that the hints of a comeback that he had often let drop in pre–All-Star interviews became louder and more frequent, punctuating even his remarks to the audience at the ceremony to retire his Lakers number ("No. 32," 1992; Springer, 1992). Speculation about Johnson's plans intensified through the summer of 1992 and his stint on the victorious U.S. "Dream Team" at the Barcelona Olympics, culminating in mid-August with his announcement that he would return to the Lakers' active roster pending the approval of his physician (Araton, "With Gold in Hand"; Heisler, "Magic's Return"). Finally, on September 29, Johnson told the press and the public that he would return to professional play on a reduced schedule, forgoing games on consecutive nights (C. Brown, "Johnson, Unbowed"; Heisler, "Magic Johnson to Rejoin Lakers").

As if to preempt concern that regular appearances on the court by an HIV-infected Johnson would compromise the game's masculine identification, numerous press pieces cited his gung-ho assertion regarding the benefits of his off-season weight-training regimen: "I'm 235 pounds now [up 15 pounds from his previous weight], with more muscles than I ever dreamed of."[28] The *New York Times*'s George Vecsey ("Magic Words"), apparently trying to buy into Johnson's own enthusiasm about his plan to return to professional play, opined: "It was the right decision because the authorities say he is not harming anybody else by taking his stricken body onto the court. . . . He threatens nobody else." Yet this very assertion, which itself seemed to constitute Vecsey's protesting too much, indicated a pervasive concern that a remobilized Johnson would, in fact, pose a threat to his fellow players. That concern, which was again focused on the possibility of Johnson's shedding infected blood into other players' wounds, inevitably implicated a fear of contamination that is routinely triggered by the known presence of communicable pathogens, particularly HIV; *New York Times* sports columnist Ira Berkow ("Unspoken Concerns") claimed to have heard a number of athletes pose some standard questions off the record: "What if [Johnson] elbowed me in the mouth, or I elbowed him in the mouth, and he bled and opened a gash in me?

Would the virus be transmitted?" Indeed, Johnson claimed that it was the response to a minor wound that he sustained during preseason play in October 1992 that precipitated his decision to retire once more at the beginning of November. "[Y]ou could see the fear upon people's faces," Johnson was quoted as telling reporter Chris Wallace during an interview broadcast on ABC television's *Prime-Time Live* on November 5. "You know," he continued, "I was there at my hotel that night, I was thinking, I said between this and all the criticism, it's just too much. It's going to happen all year long. Whether I get cut or somebody else. Boom. There's that panic. There's that fear."[29] That fear obviously stemmed from the perception that players sharing the court with Johnson risked contracting the virus with which he was infected. The terms and circumstances in which that fear was discussed, however, indicated that more than the athletes' physical health was seen as being endangered, with masculinity itself still as much an object of anxiety as it had been a year earlier, when Johnson first announced his HIV seropositivity.

A key sign of this anxiety was the fact that Magic Johnson's emergence from retirement was accompanied not only by players' expressions of concern about his possibly spreading HIV, but also by renewed speculation that he had been infected in the first place through unprotected sex with a man. Within the first month after Johnson announced that he would return to professional basketball, columnist Dave Kindred (1992) of the *Sporting News* expressed doubt that Johnson had contracted HIV through heterosexual activity. In responding to Kindred's insinuations, Johnson claimed that a player in the NBA—later reported by Long Island *Newsday* to be Johnson's one-time best friend, Isiah Thomas—had been spreading rumors of Johnson's bisexuality throughout the league.[30] Thomas denied the accusation—"Why," he is reputed to have asked, "would I want to spread rumors about [Johnson's] homosexuality when I used to be part of them?" (Araton, "Bashing and Trashing")—but its very registration in the press indicates the perceived seriousness of any challenge to an athlete's heterosexual identity. After Johnson's return to the game in 1992—as in the wake of his 1991 announcement—such a challenge seemed to be constituted by the very presence of HIV itself. It was met by a strenuous effort, not necessarily to expel Johnson, as bearer of the virus, from the league (though this was one eventual—and, I will argue, inevitable—outcome), but at the very least to configure other players' relation to HIV in terms that would not compromise their normative masculinity.

The promulgation of rumors positing Johnson's homosexual activity—whatever their source—was one aspect of this effort; another was the resurrection of the familiar practice of explicitly invoking players' heterosexuality in discussions of HIV. The effectiveness of this latter strategy lay largely in its great flexibility, whereby it could be deployed not only by those opposed to Johnson's participation in league play, but also by those who ostensibly supported it. Thus, on the one hand, one team's general manager, who requested anonymity, could couch players' fears of HIV in terms of a sensitivity for their female partners' concerns that the athletes themselves were apparently too manly to acknowledge publicly: "A lot of guys won't say it, but their wives and girlfriends are concerned. Guys get teeth marks on their heads and arms all the time. They bleed. Doctors say there is no risk, but they don't really know" (Araton, "Johnson's Return," p. S11). On the other hand, after Johnson's second retirement, his Laker teammate Vlade Divac was able to register both his support for Johnson and his own heterosexual orientation in a similarly formulated statement: "I am not scared playing with Magic. My wife was not scared . . ." (Friend, "No Anger"). I have already noted that such references to wives and female partners seem calculated to ward off the connotations of HIV that threaten conventional masculine identity, and their perceived ability to do so substantially explains their general appeal. At the same time, however, these references alone could never succeed in fully vanquishing the threats to masculinity that are at issue here, both because such challenges are by their very nature perennial and constant and, more specifically, because the heterosexually identifying references made by and about players other than Johnson are identical in kind to those made by Johnson himself, whose infection and public association with HIV mitigated their capacity to defend against the virus's connotative threat.

By the time of the debate over Johnson's return to NBA play, most observers were well aware of the centrality of his wife—Earletha "Cookie" Johnson—to his public discussion of his seropositivity. Not only did Cookie Johnson appear by Magic's side during his November 1991 announcement, but, logically, her own HIV status immediately came into question, with Magic assuring listeners at the press conference that she had tested negative for antibodies to the virus (Stevenson, "Magic Johnson Ends His Career," p. B12); she was declared definitively HIV-seronegative in December 1991 (Almond, "Johnson's Wife Tests Negative"). Further, Cookie became greatly admired by a wide segment of the public after Magic's relating, in his *Sports Illustrated* article, her indignantly loyal response to his suggestion that she might rightfully leave him upon learning of his infection: ". . . before I could get most of the words out of my mouth, she slapped me upside the head and said I was crazy" (M. Johnson, "I'll Deal," p. 20; for an extended account of Cookie's response, see Randolph, 1992). Finally, Johnson emphasized that his decision to return to basketball had been made after close consultation with Cookie over the months following the 1992 All-Star game.[31] Indeed, Magic Johnson's foregrounding references to his wife in much of his public discussion of his HIV infection could easily have served as the prototype for similar invocations by other members of the NBA in the wake of his announcement, ironically making those invocations appear merely as further evidence of the strong identification with the HIV-infected Johnson that his cohorts experienced.

Earvin "Magic" Johnson announces his return to the NBA in September 1992 while Earletha "Cookie" Johnson looks on. Photo: AP/Wide World Photos.

Perhaps the most striking illustration of this point derives from a reference by Karl Malone of the Utah Jazz, not to heterosexuality or heterosexual attachment per se, but to the normative masculinity that they supposedly signify. Malone became a focus of controversy in early November 1992, when he publicly acknowledged his fears about Magic Johnson's return to the basketball court, thus rending the veil of anonymity that had previously characterized press reports of player concern. In a conversation with the *New York Times*'s Harvey Araton ("Johnson's Return," p. S1), Malone spoke of the danger he felt in playing against Johnson: "Look at this, scabs and cuts all over me. . . . I get these every night, every game. They can't tell you that you're not at risk, and you can't tell me there's one guy in the N.B.A. who hasn't thought about it." On the day following the publication of Araton's article, Johnson announced his second retirement from the NBA, fueling widespread speculation about the role of Malone's comments in the decision.[32] So intense and long-lasting was the discussion of this matter that Malone himself eventually expressed regret over not having raised the issue privately with Johnson before going on record; had he been given the chance to do it over again, Malone said, "I would still have made the same statement, but I would have talked to him first. . . . [W]hen the dust settles . . . , I'll make the call but no one will know about it. I'll talk to him about it like a man" (Araton, "Malone Admits Error"). In thus registering his intention to confront Johnson personally with his concerns, Malone rhetorically distinguished himself from those players who would discuss their fears only under cover of anonymity, projecting a demeanor of forthrightness that he was apparently eager for observers to apprehend as intrepid "manliness." This projection, however, like players' pointed references to their female partners, closely approximated the mode of self-presentation used by Johnson himself the year before, when he proposed that his public discussion of his extensive sexual activity constituted his "being a man" at a critical juncture. Indeed, the parallel between Malone and Johnson was particularly strong, in that not only did they both posit the mere verbal acknowledgment of their problematical positions as the very essence of their masculinity, but in doing so, they obscured the existence of earlier crucial moments at which similarly forthright action might have prevented their problems from developing in the first place. After all, either Johnson's having taken safer-sex precautions or Malone's having raised his concerns in a forum for proper discussion might have been construed as alternative instantiations of the manfulness they were both so anxious to assert after the fact. As it is, the versions of masculinity that the two athletes did put forth—however limited and inefficacious they might have been—were so nearly identical as to cause us inevitably to wonder what really distinguished each man from the other at the moment of Malone's intervention.

It is precisely this possible lack of differentiation between Johnson and his NBA associates that I am suggesting generated intense anxiety once his HIV infection became public knowledge. Until that point, players in the NBA must have been as eager to be like Magic Johnson as the mother on the Southside of Chicago was for her children to "speak like" Max Robinson, given Johnson's widely acknowledged prowess on the court. Upon revealing his HIV seropositivity, however, Johnson became associated, willy-nilly, with the taint of male homosexuality and consequent inadequate masculinity that HIV has always connoted in the U.S. context, with the result that any identification with him or approximation to his status became a deeply problematic and conflictual prospect for those men who had, to adapt Byron Scott's phrase, "been with him for so long." Indeed, the near-familial attachment between Johnson and other African-American players such as Scott and Isiah Thomas would, as I have already suggested, constitute the logical site at which tensions generated by Johnson's HIV status would be manifested and played out, with the catalytic statements by Karl Malone—to whom Johnson was not so close—representing a sort of culmination in this crisis of black male mutual identification.

In the end, of course, the most significant difference between Johnson and Malone (as well as other players in the NBA) in the fall of 1992 was that the former was known to be infected with HIV while the latter was not. Johnson's statements to the media suggested that the emotional pressures that bore down on him due to this fact were so intense as to necessitate his second retirement from pro basketball despite researchers' continued assertion of the needlessness of this move (see Altman, 1992; Heisler, "Magic Johnson Retires," p. A1; Martinez, 1992, p. B9). Consequently, Johnson shed the dubious distinction of being the only active player in the NBA known to be HIV positive, with the effect that he became more markedly distinguished from his peers in the league by very virtue of the fact that he was now no longer in it. In other words, he whose masculinity had been laid open to question through his infection with HIV became disassociated from the primary context in which he had heretofore derived his indisputable masculine identification; as a result, the constituents of that context—namely, players in the NBA—became free once again of the demasculinizing taint that HIV comprises. These are the key sociocultural facts in the story of Magic Johnson's second withdrawal from professional basketball, in which sociocultural effects seem to have loomed much larger and played a much greater role than medical and scientific evidence (granting the admittedly problematic aspects of the latter), as they have throughout the AIDS epidemic. One thing that epidemic has reminded us, however (as though such reminding should have been necessary), is that sociocultural factors themselves figure heavily in and have a profound effect on the medical phenomena that we still too foolishly look to the "natural" sciences to control and combat. That scientific research has produced so few weapons in the fight against HIV is the primary reason that sociocultural intervention—specifically the halting of risky practices and the changing of behaviors—has become our primary tool. Such intervention, though, is an extremely delicate undertaking, especially insofar as behavior is closely associated with identity, and identity is experienced as precious, hard-won, and in need of constant defense. This is particularly the case for masculine identity as it is conceived and lived throughout U.S. culture, and it is precisely masculine identity that is seen as most threatened not only by HIV, but, both consequently and paradoxically, by the sexual-behavioral changes that are essential to the effort to stem its spread.

For all Magic Johnson's evident reluctance to become implicated in the questions regarding normative masculinity that societal response to HIV has forcibly raised—and it is important to note that in manifesting such reluctance,

Johnson is certainly no different from the vast majority of heterosexual men who have gone so far as to give the issue conscious thought[33]—he has nonetheless kept good on his pledge to fight AIDS by trying to effect behavioral change among key segments of the population. The evidence available so far suggests that the predominant hindrances to his conscious efforts in this area (as opposed to the unintended lessons that I have suggested he conveyed through his statements at the time of his initial retirement) have derived not from his own ignorance and prejudice about the social ramifications of HIV, but from the same official checks on the promulgation of AIDS-educational materials that have stymied so many others in the fight against HIV.[34] Always accompanying this discernible barrier, however, is one less vividly evidenced in the public record (though it can easily be teased out from between the official lines in the manner that I have undertaken here, by way of identifying and analyzing it), and that is the attitudinal block against crucial AIDS-prevention information that frequently characterizes those who strongly disavow the populations that have been most visibly affected by HIV. A major impetus for such disavowal is that a defining characteristic of one of those populations—namely, gay men—is that its members are widely seen precisely as *not men*. Indeed, it was the extension of this judgment to himself that Magic Johnson was striving desperately to prevent by so insistently and repeatedly asserting his heterosexuality in the days following his November 1991 press conference. And it was, as I have suggested, the possibility that such a judgment might be extended—through the logic of guilty association—to other players in the NBA that was undercut with Johnson's second retirement in November 1992.

With the distinction between Johnson and other members of the NBA having been underscored by his more than three-year absence from the league, one now wonders whether his return to that veritable citadel of masculinity will reaffirm for the public Johnson's conventional masculine identity, which his infection with HIV evidently put into question. If so, perhaps the HIV-prevention information that he offers will be that much more readily received by a population intensely concerned with safeguarding its own masculine identification against any possible threat—specifically, the young African-American males whom Johnson putatively most hopes to reach. Regardless, both the inevitability and the uncertainty of this proposition indicate how intractable and dangerously self-fulfilling is the logic of proof that governs dominant conceptions of masculine identity in U.S. culture, which I would argue are particularly crippling for populations of color.

It will require an immense amount of critical work—some of which I take up in the following chapters of this book—to outline the specifics of those crippling effects as well as to indicate the serendipitously productive ways in which they have sometimes been negotiated. With respect to combating AIDS among black men, however, the critical intervention must extend to an immediate and uncompromising literal revision of everything we "know" about masculine identity, in order to ensure that what we know about HIV can be effectively communicated throughout the population. Otherwise, like so many others engaged in the fight against AIDS, Magic Johnson will find that, for all the import of his message and the energy with which he propounds it, he is merely preaching to the converted or—not worse, but sadder—talking to himself.

$$\boxed{2}$$

NATIONALISM
AND SOCIAL DIVISION
IN BLACK ARTS POETRY
OF THE 1960s

Black Rhetoric and the Nationalist Call

Who is being spoken to, and how, is a key issue in the material to which I now
turn, as is the sort of dynamic of expulsion that characterized Magic Johnson's
1992 experiences in the NBA. At the same time, however, both of these issues signify differently in Johnson's situation—where they refer primarily to masculine
identification—than they do in the context I am now considering, in which masculinity gives way to—and simultaneously grounds—black identity. I have
already alluded to this process in my brief consideration of Haki Madhubuti's
"Don't Cry, Scream" (1969); and it is perfectly emblematized in Nikki Giovanni's
contemporaneous exhortation, "Learn to kill niggers / Learn to be Black men"
("True Import," p. 319), in which the accession to manhood that Giovanni
demands coincides with the achievement of "Blackness" that she extols, both
these developments deriving from the execution of cathartic violence against
those who are yet "niggers" (according to a strict reading of the first line's syntax),

by those very "niggers," who will thus emerge as "black men" (if we imagine a comma before "niggers" that renders it in the vocative case). Insofar as black identity thus depends upon identification specifically *as man,* however, then blackness will partake of the very uncertainty, tentativeness, and burden of proof that we have already seen to characterize conventional masculinity—a fact that is suggested by the nature of the distinction between "niggers" and "black men" that Giovanni invokes in the first place.

This chapter undertakes to explicate the way that distinction operates at a key moment in African-American cultural history—a moment for which the perfect epigraph might well be the one used by an influential literary figure to introduce a defining document in African-American poetics. Dudley Randall's anthology, *The Black Poets,* published in 1971, is significant not so much for the texts it provides of folk verse and literary poetry from the mid-eighteenth through the early twentieth centuries as for its canonization of poetry from the contemporaneous Black Arts movement. The concluding (and by far the longest) section of Randall's anthology is titled "The Nineteen Sixties," and it is prefaced by the short poem "SOS" by Imamu Amiri Baraka (LeRoi Jones), which is printed not in the main text but on the title page for the section:

> Calling black people
> Calling all black people, man woman child
> Wherever you are, calling you, urgent, come in
> Black People, come in, wherever you are, urgent, calling you, calling
>   all black people
> calling all black people, come in, black people, come on in. (p. 181)

Given the epigraphic function that Randall confers on it, we can reasonably conclude that Baraka's "SOS" is somehow emblematic of the poetic project of many young black writers of the late 1960s, and it is not particularly difficult to identify exactly in what this emblematic quality might consist. We know, after all, that radical black intellectual activism of the late 1960s was characterized by a drive for nationalistic unity among people of African descent. As Larry Neal put it in his defining essay of 1968, "The Black Arts Movement":

> Black Art is the aesthetic and spiritual sister of the Black Power concept. . . . The Black Arts and the Black Power concept both relate broadly to the Afro-American's desire for self-determination and nationhood. Both concepts are nationalistic. One is concerned with the relationship between art and politics; the other with the art of politics. (p. 272)

Addison Gayle also embraced the nationalist impulse in his conception of the movement, outlined in his 1971 introduction to *The Black Aesthetic.* According to Gayle, "The Black Aesthetic . . . is a corrective—a means of helping black people out of the polluted mainstream of Americanism" (p. xxiii). And in 1973, Stephen Henderson elaborated the development of this impulse through the late 1960s: "The poetry of the sixties is informed and unified by the new consciousness of Blackness . . . [, which has] shifted from Civil Rights to Black Power to Black Nationalism to Revolutionary Pan-Africanism . . ." (p. 183). Thus did three of the Black Aesthetic's most prominent theorists conceive the importance of nationalist unity to the Black Arts movement.[1] It probably goes without saying that such a nationalist impulse, having once been manifested, can develop in any number of different directions. For the sake of the present analysis, however, we can suspend consideration of this important point while we confirm the existence of that impulse, in however rudimentary a form, in Baraka's poem.

In the introduction to their authoritative anthology, *Black Nationalism in America* (1970), John Bracey, Jr., August Meier, and Elliott Rudwick identify as the basis of black nationalist thought "[t]he concept of racial solidarity," which, they assert, "is essential to all forms of black nationalism" (p. xxvi). It is precisely this fundamental impulse to racial solidarity that is manifested in Baraka's "SOS." Considered with respect to nationalism, the political import of the poem inheres not in the stridency and exigency of its appeal, but rather in its breadth, in the fact that Baraka's call apparently embraces all members of the African diaspora, as it is directed explicitly and repeatedly to "*all* black people," thereby invoking a political Pan-Africanism posited as characteristic of the Black Arts project. Moreover, the enjambment of the last two lines and their modification of the injunction definitively transform the SOS from a mere distress signal into a general summons for assembly. What is striking about Baraka's poem, however, is not that it "calls" black people in this nationalistic way but that this is *all* it does; the objective for which it assembles the black populace is not specified in the piece itself, a fact I take to indicate fundamental difficulties in the nationalist agenda of the Black Arts poets, as will soon become clear.

In the meantime, I think it is useful to consider Baraka's "SOS" as a synecdoche for all of his poetic output of the 1960s, which constituted a challenge to other African-American poets to take up the nationalist ethic he espoused. As the source of this influential call, Baraka can certainly be seen as the founder of the Black Aesthetic of the 1960s, and "SOS" as representative of the standard to which his fellow poets rallied. "SOS" is part of Baraka's collection *Black Art,* comprising poems written in 1965 and 1966, and published, along with two other collections, in the volume *Black Magic: Poetry, 1961–1967* (1969). Its message was subsequently engaged by other black writers from different generations and disparate backgrounds. For instance, in her 1972 autobiography, *Report from Part One,* Gwendolyn Brooks, who built her reputation on her expertly crafted lyrics of the 1940s and 1950s, made Baraka's enterprise her own as she described her new poetic mission in the early 1970s:

> My aim, in my next future, is to write poems that will somehow suc-
> cessfully "call" (see Imamu Baraka's "SOS") all black people: black
> people in taverns, black people in alleys, black people in gutters,
> schools, offices, factories, prisons, the consulate; I wish to reach black
> people in pulpits, black people in mines, on farms, on thrones[.]
> (p. 183)

Sonia Sanchez, on the other hand, in her 1969 poem, "blk/rhetoric," invoked Baraka's language to question what might happen after the calling had been done:

> who's gonna make all
> that beautiful blk/rhetoric
> mean something.
>   like
> i mean
>   who's gonna take
> the words
>   blk/is/beautiful
> and make more of it
> than blk/capitalism.
>   u dig?
>   i mean
>   like who's gonna
> take all the young/long/haired/
> natural/brothers and sisters
> and let them
>   grow till
>   all that is
> imp't is them
>   selves
>   moving in straight/
> revolutionary/lines/toward the enemy
> (and we know who that is)
>   like.   man.

who's gonna give our young
blk people new heros
(instead of catch/phrases)
(instead of cad/ill/acs)
(instead of pimps)
(instead of white/whores)
(instead of drugs)
(instead of new/dances)
(instead of chit/ter/lings)
(instead of a 35¢ bottle of
                    ripple)
(instead of quick/fucks
   in the hall/way of
              white/america's
                       mind)
like. this. is an S. O. S.
me. calling. . . .
            calling. . . .
                    some/one.
      pleasereplysoon.

Sanchez's call—prefaced as it is by her urgent question, and attended by the entreaty to her listeners in the final line—is more pleading than Baraka's, which is unabashedly imperative. I would suggest that the uncertainty that characterizes Sanchez's poem is the inevitable affective result of writing beyond the ending of Baraka's "SOS," which it seems to me is what "blk/rhetoric" does. By calling into question what will ensue among the black collectivity after it has heeded the general call—succumbed to the rhetoric, as it were—Sanchez points to the problematic nature of the black nationalist project that characterizes Black Arts poetry.

What remains certain, in Sanchez's rendering—so certain that it need not be stated explicitly—is the identity of the "enemy" against whom the assembled black troops must struggle. While Sanchez's elliptical reference might appear as somewhat ambiguous at this point, especially after the emergence in the early and mid-1970s of a strong black feminist movement that arrayed itself against racism *and* sexism, it seems clear enough that in the context of the 1969 Black Arts movement the enemy was most certainly the white "establishment." But this is the *only* thing that is "known" in Sanchez's poem, and while the identification of a generalized white foe is a central strategy in the Black Arts movement's effort to galvanize the black populace, here it provides a hedge against the overall uncertainty that characterizes the rest of the poem—a definitive core on which the crucial questions about the efficacy of nationalist rhetoric can center and thus themselves still be recognizable as nationalist discourse.

With its counterbalancing of fundamental inquiries about the future of the black nationalist enterprise by recourse to the trope of the white enemy, Sanchez's "blk/rhetoric" verges on the problematic that I take to be constitutive of the Black Arts project. Insofar as that project is nationalistic in character, then its primary objective and continual challenge will be not to identify the external entity against which the black masses are distinguished—this is easy enough to do—but rather to negotiate division within the black population itself. I specifically invoke *negotiation* here and not, for instance, *resolution* because I want to claim that the response of Black Arts nationalism to social division within the black populace is not to strive to overcome it, but rather repeatedly to articulate it in the name of black consciousness.[2]

Antiwhite Sentiment and the Black Audience

It has been widely held that the fundamental characteristic of Black Arts poetry is its virulent antiwhite rhetoric. For instance, as Houston Baker (1988, p. 161) has noted, the influential black critic J. Saunders Redding disparaged the Black Aesthetic as representative of a discourse of "hate," a "naive racism in reverse." And it is true that Baraka himself became known for a generalized antiwhite sentiment, often manifested in highly particularized ethnic and religious slurs, especially anti-Semitic ones. His "Black Art" (1966, 1979) provides an exemplary litany, calling for

> ... [p]oems that wrestle cops into alleys
> and take their weapons leaving them dead
> with tongues pulled out and sent to Ireland. Knockoff
> poems for dope selling wops or slick halfwhite
> politicians Airplane poems ...
> ... Setting fire and death to
> whities ass. Look at the Liberal
> Spokesman for the jews clutch his throat
> & puke himself into eternity ...
> ... Another bad poem cracking
> steel knuckles in a jewlady's mouth[.] (p. 224)

"Black People!" calls for the "smashing [of] jellywhite faces. We must make our own / World, man, our own world, and we can not do this unless the white man / is dead. Let's get together and killhim [*sic*] . . ." (pp. 226–27). Similarly, Nikki Giovanni, in the poem to which I have already referred (and to which I shall turn again soon), inquires urgently of the "nigger" she addresses, "Can you kill . . . / . . . Can you poison . . . / . . . Can you piss on a blond head / Can you cut it off . . . / . . . Can you kill a white man" ("True Import," p. 318).

While the affective power of such antiwhite sentiment in much of the poetry certainly cannot be denied, it seems to me that the drama of interracial strife that this rhetoric represents also serves to further another objective of Black Arts poetry—the establishment of *intra*racial distinctions that themselves serve to solidify the meaning of the Black Aesthetic. We can clarify this point through reference to a few poems that, while their authors may have since taken disparate poetic paths, function as archetypal Black Arts works: Baraka's "Poem for Half White College Students"; Giovanni's "The True Import of Present Dialogue: Black vs. Negro"; "Move Un-Noticed to Be Noticed: A Nationhood Poem," by Haki Madhubuti (Don L. Lee); Sanchez's "chant for young / brothas & sistuhs"; and "Okay 'Negroes,'" by June Jordan. These five poems (which are presented in their entirety in this book's appendix) have been widely anthologized as exemplary of the Black Arts project, yet I would argue that they are exemplary not because they are *representative* of the poetics deployed in most Black Arts productions, but rather because they expose the logic of the Black Arts ethic that governs work from the movement generally, though its operation is carefully suppressed in most of that material.

These pieces certainly present disparaging references to white society—Jordan's "male white mammy," Sanchez's rendering of the heroin high, Baraka's invocation of film celebrities as representative of the shallowness of Euro-American culture—all of which fit neatly into characterizations of Black Arts poetry as essentially antiwhite. But while these works might engage conceptions of white America as a negative force, the rhetoric of the pieces is not addressed—not directly, at any rate—to the white society that is the ostensible target of their wrath. Rather, all the poems employ the second-person pronoun *you* in ways that are clearly meant to conjure a specifically black addressee, and thus to give the impression that the poetic works themselves are meant for consumption by a specifically black audience. In other words, the rhetoric of Black Arts poetry, in conjunction with the sociopolitical context in which it is produced, works a twist on John Stuart Mill's (1833, 1979, p. 1055) proclamation that "poetry is overheard," as it seems to effect a split in the audience for the work. Because of the way the poetry uses direct address and thus invites us to conflate addressee and audience, it appears that the material is meant to be *heard* by blacks, and *over-*

heard by whites, who would respond fearfully to the threat of mayhem it embodies. I think that this is appearance only, however, and it will be a secondary effect of my argument to demonstrate that, while Black Arts poetry very likely does depend for its power on the division of its audience along racial lines, it achieves its maximum impact in a context in which it is understood as being *heard* directly by whites, and *over*heard by blacks.

Clarification of this last point is forthcoming. In the meantime, it is necessary to acknowledge the substantial polemical effect that is achieved through the *presentation* of Black Arts poetry as meant for black ears only, for it is this presentation that commentators have seized on in characterizing the Black Arts movement as representing a completely Afrocentric impulse. As Gayle, for instance, put it in his introduction to *The Black Aesthetic* (1971, pp. xxi–xxii), the black artist of the 1960s "has given up the futile practice of speaking to whites, and has begun to speak to his brothers. . . . to point out to black people the true extent of the control exercised upon them by the American society. . . ." Gayle's claim is, in itself, not earth-shaking; it typifies contemporary conceptions of the Black Arts movement's significance in African-American cultural history. What *is* notable is that Gayle's statement, in positing the Black Arts strategy as historically unique, established itself as a historical repetition, insofar as, nearly fifty years before, a black theorist of the Harlem Renaissance made a very similar claim about the nature of that movement. In his 1925 article on the contemporary flowering of African-American art, "Negro Youth Speaks," Alain Locke insisted that "[o]ur poets have now stopped speaking for the Negro—they speak as Negroes. Where formerly they spoke to others and tried to interpret, they now speak to their own and try to express" (p. 18). The full irony of this repetition lies in the fact that it was precisely on the basis of the perceived failure of the Harlem Renaissance to engage African-American interests that Black Arts theoreticians found fault with the earlier movement. Larry Neal (1968, p. 290) specifically charged that the Harlem Renaissance "failed" in that "[i]t did not address itself to the mythology and the life-styles of the Black community." Clearly, there is an anxiety of influence operative here, manifested in the powerful need among the Black Aestheticians to disassociate themselves from the Harlem Renaissance; and this disassociation would evidently be achieved through the later movement's presumedly uniquely effective manner of addressing itself to the interests of black people. By examining this strategy, we can see more clearly both how social division within the black community is fundamentally constitutive of Black Arts nationalism and, relatedly, why it *is* so difficult for the Black Arts movement to postulate concrete action beyond "black rhetoric," to project beyond the "call" manifested in Baraka's "SOS."

Blacker Than Thou

What is most striking about the way the poems under consideration—which I have suggested distill the logic of the Black Arts project—address themselves to the black community is their insistent use of the second-person pronoun. This aspect of the poetry is notable not only because it indicates both the Black Arts poets' keen awareness of issues of audience and their desire to appear to engage their audience directly (both of which I have already alluded to), but because the *you* references also—and paradoxically, given the Black Aesthetic's nation-building agenda—represent the implication of intraracial division within the Black Aesthetic's poetic strategy. It is clear, of course, that the use of the second-person pronoun of whatever number implies less inclusiveness than would, say, the use of the first-person plural, *we*. What remains to be explored is exactly on what this apparent exclusivity—this implicit social division—is founded, both grammatically and historically, in order for us to grasp more fully the significance of Black Arts poetics.

Theoretical work in the grammar of the linguistic "shifter"—of which pronouns are one type—has illuminated the peculiar character of the second-person singular pronoun, *you,* and its difference from *he, she,* or any other "third-person" entity. The pertinent findings of this work can be put fairly simply: Because it conjures an addressee to whom an iteration is directed, the invocation of *you* also necessarily implies a producing *source* of that iteration—namely, an *I*—against which *you* itself is defined; as linguist Emile Benveniste (1971, p. 201) has put it, *you* constitutes specifically and emphatically "the non-*I* person." And, because *you* thus exists in a contrastive relationship with *I,* any assertion made about *you* implies a converse characterization of *I*. Indeed, a statement about *you* can actually more effectively limn the traits of an iterating *I* than can a bona fide first-person proclamation since, to adduce one of the lessons of post-structuralist theory, the latter always implicates a disjuncture between the *I* who *issues* it and the *I* that is *represented in* it: in the Lacanian-influenced formulation of Antony Easthope (1983, p. 44), "the 'I' as represented in discourse . . . is always sliding away from the 'I' doing the speaking," rendering impossible any stably accurate first-person characterization.

Numerous commentators have discussed the ramifications of such post-structuralist–informed analysis for socially marginalized groups, whose political agendas have often been considered as based on a primary need to forge stable identities in the first place, and not on the deconstruction of such identity.[3] Certainly, the Black Arts movement can easily be understood as an attempt to establish a positive African-American subjectivity—based on nationalist ideals—in the face of major sociopolitical impediments to its construction. But post-structuralism's calling into question the unitary stability of the subjective *I* does not, I think, *prohibit* the Black Aesthetic's construction of a powerful black nationalist subject; it merely stipulates that such construction is possible only from a position externally and obliquely situated with respect to the discursive *I*. In that case, however—and in light of the analysis just presented—it is impossible for the Black Arts work examined here to posit an effective black nationalist *collectivity*. This is because the strategy necessarily deployed by Black Arts poetry to establish a strong black nationalist subject—and through which it derives its meaning and power—is founded on the oppositional logic that governs the pronominal language characteristic of the work. That opposition is thematized in the poetry, not in terms of the "us versus them" dichotomy that we might expect, however, with *us* representing blacks and *them* whites; rather, it is played out along the inherent opposition between *I* and *you,* both of these terms deriving their referents from within the collectivity of black subjects.

Thus the project of Black Arts poetry can be understood as the establishment of black nationalist subjectivity—the forcible fixing of the identity of the "speaking" *I*—by delineating it against the "non-*I* person," the *you* whose identity is clearly predicated in the poems we are considering. So the *you* in Baraka's "Poem for Half White College Students" is the African American who identifies with the Euro-American celebrity, against which the speaking *I* of the poem is implicitly contrasted. In Giovanni's and Lee's poems, *you* represents the Negro subject whose sense of self-worth and racial pride has yet to be proven. In Sanchez's "chant," *you* is the black junkie who finds solace in the "wite" high of heroin, which is clearly associated with Euro-American corruption. And in June Jordan's "Okay 'Negroes,'" *you* is the African American who has not yet developed an understanding of the raciopolitical forces that impinge upon black subjectivity. Clearly, I oversimplify to the extent that the referent of any given *you* might well vary even within a single poem. But my point is that because, in spite of these shifts, the second person is much more readily identified than the speaking *I* for any utterance, any *you* that these Black Arts poets invoke can function as a negative foil against which the implicit *I* who speaks the poem can be distinguished as a politically aware, racially conscious black nationalist subject. It is this intraracial division on which the Black Arts project is founded, and not any sense of inclusiveness with respect to the African-American community that we might discern in Baraka's "SOS," which fact greatly problematizes the possibility of effective communal action after the issuance of Baraka's call.[4]

Indeed, once we have clarified the *I–you* division that underlies the Black Arts concept of African-American community, we can better understand the intraracial division that is implicit in movement references to the "black" subject itself. If it appears to us that Baraka's "SOS" embraces all members of the black diaspora, this is only because we are forgetting something that Lee's poem, on the other hand, usefully reminds us—that the designation *black,* from the middle 1960s through the early 1970s, represented an emergent identification among nationalist activists and intellectuals, and not a generic nomenclature by which any person of African descent might be referenced. Consequently, if Baraka is calling "all black people," he is already calling only those African Americans whose political consciousness is sufficiently developed for them to subscribe to the designation *black* in the first place. All others—designated by *you* in the poems that utilize the pronominal rhetoric—will be considered as *negroes,* as in the titles of Giovanni's and Jordan's poems—a term that is pointedly transmuted into *niggers* in Giovanni's text.

Anxious Identities and Divisional Logic

Having detailed these poems' method for authorizing their own black nationalist rhetoric, we must now consider how to account for it, since the intraracial division that it comprises evidently runs counter to the solidarity we have taken to found black nationalism. Undoubtedly, a number of specific, local contingencies contributed to the development of the Black Arts movement's agenda and practice. At the same time, it is possible, within the analytical context set up here, to identify a key concern that informed the enactment of its signal strategies. We have already noted that whatever political solidarity characterized the Black Arts movement did not necessarily bind it to its historical precursor, the Harlem Renaissance, whose cultural politics Black Aestheticians repudiated even as they recapitulated its rhetoric. That repudiation, as instanced in the writings by Larry Neal that we have examined, was based specifically on the sense that Harlem Renaissance artistic practice was fundamentally estranged from the concerns of the black community—that "[i]t failed . . . ," in Neal's (1968, p. 290) words, "to link itself concretely to the struggles of that community. . . ." By apparent contrast, rootedness in the day-to-day exigencies of black life was regularly invoked as a prime characteristic of Black Arts practice, with Baraka ("The Black Aesthetic," p. 5), for instance, coining alternative etymologies and manipulating typography to assert the essential groundedness of the Black Aesthetic: "What does aesthetic mean? A theory in the ether. Shdn't it mean for us Feelings about reality! . . . About REality." Thus commitment to black empowerment was conceived specifically in terms of engagement with the "hard facts" of African-American existence (to invoke a term with which Baraka was later to title a collection of his poems; see *Selected Poetry,* 1979, pp. 235–73), as opposed to the rather more "ethereal" concerns that putatively occupied the writers of the Harlem Renaissance.

And yet, four years prior to the 1969 publication of his "Black Aesthetic" essay, Baraka had already characterized as problematically *disengaged* from "reality" not the "Literary Negroes" he excoriated in that later piece (p. 6), but the entire class of *white men*, who, he charged, "devote their energies to the nonphysical, the nonrealistic," thereby becoming "estranged from" the physical and the real—evidently conceived here as one and the same (1965, 1966, p. 216). Anticipating the "Primeval Mitosis" analysis of Eldridge Cleaver's *Soul on Ice*, Baraka posited this estrangement not only as the critical and debilitating "alienation" frequently invoked by Euro-American intellectuals themselves (1965, 1966, p. 218), but specifically in terms of a failed masculinity the recognized horror of which powered the shock effect of his opening lines: "Most American white men are trained to be fags. For this reason it is no wonder their faces are weak and blank, left without the hurt that reality makes. . . . That red flush, those silk blue faggot eyes" (1965, 1966, p. 216). Given this categorical invalidation of Euro-American manhood by virtue of a perceived disengagement from the pressing demands of the physical world that supposedly constitute "real life," the comparable disengagement that Black Aestheticians discerned in the Harlem Renaissance (for instance) would indicate not only an inadequately developed black consciousness (particularly insofar as that disengagement would apparently constitute the adoption of a recognizably white social disposition), but a similarly inadequate masculinity that is coextensive with it. (This analysis is especially plausible with respect to the Harlem Renaissance itself, in light of the widely recognized—though generally only coyly acknowledged—homosexual orientation of many of its key male figures, including Countee Cullen, Wallace Thurman, and Alain Locke himself. See Rampersad, 1986, pp. 66–71, 165.) This logic allowed for Black Arts judgments of insufficient racial identification to be figured specifically in terms of a failed manhood for which homosexuality, as always, was the primary signifier. Baraka's scathing "CIVIL RIGHTS POEM" is a quintessential case in point:

> Roywilkins is an eternal faggot
> His spirit is a faggot
> his projection
> and image, this is
> to say, that if i ever see roywilkins
> on the sidewalks
> imonna
> stick half my sandal
> up his
> ass

Indeed, so well understood was the identification between inadequacies of man-hood and black consciousness in the Black Arts context that this poem needed never render explicit the grounds for its judgment of NAACP leader Roy Wilkins, for the perceived racial-political moderation of both him and his organization clearly bespoke his unforgivable "faggotry."

The Black Aestheticians' development of such a potent gender-political rhetoric through which to condemn perceived failures of black consciousness is significant for my analysis here for at least two reasons: First, it can clearly be seen as establishing a circular dynamic whereby Black Arts writers' own need not to be deemed racially effeminate fueled the ever-spiraling intensity of their repudiative formulations, including the divisional *I–you* constructions that we have exam-ined;[5] second, it indicates the Black Aestheticians' preexistent anxiety regarding their own possible estrangement from the very demands of everyday black life that they repeatedly invoked as founding their practice. If the routine figuration of such estrangement as a voluntary and shameful effeminization was a powerful signal practice in Black Arts poetics, this may well be because the estrangement itself was experienced as the unavoidable effect of inexorable social processes—specifically, the attenuation of the Black Aestheticians' *organic* connection to the life of the folk (to invoke the Gramscian concept) by virtue of their increasing engagement with the *traditional* (Euro-American) categories of intellectual endeavor, through which they largely and inevitably developed their public pro-files in the first place. The degree to which such *ressentiment* characterized Black Arts writers' relation to their undertakings in literature, say, or in the academy is suggested (for instance) by A. B. Spellman's arguably disingenuous condemnation of the emergent black-studies movement of the late 1960s and early 1970s as unacceptably "bourgie" (cited in Emanuel, 1971, p. 220). And the danger that the Black Aestheticians, in particular, might be accused of an intellectualized disen-gagement from concrete reality was evidenced as early as 1966, with Stokely Carmichael's highly charged proclamation: "We have to say, 'Don't play jive and start writing poems after Malcolm is shot.' We have to move from the point where the man left off and stop writing poems" (p. 472). Such suspicion regarding black intellectualism accounts for the will to linguistic performativity that characterizes Black Arts rhetoric—the anxious insistence that Black Arts verse constitutes sub-stantive intervention in "real-world" affairs. Indeed, Baraka ("The Black Aes-thetic," p. 6) tried mightily to disassociate the Black Arts movement from the inef-fectuality connoted by "poetry": "Poetry is jingling lace without *purpose*. . . . We are 'poets' because someone has used that word to describe us. What we are our children will have to define. We are creators and destroyers-firemakers, Bomb throwers and takers of heads"; and the poetry itself often seeks to instate the distinction, as when Nikki Giovanni considers her inability to produce a "tree poem" or a "sky poem" in "For Saundra" (1969, 1971, p. 322):

> so i thought again
> and it occurred to me
> maybe i shouldn't write
> at all
> but clean my gun
> and check my kerosene supply
>
> perhaps these are not poetic
> times
> at all

Giovanni herself provides a good indication, not only of the extent of the Black Arts poets' concern about their relation to the black "community," but of the degree to which that concern was figured in terms of an anxiety regarding masculine potency. For while it is a truism that discussion of intraracial gender politics was generally suppressed in the Black Power context, indicating women's contested position within the movement,[6] Giovanni's work (as contrasted with that of Sanchez and Jordan, for instance) so insistently invokes a phallic standard of political engagement (the demand for avenging "Black men" in "True Import"; the reference to Richard Nixon as "no-Dick" in "For Saundra") as to suggest that no other term was available—not even to her who, in 1968, explicitly referenced herself as a "black female poet" ("My Poem," 1971, p. 319).

On the other hand, just beneath what appears as the all-too-uniformly status-anxious surface of the Black Arts poetic lurks a more profound wariness regarding the significance of the movement's own invocations—a wariness rendered explicit by Sonia Sanchez's worry that black-power rhetoric will lead only to "blk/capitalism." It seems to me that it is the threatening unpredictability of exactly what *will* issue from the essentially contradictory nationalist urge that accounts for Baraka's decision not to project beyond the call manifested in "SOS," with the result that the poem is driven by its first-order nationalist impulse rather than dissipated in the ambivalence with which that impulse would inevitably be followed up.

Ambivalence can have no place, after all, in the prosecution of such a revolutionary political program as the Black Aesthetic was supposed to represent. Indeed, the need to quell potential ambivalence might well explain the violent rhetoric that so much of the work employs, the extreme nature of which seems meant as much to desensitize black audiences to the contradictions of nationalist logic as to effect fantasmatically the white enemy's demise. At the same time, it is the fantasy of linguistic performativity apparently informing these invocations of violence that suggests that Black Arts poetry, as I have already proposed, is intended to be *heard* by whites and *over*heard by blacks. For according to this fantasy, not only would to be *heard* be to annihilate one's oppressors, but to be *over*heard would be to indicate to one's peers just how righteous, how nationalistic, how potently Black one is, in contradistinction to those very peers, who are figured as the direct addressee of the Black Arts works. And insofar as that Blackness is conceived in anxiously masculine terms, then the pronominal construct through which it is registered suggests, "*I* am a man, but *you* . . . ?"

All of which is to say that Black Arts rhetoric, whose ostensible objective is to promote racial solidarity, actually engenders a *division* among blacks that is paradoxically necessary to the nationalist project—a division that, furthermore, is predicated on a profoundly problematic masculinist ethic. While Black Arts politics—the most recent fully theorized version of African-American nationalism—is now a quarter-century old, its continuing import can be discerned in a range of rather more current phenomena, from the interest in accounts of the Black Power era by such authors as Elaine Brown, David Hilliard, and Hugh Pearson, to Afrocentric educational movements and certain aspects of hip-hop culture. It is as crucial as ever, then, to offer a cogent critique of black masculinism and the nationalist impulse. The point, of course, as is already clear, is not to sacrifice the one for the other—a practical impossibility in any event—but, by fully analyzing the workings of both, to expose and abolish the limits they present in promising liberation for "all black people," but not, evidently, for "you."

WHAT'S MY NAME??

Designation, Identification,
and Cultural "Authenticity"

Designatory Reference and Social Effects

The manipulation of personal pronouns is not the only means by which an articulate black subject might stake out a political position relative to other persons of African descent. Powerful political statements can also be registered through the designatory terms by which individuals reference themselves and other black people. We have noted, for instance, the emergence in the late 1960s of the word *black* as the chosen designation for a nationalistically conscious intelligentsia; later, of course, the political resonances of the term would be diminished somewhat as it came into general use to refer to any and all persons of African ancestry. More recently, *African-American* has gained widespread usage, its supposed desirability over other available terms deriving from its vaunted capacity to signal such ancestry explicitly.

The putative advantages of the new designation notwithstanding, a number of commentators questioned the appropriateness of a focus on nomenclature at the time of its emergence, fearing, as the *New York Times* noted in January 1989, "that the debate over a new name draws attention away from problems like unemployment and drug abuse" (Wilkerson, "'African-American,'" p. A1). Indeed, in a July 1989 *Ebony* magazine forum on the question of "African-American or Black," the Rev. Joseph Lowery of the Southern Christian Leadership Conference unequivocally recast the terms of discussion along precisely such social-welfare lines. Claiming to like the one term "for its historicity and the other for its poetry," Lowery went on to declare:

> I reject the debate. Instead, I choose to direct my interests and ener-
> gies toward resisting the assault on our efforts to achieve economic
> justice. I will expend my energies on plans to fight in the voting
> booths and in the streets for economic parity, and shall not rearrange
> my priorities or be diverted from the continuing struggle for afford-
> able housing, job training, jobs, adequate health care, quality educa-
> tion and justice for all Americans. ("African-American or Black,"
> 1989, p. 80)

Others were even more blunt. African-diaspora scholar Ruth Hamilton was identified by the *Los Angeles Times* as "willing to call herself African-American," but she nonetheless insisted that "the critical question is: So what? . . . Does it really change the social conditions and consciousness of people[?]" (Njeri, 1989, p. 4). And with typical irascibility, cultural critic Stanley Crouch declared, "Any [term]'ll do for me; *Negro, Afro-American,* African-American—I don't care"; and he warned against distracting attention from such issues as "crack, AIDS, teenage pregnancy, the collapse of our public schools [and] lower voter registration" (quoted in Giordano, 1989; italics and brackets in original).

However much some observers might doubt the significance of group designation to blacks' social and political well-being, though, others are very clear on its import, tracing it to the constitutive effect of language on the social order. Geneva Smitherman (1991, p. 117) provides the most concise exposition of this view in her assertion that "language . . . play[s] a dominant role in the formation of ideology, consciousness, and class relations[,]" and, therefore, that "consciousness and ideology are largely the products of what I call the SOCIOLINGUISTIC CONSTRUCTION OF REALITY." At the same time, however, Smitherman also offers what should function as a monitory caveat on sociolinguistic constructionism, noting that "linguistic form exists in a dialectical relationship with social cognition and social behavior," and thereby hinting at a degree of mutualism in the constitutive relation between language and "reality" that must inevitably render problematic questions of ultimate cause and effect (1991, p. 117). This problematic quality emerges in the discourse of the most recent terminological debate, in ways that bear interestingly on the gender-political concerns I address here. In order to help us understand exactly how that is so, let us quickly review the history of group-designatory terminology within African-American culture prior to the latest development.

Sticks, Stones, Bootstraps

While by the sixteenth century a variety of European-derived terms were used by English-speaking whites to characterize dark-skinned persons of African descent, the Spanish and Portuguese *negro* (meaning "black") soon eclipsed such alternatives as *blackamoor, black, moor,* and *neger* to become the dominant designation in American usage. Because the term was evidently not properly descriptive, however, but rather imbued with negative assessments as to the humanity of those made to bear it, it was staunchly resisted by literate blacks through the eighteenth century. Surviving documents from the period indicate that, whenever possible in referring to themselves, such persons opted for *African* or, in what might be considered an instance of ironic signification, the closest Anglo-Saxon approximation to "negro"—*black.*

At the turn of the nineteenth century, however, the preference for the term *African* among blacks in the United States began to wane, as free blacks resisting emergent efforts to relocate them to the continent turned to *colored,* by way of deemphasizing their African identification. *Colored* held sway for the next hundred years or so, though *negro* was also regularly used by a number of prominent blacks, including Frederick Douglass and Booker T. Washington. Apparently by sheer dint of increasing public usage by such figures and leading whites alike, *negro* began to supplant *colored* as a term of dignity and respect by the end of the nineteenth century, with the 1909 founding of the National Association for the Advancement of Colored People marking the last prominent official use of the obsolescent term.

By the 1910s, black activists' efforts at linguistic reform were focused primarily in a campaign for the capitalization of *negro* in the print media—a campaign whose success is generally identified with the official adoption of *Negro* by the *New York Times* in 1930.[1] The rejection of the term during and after this period by such figures as Adam Clayton Powell and Elijah Mohammed signaled their relatively militant racial-political stances, along the lines of what would later be adopted and adapted by proponents of Black Power in the 1960s.

These latter activists' promotion of *black* over *Negro* sparked a debate among African Americans whose terms anticipated the more recent controversy, with a sizable group citing the effects of a name change as irrelevant to African Americans' pressing material concerns. Advocates for the use of *black,* on the other hand, invoked precisely the sociolinguistic-constructionist argument that Geneva Smitherman would later elaborate: in the characterization provided by historian Lerone Bennett, Jr. (on whose classic 1967 account the preceding genealogy is based; see pp. 46–52), this group insisted that "names are of the essence of the game of power and control" and that "a change in name [would] short-circuit the stereotyped thinking patterns that undergird the system of racism in America" (p. 47). Bennett's reference to "short-circuiting" here suggests the degree to which proponents of *black* understood as interrelated two "systems" that their opponents saw as relatively distinct—to wit, the system of social relations in which racism holds sway, and the system of language whose signifying elements are fundamentally arbitrary.[2] Bennett claimed that it was precisely the arbitrariness of the linguistic sign that had led some to conclude that there is in fact no constitutive relation, one way or the other, between language and social structures, a position he saw as exemplified in W. E. B. Du Bois's 1928 defense of the term *Negro,* excerpted here:

> Names are only conventional signs for identifying things. Things are the reality that counts. If a thing is despised, either because of ignorance or because it is despicable, you will not alter matters by changing its name. If men despise Negroes, they will not despise them less if Negroes are called "colored" or "Afro-Americans." ("The Name 'Negro'"; quoted in Bennett, 1967, p. 51)

The fault in Du Bois's argument, Bennett pointed out, lay not in his "correct premise that names are *objectively* unimportant," there being "no necessary connection between the name and the thing," but rather in his conclusion that, consequently, names are "unimportant *to people*" in social terms (p. 52). Indeed, it was precisely in recognition of language's social-collectivist import that 1960s opponents of the term *Negro* rejected such individualist arguments as that propounded by psychiatrist Jeanne Spurlock, who, according to Bennett, doubted "that a change in name [would] change the way Negroes experience themselves and the way others experience them," precisely because, as she herself put it, "The word 'Negro' means different things to different people, depending on so many things in their individual backgrounds" (p. 52). By contrast, proponents of the term *black* cited Whorfian linguistic research by way of asserting the impact not of individual "background," but of sociolinguistic *context* on people's conceptual experience. Bennett himself asserted that "modern linguistic scholarship is virtually unanimous in its findings that names and words determine, to a great extent, what we see and what we feel" (p. 52). That such determination must be considered a properly *social* effect, rather than a function of the linguistic sign per se, was suggested by the claim of pro-"black" activist Keith Baird that "[a] name can determine the nature of the response given to it by virtue of the associations which its use conjures up" (quoted in Bennett, 1967, p. 52), where "associations" are understood as deriving not from idiosyncratic individual psychology, but from lived relations in the larger arena of human interaction. It is this understanding that led Baird to his pithy assertion:

> The very act and fact of changing the designation . . . will cause the individual to be redesignated to be reconsidered, not only in terms of his past and his present but hopefully in terms of his future. . . . Designation has an important bearing on destiny. (quoted in Bennett, 1967, p. 52)

This latter claim, which is largely consonant with Smitherman's sociolinguistic-constructionist outlook, has been a significant element in discussions of group designation among African Americans since the 1960s, manifesting in the most recent debate primarily as an assertion of the positive effect of *African-American* on the psychic well-being of those so designated.[3] Historian Mary Frances Berry, for example, while warning that the adoption of the term "doesn't mean that everything will be wonderful and all the poor people will get taken care of," nonetheless proposed that "with the devastating problems in the community now, building self-esteem can't be all bad" (Wilkerson, 1989, p. A14). And that self-esteem has generally been posited as deriving from the term's invocation of cultural heritage and geopolitical history, which, according to educator Mary Futrell, "is very positive for young people," giving them "a sense of pride" ("African-American or Black," 1989, p. 78).

However this may be, whether the development of such "self-esteem" and "pride" will necessarily accrue to an improvement in African Americans' sociopolitical situation remains profoundly uncertain (as Berry was careful to indicate), with the question of *how* it might do so remaining wholly unelaborated—largely, I think, because of the difficulty of explicating the relation between individual psyche and social collectivity on which such an elaboration itself depends. Indeed, Baird himself emphasized that a change in designation would bring about a "reconsideration" specifically of the *individual,* demonstrating the ease with which even the most committed adherent of social-collectivist analysis can slip into an individualist rhetoric without accounting for the nature of the relation between individual experience and sociopolitical disposition. The significance of such slippage becomes particularly clear when we consider its implication in another crucial undertheorization—that of the relation between politics and culture, the extreme complexity of which is belied by the simple insistency with which the proponents of designatory change have repeatedly *invoked* it in their calls for the adoption of *African-American.*

The rhetoric of those calls has generally bespoken their issuers' strong belief in a well-nigh causal association between cultural practice and sociopolitical relations whereby the former largely determines the latter. National Urban Coalition president Dr. Ramona Edelin provided the most striking articulation of this view in her 1989 declaration that "[o]nly culture moves people forward"—a claim she elaborated by suggesting that "to consistently refer to ourselves as African-Americans and to understand the tie we have to African people around the world" would help blacks develop a "cultural context" in which to "move . . . forward, reclaim our children, create markets and jobs so that we don't continue with poverty, ignorance, poor health—all the conditions that we face right now . . ." (quoted in Njeri, 1989, p. 4). Elsewhere, Edelin proposed flatly that "[o]ur cultural renaissance can change our lot in the nation and around the world" ("African-American or Black," 1989, p. 76).

As I have already indicated, such proclamations as Edelin's provide no explanation as to *how* developments in the cultural realm might effect desirable change in blacks' sociopolitical status, but my concern here is less with the specific details of this extraordinary process than with the implications of its supposed general character, discernible from the terms in which it is invoked by its staunchest exponents. Those terms are exemplified in Jesse Jackson's suggestion that the adoption of the new designation constitutes an "attempt to lift our children by the power of their culture" (cited in Peretz, 1989), where "culture" evidently comprises both such discrete formations as the term *African-American* itself and the collective heritage that the designation invokes. Beyond the collectivizing function that the term clearly serves, though, by conceiving U.S. blacks as members of a global African diaspora, it also, according to Jackson, puts the group on par with other actors in the international political theater in a way that alternative designations do not: "Black," Jackson declared by way of making this point, "tells you about skin color and what side of town you live on. African-American evokes discussion of the world" (quoted in Wilkerson, 1989, p. A14). Thus, not only does the invocation of collective heritage comprised in the term *African-American* accrue to the enhanced self-esteem of those so designated, as Mary Futrell suggested, but the general reconsideration of black identity that such enhancement implies issues in African Americans' ameliorated sociopolitical status both at home and abroad. It is in the exposition of these dual developments—the precise mechanics of which, it must be reemphasized, are never explicated by the proponents of *African-American*— that we can see implicated what I have referred to as a noteworthy "slippage" between a social-collectivist and an individualist ethic on the part of advocates for the terminological change. For if the influential associations attending any given designatory form—*African-American* in this instance—derive from the properly social context in which linguistic meaning in general is forged, the "self-esteem" that they are believed to enhance must be conceived as a fundamentally individualized psychic effect on which is grounded, in turn, the political advancement of the entire African-American collectivity.

I point out the operation of this slippage not to indicate logical contradictions that undermine the validity of arguments for terminological change, but rather to identify one instantiation of the *dialectical relationship* in which Smitherman suggests sociolinguistic constructionism is implicated, whereby "linguistic form" both conditions *and reflects* "social cognition and social behavior."[4] In other words, to focus on the case at hand, not only does the social significance of *African-American*—or, before it, of *black*—enhance the standing of those so designated, but the very use of the term itself evidences the fact of that enhancement. However much this mutualism might objectively characterize the relation between the constructionist and the reflectionist functions of language, though, it is not necessarily recognized in polemical presentations that nonetheless insist on language's social import. Rather, such presentations often suppress the mutual constitutiveness of linguistic form and social fact by way of making a point that, ultimately, depends for its validity on that very mutualism.

For example, in an article written in the mid-1980s, before the general adoption of the term *African-American*, K. Sue Jewell (1985) reviewed the displacement of *Negro* by *black* in the late 1960s and early 1970s. Early in her analysis, Jewell clearly suggests that language has a constitutive effect on blacks' social experience, charging that *Negro* "designat[ed] the inferiority and pathology of African-Americans" and thus "resulted in the[ir] . . . stereotypic treatment" (pp. 59, 60); at the same time, she also implicitly acknowledges that social experience can determine linguistic form, asserting that the emergence of *black* "symboliz[ed]" African Americans' achievement of "race consciousness and unity" and thus "marked a progression toward . . . self-improvement" (p. 60). If this account implies that Jewell recognizes linguistic form and social experience as being mutually constitutive, however, her consideration of the significance of group designations in use at the time of her writing most emphatically does not. More than simply discerning a "pronounced Afrophobia" and lack of African cultural identification among those who fail to proclaim their "African" heritage, Jewell also charges that self-described "blacks," by choosing a designation that makes no reference to "America," betray a sense of not being entitled to the rights and privileges of U.S. citizenship (p. 64). According to Jewell, then, in the 1980s *black* implied only the psychic deficiency of those who subscribed to it—a profoundly ahistorical assessment that discounts the prideful race consciousness that Jewell herself claims was connoted by *black* in consequence of various sociopolitical developments of the 1960s. Jewell's suppression of this connotation serves not to clarify the long-term effects of those developments—her ostensible objective—but only to buttress the argument for the general adoption of *African-American* that she is evidently concerned to make. At the same time, however, if *African-American* itself connotes simultaneous identification with African heritage and entitlement to the benefits of U.S. citizenship, this is only because those significances have accrued to the term (or to the two elements comprised in its compound structure) by virtue of the same process of social sedimentation that Jewell implicitly denies conditioned the meaning of *black* up through the 1980s.[5]

Polemical efficacy, then, can apparently dictate the discursive suppression of key aspects of sociolinguistic effect; and the specific character of that suppression can itself indicate the polemical stake implicit in what purports to be a merely expository presentation. Or, alternatively, when the polemical quality of the presentation is clear, such selective suppression can indicate an author's investment in multiple points whose implications are actually contradictory. For example, like Du Bois's essay of sixty years prior, a February 1989 *Newsweek* opinion piece by Barbara Lyles takes the arbitrariness of names as signaling their relative inconsequentiality, in comparison with the evidently more substantive fact of noteworthy "achievement": "Forget the semantic absurdity of what to call people of color and get on with the business of achieving. If attention is drawn to what is done rather than who does it, names won't matter" (p. 9). Even were it possible to consider achievement as an abstract effect distinct from the agent who accomplishes it, however, elsewhere in the same essay Lyles betrays her own stated investment in this project, emphasizing the key identity trait of those whose achievement she wants to recognize even as she denies the significance of the various terms used to designate it:

> As a kid, I was a "negro." My father often admonished us that "colored people" were never to be referred to in his house as "niggers." Daddy required that we familiarize ourselves with Carter G. Woodson, W. E. B. Du Bois, George Washington Carver, Paul Laurence Dunbar, Countee Cullen and lots of other renowned "negroes." I now realize that, having been exposed to "negroes" in history and "people of color" in antiquity, I had had a prefashionable instruction in the positive meaning of being colored. (p. 8)

This passage belies Lyles's insistence on the valuation of deeds over identity, insofar as her lessons in "the positive meaning of being colored" necessarily derive from her education in the achievements *specifically of* those identified as "negroes" and "people of color," the varying designations for whom, moreover, clearly do not indicate the inconsequentiality of names per se or Lyles's father would not have adamantly banned the word *nigger* from his house.

It is, additionally, precisely Lyles's invocation of her father that further indicates and specifies her stake in identifying the agents of commendable achievement, her assertions to the contrary notwithstanding, for the particularity of the father's identity is of primary importance in her rendering: "The point is also to be made," she remarks, "that Daddy was *there:* colored? negro? Negro?; a male image with undeniable positive influence" (p. 8). Whatever the significance of her father's maleness during the period of his most profound "influence" on her, Lyles's invocation of it in her essay indicates her implication in a contemporary discursive context in which the viability of a "positive" black male subject is so intensely contested an issue as to warrant Lyles's apparent abandonment of her program to deemphasize agential identity in favor of a focus on "achievement" per se. Indeed, the very intensity of that contestation—along with the example of Lyles's contradictory line of argument, for which it evidently partly accounts—suggests the need for further exploration of gender politics in the designatory debate, by way of determining to what extent the latter is propelled and shaped by anxiety over the status and significance of black masculinity.

Masculinity, the Black Elite, and Cultural "Authenticity"

The potential implication of such anxiety in even the most seemingly innocuous aspects of the recent terminological discussion can be divined from the fact that it is Jesse Jackson who is most extensively credited with (or blamed for) promoting the adoption of *African-American* among the general population, even though, as at least a few observers have noted, it was actually Ramona Edelin who proposed the move at a December 1988 meeting of black policy makers in Chicago (see Lacayo/Monroe, 1989; Njeri, 1989, p. 1; Smitherman, 1991, p. 115). Indeed, the specific context in which Edelin made her proposal is so breathtaking in its stereotypic manifestation of gender politics as absolutely to compel our analytical attention. According to the *Los Angeles Times,* Edelin suggested that the Chicago conference employ the term *African-American* when Jackson "*asked her to act as official scribe for the meeting*" (Njeri, 1989, p. 1, emphasis added), a fact that was not registered in the majority of press accounts, which generally identified Jackson himself as the source of the proposal.[6] This classic development—whereby a woman's effective policy-making role is embedded in (and obscured by) her secretarial function, and concomitantly ascribed to the man recognized as being in charge of the proceedings—is of course largely explained in this case by the significantly more prominent public profile Jackson enjoys, relative to Edelin; but rather than neutralizing the gender-political significance of that development, this fact (which itself is not gender-politically innocent), actually underscores its implication in a crucial problematic that Edelin herself saw as characterizing the push for the adoption of *African-American*. Sensitive to criticisms that that push represented willful imposition by a black intelligentsia rather than a more "organic" cultural emergence, Edelin told the *Los Angeles Times*, "We don't pretend that anyone cares about a name change, in and of itself, just because some elite proposes it" (Njeri, 1989, p. 4). Indeed, such elite status as Jesse Jackson, especially, enjoys has been as much an object of anxiety in discussion of the adoption of *African-American* as I am suggesting has black masculinity itself, with the vulnerability of the latter seen largely as a troubling ramification of the former, which thus must be carefully managed so as not to undermine the "authenticity" of blackness, of maleness, or of African-American culture in general.

This latter claim is substantiated by the degree to which one writer, at least, has strived to posit Jesse Jackson not as *originating* the use of *African-American* (which function on Jackson's part appears to be at stake in his eclipsing of Edelin in the public eye), but rather as merely engineering its spread throughout the general culture. Writing explicitly against such claims as Stephan Thernstrom's (1989, p. 10) that, if the term *African-American* takes hold, "it will be the first time in U.S. history that an ethnic leader has single-handedly changed the name commonly applied to his or her group," linguist John Baugh (1991) is equally concerned with countering the notion that the new nomenclature first emerged specifically among a black social and cultural elite, implied, for instance, in Isabel Wilkerson's (1989) assertion that "[t]he term, used for years in intellectual circles, is gaining currency among many other blacks . . ." (p. A1).[7]

Recognizing that the conception of Jesse Jackson as the founder of the terminological shift is rooted largely in media coverage of the December 1988 press conference in which he announced, "Just as we were called colored, but were not that, and then Negro, but not that, to be called black is just as baseless" ("Jackson and Others"), Baugh begins his analysis by addressing the claim that for Jackson "to imply that these labels were imposed by outsiders is unfair," since each was at some point adopted by African Americans themselves (Baugh, 1991, p. 134; for a typical instance of this charge against Jackson, see Thernstrom, 1989, p. 10). By way of refuting this suggestion, Baugh asserts that the validity of Jackson's claim was grounded in the function of certain social divisions whose existence was elided in Jackson's oft-quoted statement. Baugh argues that, in that statement, Jackson

> accuses no one of imposing terminology, but, because his comments were addressed to all Americans, he failed to make critical social and ethnographic distinctions between those who are familiar with VAAC and others who have little or no contact with ASD. (p. 134)

VAAC and *ASD* are abbreviations for *vernacular African-American culture* and *American slave descendants*—terms coined by Baugh to denote, in the first case, "the African American cultural traditions that have been developed in racial isolation from the majority culture" (p. 144 n. 2), and, in the second, U.S. citizens of recognized African lineage whose forebears were held as slaves in America. These formulations themselves implicate the social and ethnographic distinctions to which Baugh refers, inasmuch as *ASD* not only represents his acknowledged attempt to achieve "neutrality" in his references to the black American population (p. 144 n. 1), but also serves as his genericizing designation for the entirety of that population, many of whose members, by contrast, either are not "active members of VAAC" or "have limited contact with" it, according to his conception (p. 144 n. 2).

The problematic quality of Baugh's deployment of these ethnographic categories in his defense of Jackson's claim (which I will soon explicate more fully) is foreshadowed in the faults of the categories themselves, which, it must be said, indicate less any failing on Baugh's part than the overwhelming difficulty of comprehensively characterizing African-American society and culture.[8] *ASD* presents the most immediate case in point. Adopted, Baugh tells us, with the intent of excluding from its field of reference such cynically mocking individuals as Edmund Morris—a white native of Kenya and naturalized U.S. citizen who in a 1989 *Washington Post* editorial laid claim to the term *African American* (Baugh, 1991, p. 144 n. 1)—the designation also excludes *black* native Africans now settled in the United States, citizens of black-African descent from other non-American locations, and U.S. descendants of the free African populations that existed on the continent throughout the American slavery era, all of whom, arguably, one would want to conceive as constituents of contemporary African-American society. Given this fact, Baugh's conception of that society is only relatively less exclusive than what he posits as vernacular African-American culture, and it is precisely the principle of exclusivity evidently at work in both these conceptions that at once grounds his defense of Jackson's proposition and renders it problematic.

When Baugh says that Jackson "failed to make critical social and ethnographic distinctions between those who are familiar with VAAC and others who have little or no contact with ASD," he implies that ambiguity characterizes both the "we" that Jackson claims has wrongly been called "colored," "Negro," and so forth, and the anonymous subject who has performed that calling. It was as a result of this ambiguity, he suggests, that Jackson appeared to be accusing those outside African-American society of "imposing terminology" on U.S. blacks. If, however, we take into account the distinction Baugh asserts between blacks who participate in vernacular African-American culture and those who do not, then Jackson's claim that "we" have been wrongly designated can appear less as an interracial indictment than as the more "objective" recognition of *intraracial* social divisions whereby blacks outside of the vernacular African-American cultural context have consistently continued to employ the supposedly inaccurate self-designations well *after* they have been displaced in the vernacular, most recently by *African-American.*

Baugh makes this point (and thereby attempts to undermine the widespread notion that the impetus for the adoption of *African-American* originated with Jackson's authoritative decree) through recourse to an interview with a group of young African-American men from East Austin, Texas, conducted in 1987, *well before Jackson's statement to the press.* Baugh (1991) himself introduces an apposite quotation from the interview, pointing out that, "[i]n contrast with Jackson's argument, the Brother takes umbrage at the label *Afro-American*":

> We ain't no abbreviated people. It ain't no "Italo-Americans," or
> "Japo-(A)mericans," and they ain't no "Mexo-(A)mericans" neither.
> We the only ones they done abbreviated. That's bull shit! [I hear you.]
> . . . Black people are Africans in America. Ain't nobody from no place
> else had to deal with slavery, and that's why they done tried to abbre-
> viate us. But I'll tell you this about that. [What's that?] We all came
> here in chains, baby, but we all came from Africa. We got just as much
> right as anybody else to demand dignity and self-respect and that's
> why I say I'm a African American! [Other men convey verbal and
> nonverbal approval.] (p. 135, brackets in original)

The "contrast" with Jackson that Baugh invokes apparently has to do with the fact that, as he notes after citing this conversation, "[t]he Brother makes no reference to 'baseless' terms," and actually uses the designation *black* in his own discussion, which fact (in conjunction with the early date of the interview) Baugh offers as evidence that the interviewee was following neither the lead nor the logic of Jackson's declaration; indeed, this is Baugh's primary point, the import of which I will consider shortly. First, though, it is important to recognize an alternative significance of the "contrast" that Baugh references, which derives from the very syntax of his own proposition. In light of his prior comments on the nature of vernacular African-American culture and without benefit of the explication that he offers only after the quotation, Baugh's assertion—"In contrast with Jackson's argument, the Brother takes umbrage at the label *Afro-American*"—suggests that his interviewee's position diverges from Jackson's both because he recoils specifically from *Afro-American* (a term to which Jackson did not refer in his initial public remarks) and because that very recoiling implies that this man *has not* passively "been called" by any offending designation, since his putative "isolation" from "mainstream" culture effectively exempts him as a meaningful referent for any term invoked within it, and the racial consciousness that characterizes him and his social circle precludes his being offensively referenced within the vernacular context. In other words, the implication of Baugh's various claims is that the improper "calling" to which Jackson referred has been performed not by nonblacks who "imposed" the terminology on African Americans generally, but rather by blacks who "are not active members of" and "have limited contact with" vernacular African-American culture, and who took on the faulty terms as *self-designations*. Furthermore, given the ramifications of Baugh's assertions that I have teased out in the foregoing analysis, the ambiguity of the "we" that Jackson claimed had been wrongly designated stems from its referential oscillation between, on the one hand, black nonparticipants in vernacular African-American culture who have inaccurately self-identified and, on the other hand, black participants in the vernacular whose alternative self-designations are set up in resistance against the hegemony of nonvernacular designatory terms. Thus the overall effect of Baugh's presentation is implicitly to establish the African-American vernacular context as both the origin for black social resistance and the locus of cultural authenticity vis-à-vis conscious identification with the heritage of Africa.

The validity of Jesse Jackson's public intervention, according to Baugh's view of the matter, derived precisely from its supposed grounding in this originary site, a keen awareness of which Baugh (1991) imputes to Jackson himself, noting that the 1987 interview he cites

> proves that Jackson did not start this process; debates concerning appropriate terminology among ASD continue to spread by word of mouth, as they have since the inception of slavery. Clearly, Jackson sensed the changing linguistic tide of self-reference toward *African American,* and he used his . . . pulpit to launch this debate into the broader public forum. (p. 135)

Later, after presenting the results of a quantitative study by way of substantiating his claims, Baugh reiterates the point: "there can be no doubt that the trend toward the adoption of *African American* was growing in the ASD/VAAC community before Jackson's comments, and it is in this context that others more qualified than I can evaluate his motives" (p. 142).

While I do not pretend any more than does John Baugh to be able to account for Jackson's "motives," I do think that the key cultural *effects* of his declaration derive from the authenticating function performed by the African-American vernacular in the type of situation at issue here, in conjunction with the gender-political significance that is tacitly imputed to that vernacular context.[9] Indeed, John Baugh himself takes notable recourse to the black vernacular tradition in the pages of his essay, explaining his references to the "Brother" he interviewed in 1987 by pointing out: "Black people commonly refer to each other as *Brother* or *Sister* as signs of racial solidarity. In this vein, I use the words here as terms of respect for fellow African American men and women" (p. 145, n. 5). Yet Baugh *does not* use both words in his article, invoking only the term *Brother;* and it is only one of his group-interviewees whom Baugh thus "respectfully" references, and not the various other African-American men whom he cites or discusses, whether Jesse Jackson, journalist William Raspberry, or the colleague to whom he anonymously refers (p. 137).·

Not only does this apparently represent a slip on Baugh's part, whereby rather than acknowledging the specifically vernacular context in which he chooses to make his "Brother" reference he instead suggests that such invocations are embraced across all of African-American society (in clear contradiction to his own observations on that society's subdivision), but it also seems to constitute Baugh's anxious insistence on his own identification with and intimate relation to his interviewees, whose vernacular "brotherhood" specifically functions as the site of the authentic African-American culture from which Baugh's professional status and practice constantly threaten to alienate him. Indeed, in this light, Baugh's claim that he himself "began to reintroduce the term *African American* before the Rev. Jesse Jackson formally called for this adoption" (p. 133) seems meant to signal, not his membership in an elite intellectual avant-garde, but rather his grounding in the black-masculine vernacular culture that he posits as a primary site of the new terminology's emergence.

The move to adopt *African-American* does not represent the first time that self-designatory change among U.S. blacks has been implicated in a project to recuperate the viability of black masculinity. This impulse can be traced at least as far back as Stokely Carmichael, whose 1966 Mississippi speeches for the Student Nonviolent Coordinating Committee have been credited with driving the shift from *Negro* to *black* ("Identity Crisis," 1969; for an account of the logic of this shift, see Carmichael and Hamilton, 1967, pp. 37–39). It has perhaps been most strikingly elaborated, however, in a statement composed by playwright and actor

Ossie Davis for *Ebony* magazine and printed as part of Lerone Bennett's 1967 article. The gist of Davis's statement is comprised in the key definitions that it offers; first, the definition of a Negro:

> I am a Negro. I am clean, black and I smile a lot. Whenever I want something . . . I go to white folks. White folks have money. I do not. White folks have power. I do not. All of my needs . . . I must depend on white folks to supply. That is what is meant by being a Negro.

Then, in contrast to this and by means of a concrete example, the characteristics of black identity:

> Malcolm X used to be a Negro, but he stopped. He no longer depended on white folks to supply his needs. . . . Most of all, he did not need them to tell him who he was. . . . That was why Malcolm was no longer a Negro. Malcolm was a man, a black man! A black man means not to accept the system as Negroes do. . . . It can be dangerous. Malcolm was killed for it. Nevertheless, I like Malcolm much better than I like myself. (printed in Bennett, 1967, p. 54)

This statement—the extraordinary power of which derives principally from the highly personalized manner in which it demonstrates the depth of "Negro" self-loathing—is notable here primarily for the curious conflation that characterizes it, whereby subscription to black identity itself bespeaks a masculine status because the courage thus to claim social autonomy is precisely what constitutes conventional manhood, no matter what the racial context. Given the racio-*political* context operative in the United States since the moment of its founding, in which the denial of social autonomy has itself been a defining characteristic of African-American experience, it is not surprising that such reclamation of that experience as was represented in the Black Power movement should be conceived in terms of accession to a masculine identity, the problematic quality of those terms notwithstanding. What our examination of John Baugh's text suggests, however, is that the cultural-political reclamation supposedly represented by the widespread adoption of the term *African-American* is *also* seen as constituting the achievement of manhood, a good twenty-five years after the similarly significant advent of *black*. That a concern with the tenability of conventional masculine identity among African-American men should at this juncture be the implicit burden of any given discussion or development in African-American society is troubling, both for the blindness to other crucial issues (which, however interrelated they may be with the challenges of black masculinity, should not be collapsed into them) that such an unwavering focus can entail, and—what may well amount to the same thing—for the degree to which it encourages the unexamined acceptance and promulgation of conventional masculinity's most deeply problematic features, in the name of racial progress.

Alliance, Identification, Displacement

Such "progress," as I have indicated in the preceding chapter, can be predicated on invidious intraracial division that actually belies the collective advancement that is being proclaimed. Since the transition from the standard usage of *black* to the relatively widespread usage of *African-American* has been pretty much unmarked by explicit intraracial conflict over the term, there is little in the public record to attest to the divisional tensions that have nonetheless characterized the development. Still, it is possible to find material that evidences such tensions, with the putative point of difference located in the comparative levels of pride in African cultural heritage that the various designatory terms supposedly indicate, along the lines sketched out in the analysis by K. Sue Jewell that we have already reviewed. Given the mode of its production and distribution, it is not surprising that popular music should offer one of the more broadly disseminated examples of such material, the potential influence of which is suggested by precisely that breadth of dissemination.

The 1992 song "People Everyday," by the rap group Arrested Development, clearly indicates what it is refusing to be in the terms by which it asserts what it is—namely, an effective inversion of the 1969 Sly and the Family Stone hit "Everyday People," which it both samples and rewrites. While the sociocultural import of the earlier recording lay precisely in its Woodstock-era embodiment of interracial harmony and melodic universalism, the later one explicitly promulgates a sort of new-wave black nationalist vision informed by 1990s Afrocentrism and post-urban sensibility; where Sly and the Family Stone engineered a gently ironic critique of interracial prejudice, Arrested Development specifies and evaluates different registers of cultural blackness offered by the contemporary context. A synoptic account of the more recent song's narrative will have to serve as the basis for analysis.[10]

The differentiation of various orders of blackness occurs in "People Everyday" when the song's first-person narrator—rapper and group leader Speech—and his love are interrupted in their idyllic outdoor encounter by a group of black men first presented as "brothers," but whose status as inferior "niggers" is soon indicated by their loudness and their public drinking of malt liquor. When these men accost the couple, the rapper initially exhibits patience and restraint, indicating his forbearance by tentatively positing them as fellow "Africans." Once members of the group begin to insult his mate, however, going so far as to fondle her person, the rapper lets loose, returning the men's offenses with a physical violence that betrays as merely wishful the song's closing injunction for "Africans" to manifest mutual love; according to the ethic that "People Everyday" propounds, the song's protagonist might be a respectable "African," but his *an*tagonists very clearly are not.

The "African/nigger" distinction that "People Everyday" thus draws clearly differentiates it from "Everyday People," as is indicated in its arrangement of the refrain line that it lifts from the earlier recording. In the Sly and the Family Stone production, this line introduces the critique of interracial intolerance that is the song's signal feature: the lead vocalist's assertion that he is "everyday people" is regularly followed by a choral narrative describing the procession of variously hued, shaped, and materially-endowed individuals comprised in the great society; and the repeated declaration that a pointedly collective "we" must necessarily coexist implicates the singularized lead vocalist within the diversity of subjects invoked by the chorus. In "People Everyday," by contrast, "everyday people" status—though asserted by a backing chorus whose collective character would seem to mitigate the refrain's grammatical singularity—appears to be enjoyed only by the lone rapper, both because the chorus posits it in apposition to his individualistic first-person narrative and because the singularistic assertion itself is not attended by the collectivizing choral refrain and lead-vocal declaration offered by Sly and the Family Stone.

More than this, though—and especially noteworthy for my purposes here—the individuation that drives what we might consider the song's *implicit* moral (as opposed to its *explicit* injunction) is itself a function of the superior racial-political consciousness that the "African" rapper is represented as having, proof of which consists in nothing other than his besting his opponents in the stereotypically masculine activity of physical combat (by way of avenging his woman's honor), even after he has tacitly derided their apparent need to challenge his "manhood." This racial-political superiority is manifested as well in other of Arrested Development's work, notably the breakthrough hit "Tennessee," in which Speech wonders why he alone, of all his people, has been granted crucial moral insight; and it has already been remarked by commentators on hip-hop culture (see D. Smith, 1994, p. 58). That an unreflective masculinism is the vehicle of that superiority has gone largely unnoticed, however, despite the great degree of attention that has been paid to the gender politics of rap per se.[11] The manifestation of that masculinist vehicle in the work of Arrested Development is particularly significant, though—indicating the importance of further analysis of it—because the mode of its elaboration there complicates the class politics that we have heretofore seen as characterizing the promulgation of "authentic" African-American culture. By presenting that authenticity as an effect *not* of black urban "street" life—indeed, it is the bottle of malt liquor, conventional symbol of the street context, that gives away the antagonists in the narrative as "niggers"—but rather of Speech's more classically "folk" intellectualism, "People Everyday" demonstrates the degree to which the chauvinism of masculine identification can hold sway across the various divisions that articulate the broader society.[12] This demonstration, in turn, suggests the full expanse of the sociopolitical field on which "chauvinism" in general might play, and thus provides us with one final indication of the potential problems associated with unconsidered "African-American" identification in the contemporary context.

The significance of such "chauvinism" as I have identified at work in "People Everyday" derives not only from the problematic gender politics that it indicates is comprised in the contemporary push for "African" identification among U.S. blacks, but, further, from its (ironic) implication of an equally worrisome ethnic myopia whose emergence was underwritten by the success of that campaign. For example, the *New York Times* reported in January 1989 that the black-owned New York City radio station WLIB had in the preceding month "broadcast a report that referred to a woman with a dark complexion and a Hispanic surname. 'Everybody in the newsroom was struggling with what to call her,' [the program director] said. 'They decided on African-Latino'" (Wilkerson, 1989, p. A14). The fact that an anonymous, authoritative "they" "decided on" the designation is somewhat sobering, since it is precisely the indignity of improperly speaking for others (or of being thus spoken *for*) that was supposed to be alleviated by the switch from *black* to *African-American*. Further, this anecdote indicates the saliency of a point touched on by scholar Ruth Hamilton in her remarks to the *Los Angeles Times* in January 1989—that any group designation employed in the United States is bound to suppress certain significant lines of cultural identification in the "name" of emphasizing others. As Hamilton's observation was rendered by reporter Itabari Njeri (1989, p. 4), "African-Americans have 'competing identities.' . . . They have 'their Southern roots, their Brooklyn roots, their Caribbean roots, which may be more important for them as a primary identity' than their African heritage."

Hamilton's claim obviously verges on the same individualist ethic that activists such as Keith Baird criticized in the 1960s, especially in that it does not acknowledge the degree to which African heritage *specifically* has constituted both the justificatory trigger for blacks' systematic oppression in U.S. society and the object of that society's most brutally repressive activity. At the same time, however, Hamilton's assertion importantly admits of the degree to which African identification among U.S. blacks—like many instances of ethnic identification throughout the U.S. context—is a profoundly subjective undertaking. Consider, for instance, the claims of Nur Ali, an African-American woman whose commitment to living an "Afrocentric" life Rosemary Bray outlines in her article, "Reclaiming Our Culture" (1990). Insisting that "[w]e just can't be 'Black' all our lives, whatever that is," Ali is definitive in her estimation of "the hardest thing, our next level of development: to finally become African"; and Bray cooperatively indicates the extent to which Ali herself has apparently succeeded in this project, asserting that, "amid the cheerful clutter of her mission shop, . . . [d]ressed in a bubah and head wrap of African print, [Ali] is a modern, urban market woman, not terribly different from her sisters in Accra or Dakar or Abidjan." Indeed, Ali goes so far as to suggest her fundamental *identity* with those "sisters," asserting that "[w]hat one African can do, another African can do. . . . I just happen to be an African born in Brooklyn" (p. 84). While obviously indicating the primacy that Ali grants to her "African heritage," this statement no less clearly bespeaks her "Brooklyn roots" inasmuch as the need for voluntaristic identification with Africa that it denotes arises specifically out of the geographic displacement that founds African-Americans' unique historical experience. That voluntarism itself is potentially problematic, moreover, in that, irresponsibly deployed, it is apt to issue less in productive diasporic alliance than in the mere solipsistic assertion of one's own "identity," and this at the cost of eliding the specific histories and experiences of those with whom one supposedly most wants to *identify*. A particularly striking instance of such elision occurred in April 1993, during a segment on the films of actor Sidney Poitier broadcast on Black Entertainment Television's *Conversation with Ed Gordon*. In a short account of the movie *To Sir, with Love*, a BET correspondent reported that in it, Poitier portrays an "African-American" schoolteacher, not only misidentifying the nationality of the character, but thereby crucially misconstruing the political significance of the film's story line, which specifically interrogates the relation between England and its Caribbean colonies by detailing the experiences of a West Indian teacher in a working-class London high school. Indeed, the anxiously self-conscious designation of the character as "African-American" constitutes a classic case of linguistic hypercorrection, in that the error thus made actually recapitulates the original "fault" whose correction was intended, comprising the same type of geopolitical "misidentification" historically suffered by U.S. blacks, which the adoption of the term *African-American* was meant to rectify.

What this anecdote demonstrates, then, is the degree to which the cultural-identificatory significance usually ascribed to this "new" term might actually represent a wishful misrecognition: However much U.S. blacks might want to underscore our "identification" with "Africa" (a concept whose highly problematic character I leave almost entirely aside in this analysis[13]), it seems likely that the widespread adoption of *African-American* bespeaks much more loudly our pecu-liarly—and *narrowly*—"American" disposition, much as the conventional use of *American* itself overprojects the political-geographical significance of the United States. The analysis I have undertaken here suggests the degree to which such ego-tistic overprojection generally might be a function of a masculine anxiety that is rendered no less potentially oppressive by the sense of vulnerability it so clearly conveys. Given this, before we submit to the impulse toward African-diasporic "identification," we would do well to consider not merely the boost to our own "self-esteem" that such identification might effect, but the processes of cultural and historical *suppression* that it might entail. For the primary objects of that sup-pression would likely be the very peoples with whom we want most closely to identify, but whose experiences, therefore—since they are not our own—we would be wise not to presume to name, claim, or speak.

CLASS ACTS

The "Street," Popular Music, and Black-Cultural Crossover

White Tradition and Black Breakthrough: The Construction of Pop-Music History

Such politically specious "identification" as I have suggested characterizes U.S. blacks' adoption of the term *African-American* is by no means unique to that particular context. Indeed, we can arrive at a fuller sense of its potential offensiveness if we consider its manifestation in a rather more "classic" scenario, without for a second suggesting the commensurability of the two instances. In a November 1986 article titled "The King of Rap," *Village Voice* reporter Barry Walters chronicled the professional rise of Rick Rubin, the young white music producer who had just recently drawn upon his interest in and knowledge of African-American musical culture, his entrepreneurial bravado, and his family's money to help effect the "crossover" of rap music from the ghetto of black hip-hop culture into the "mainstream" of the pop-music recording industry. In an economical allusion to the specific quality and import of Rubin's cross-racial identification, Walters asserted that "by talking black and being white, Rubin has brought together the intemperance of heavy metal and the braggadocio of rap—a lucrative marriage" (p. 20). In most cursory, folk-wise considerations of this proposition it would undoubtedly be precisely the *lucrativeness* of Rubin's undertaking (indeed, a year before Walters's writing, Rubin and then-partner Russell Simmons signed a deal with CBS whose value, according to Rubin, was "in the millions"; see Walters, 1986, p. 19) that would signal its suspect character, apparently indicating the degree to which his *identification* with black music predicates his *capitalization* on it, and thus implies his *exploitation* of both black musicians and the black record-buying public. Such an analysis does not take us very far, however, toward understanding either the extremely complex phenomenon of pop-music crossover or, more pertinent to my concerns in this volume, its social significance with respect to racial, gender, and class identities. In order to achieve such an understanding, we will need to move beyond a focus on Rick Rubin per se, to consider the pop-musical epoch marked by his rise, itself a landmark in the career of crossover.

In terms of crossover—the transdemographic, often trans*racial*, commercial success of a theretofore categorically bounded act or musical genre—the most significant mid-1980s development for Rick Rubin was not his and Simmons's deal with CBS, but rather the double-platinum sales of the 1986 album *Raising Hell*, by the rap group Run-DMC, which the two partners produced (Walters, 1986, p. 19). Propelled by the summer success of the single "Walk This Way," *Raising Hell* sold more than two million copies between the time of its

Run-DMC (left to right: DMC [Darryl McDaniels], Jam Master Jay [Jason Mizell], Run [Joseph Simmons]) in performance in 1985. Photo courtesy of Photofest.

spring release and mid-autumn, implying an incursion into the white record-buying market that was unprecedented for a rap production. At the same time, certain factors in the album's success both indicate its implication in a long history of black-cultural crossover and continue to underwrite the significance of such crossover in the contemporary context, so it will be useful to examine them with some care.

By now the general contours of rap music's history are well known. Emerging in the South Bronx in the mid- and late 1970s, rap developed from the distinctive, often Caribbean-influenced, practices of neighborhood DJs to incorporate, eventually, the "sampling" and electronic manipulation of instrumental and vocal riffs from extant recordings; the unique percussive effects achieved by "scratching," or quickly turning a record to and fro on a stereo turntable so that the needle rides back and forth in a chosen groove; and, of course, the rhythmic chanting of rhymed vocals typically characterized by hyperbolic braggadocio and reflections on African-American life in the contemporary urban context.[1] It did not take long for the form to circulate in a wider arena, with the release of the Sugar Hill Gang single "Rapper's Delight" at the turn of the decade introducing listeners across the country to its style and techniques (T. Rose, *Black Noise*, 1994, p. 56), and the *New York Times* citing a rap recording—"The Message," by Grandmaster Flash and the Furious Five—as "the most powerful pop single" of 1982 (noted in Adler, 1983, p. 42). Indeed, the influence of rap beyond a specifically African-American milieu was indicated as early as 1981, when the single "Rapture" by the new-wave group Blondie became a "hit" on *Billboard* magazine's Hot 100 pop singles chart (Bronson, 1991, p. 287). Still, the massive sales of *Raising Hell* and, especially, "Walk This Way" represent a watershed in the rise of rap, for reasons that could not possibly have been anticipated at the time of the form's emergence.

The crossover success of "Walk This Way" derived primarily from three interrelated factors that bear careful consideration. The first is that the song was not originally recorded by Run-DMC, but by the white "hard rock" band Aerosmith, who released it in 1975; the second is that the Aerosmith members who wrote the song, Steven Tyler and Joe Perry, give performances on Run-DMC's recording of it; and the third is that the video for Run-DMC's cut, which also features Tyler and Perry, received massive airplay on the Music Television cable station—better known as MTV—throughout the summer of 1986 (Palmer, 1986, p. 23). The significance of this last fact could easily be overlooked from a contemporary perspective, given the preponderance of black hip-hop acts whose music videos are now featured on both MTV and the various newer stations that roughly duplicate its format and function. In 1986, however, the very appearance on MTV of a video by a black act was still so rare as itself to constitute that act's noteworthy crossover into what had seemed a practically impenetrable arena.

This fact was actually figured in Run-DMC's "Walk This Way" video, which, as the *New York Times*'s Robert Palmer commented in September 1986, "seems deliberately symbolic." As Palmer described the narrative presented in the video:

> Aerosmith's Steve Tyler and Joe Perry perform a concert on one side of a wall while Run-DMC tries to make a record on the other. . . . But the sounds are too powerful; each side hears what the other is doing. Finally, the rappers rip through the wall and step into the rock performance, which becomes a rocking celebration of the song's biracial and musical fusion. (p. 24)

The "biracial" quality to which Palmer refers characterizes not only the "song" featured in the video, but Run-DMC's appearance both *with* Tyler and Perry and, more significantly, *before* the audience for the performance, every single member of which (as far as can be determined from the fleeting glimpses offered by the video) is white. This characteristic of the audience *in* the video makes it an effective figure for what company executives envisioned as the likely audience *for* a video aired on MTV, which from the time of the station's inception in 1981 was not only white, but also relatively young (ages 12–34) and predominantly male, thus constituting a prime target market for producers of the specifically "rock"-oriented music and videos that MTV programmers had decided to feature.

Of course, that decision, which substantially shaped MTV's audience in its early years, was itself attributed by station executives to constitutional factors that they saw as objectively manifest in a *preexistent* audience that they wanted to tap. For MTV was one of the television industry's most successful early subscribers to the demographically engineered strategy known as "narrowcasting," whereby the station's appeal to financial backers, rather than deriving from its capacity to "broadcast" programming to the widest possible audience, on the contrary issued from its ability to target a sizable yet relatively homogeneous viewership. Given certain obvious demographic data for the United States, it is fairly easy to deduce that the optimum—because most lucrative—coincidence of such homogeneity and sizability would inhere in precisely the young, white, male collectivity eventually conceived by station executives as the "MTV audience."

More questionable, however, are the uniformity of musical interests and the affective characteristics that station management attributed to that "audience" as it cultivated its programming strategy. Not only did MTV programmers see their constituency as unalterably in thrall to conventionally white-oriented, classic "hard-rock" music, but also as almost fanatically enthusiastic about it, a trait that was posited as highly appealing to industry marketers. According to MTV founder Bob Pittman, who consistently defended the station against charges of racism in the composition of its playlist, when the programming design was being drafted, "[t]he mostly white rock audience was more excited about rock than the largely black audience was about contemporary rhythm and blues," impelling the station to target this apparently exuberant white market. What's more, according to the *New York Times*'s rendering of a Pittman statement, the station was responding not only to the supposed enthusiasm of the white rock audience, but also to the "innovative" quality of rock culture itself, as evidenced in the rock-music press; by contrast, Pittman discerned no comparable innovativeness in the print media attendant to black popular music (Levine, 1983, pp. 55–56). Thus, according to Pittman, black pop-musical culture is definitionally relatively *conservative,* which characteristic apparently made it unsuitable for engagement by the implicitly progressive medium that was MTV in the early 1980s.[2]

It is important to note that MTV's relatively exclusive telecast roster was not anomalous in the larger scheme of things. Rather, it strongly recalled the airplay policies of any number of radio stations across the country featuring an "album-oriented rock" (AOR) format—a key factor in the ongoing exclusion of African-American artists from "mainstream" radio playlists. Developed in the early 1970s in response to Nixon-era threats against putatively subversive "freeform" FM radio, AOR stations play little or no music by blacks, fairly indicating the increasing disassociation of African-American music from the "rock" designation since the term gained popular currency in the 1950s.[3] That disassociation, effected through industry practice itself, long served to justify radio stations' own narrowcasting policies, and thus to prevent black artists from gaining exposure to the young, white audiences AOR stations target. Consequently, African-American musicians desiring to expand their market—as any of them might logically want to do—have long been forced to seek exposure through means other than radio airplay. Clearly, music video could have constituted just such an alternative for black musical acts in the early 1980s but for the fact that MTV, which enjoyed a virtual monopoly on the telecast of the new genre, effectively replicated the playlist policies of AOR radio itself (see Zeichner, 1982, p. 39).[4]

Nevertheless, it is clear that Run-DMC's video for "Walk This Way" conformed to whatever programming criteria were operative at MTV by the summer of 1986 (after which, incidentally, Pittman made a departure from the station; see DeCurtis, 1986), potentially indicating that the hard-rock material that the group adopted and adapted worked a sort of progressivizing function on the African-American rap form whereby the latter became suitable for the "innovative" context that the station represented. To accept this, however, would be to grant Pittman's claim about the conservatism of black pop-musical culture—certainly not the inclination of Rick Rubin, who traced his interest in black music to his days in high school, where, he told Barry Walters, his black classmates' musical tastes were uniformly more "progressive" than those of his white peers (Walters, 1986, p. 23). In the same vein, *Rolling Stone* critic Mark Coleman suggested that, rather than benefiting from the "innovative" quality of Aerosmith's 1970s composition, Run-DMC's cut actually *modernized* the rock band, "drag[ging] guest stars Steven Tyler and Joe Perry into the Eighties, kicking and screaming." The mutually substitutable character of judgments about the relative "conservatism" or "progressiveness" of different musical styles suggests fairly clearly, I think, their speciousness and lack of critical utility. Nonetheless, the nature of the evidence on which they are based indicates certain crucial facts about the racial politics of the contemporary pop-music industry, some consideration of which will help us grasp the import of Run-DMC's 1986 appearance on MTV.

Barry Walters (1986) has made a useful point by way of explicating Rick Rubin's claim that his black classmates were more musically "progressive" than their white counterparts:

> The music industry treats white music as an ongoing history, and
> black music as just the latest thing. Many record companies will keep
> in print the entire catalog of white acts that don't sell big numbers
> and delete product by all but the biggest-selling black acts. . . . In
> other words, black kids are "progressive" because they've got no
> choice. (p. 23)

This is a trenchant observation, and it helps tremendously in contextualizing MTV with respect to the larger pop-music industry, whose conceptualization of white rock-and-roll as a sustained, coherent tradition is indicated by certain peculiarities in the recognized barometer of the contemporary music scene, the "hit" charts published in *Billboard* magazine.

As of November 1986, when the popularity of Run-DMC's *Raising Hell* album had begun to be fully registered, *Billboard* published record charts under two categories—Albums and Singles. Singles charts covered the areas of Adult Contemporary, Country, Dance/Disco, and Black Music, and the supposedly cross-generic "pop" ranking called the "Hot 100." Under the Album category fell eight different charts, those for Jazz, Country, Classical, Latin, and Black music, a "pop" listing corresponding to the "Hot 100" for singles, a list of top-selling compact disc recordings, and a chart titled "Rock Tracks." The most notable aspect of this last chart is that it wasn't a list of albums at all, but rather of single cuts played on "album-oriented rock" radio stations. Nevertheless, it was clearly identified as an "album" chart in *Billboard*'s table of contents. The implication is that a "rock track," though technically a single song, is part of a larger artistic work comprised in an album and that, although for airplay purposes singles must be used to represent the complete work, the album ought not be dissected into its constituent songs if one is to appreciate the artistic integrity of the whole. This, apparently, is not true of the other categories for which singles charts were published, and certainly not for "Black" songs, which evidently do not cohere as conceptually integrated albums and thus are easily pegged as discrete "singles" whose rise up the charts is always contingent and anomalous, just as more general black-musical developments, as Walters points out, constitute an unaccountable "latest thing." Moreover, of the *Billboard* charts that recorded the "popularity" of actual singles, only the "Rock Tracks" and "Adult Contemporary" rankings were based solely on reports of radio airplay, while all the others were based upon the dual criteria of airplay and retail sales. Since commercial radio stations had had restrictive playlists—based on policies similar to that of MTV—for much longer than MTV had even been in existence in 1986, the likelihood of the "Rock Tracks" chart's representing "public" opinion about contemporary releases seems nil. The use of retail sales figures in the compilation of most of the other charts at least provided the illusion that audience tastes contributed to a record's ranking, though the fact that such tastes are themselves conditioned by radio station airplay decisions makes even this criterion questionable.

Thus, insofar as the music industry itself operates in such a way as continually to reaffirm the overall integrity of white-oriented rock music, the potential appearance of any black musical production amid the white rock context must necessarily figure as the irruption of a completely unaligned, free-floating agent into the coherency of that music's artistic "tradition." Given this, Run-DMC's use of Aerosmith's material and the rock musicians' appearance in both the audio and video versions of the rap group's recording must be seen as crucial to the rappers' admission onto MTV, serving a function at once inoculatory and disciplinary whereby Run-DMC was made both "presentable" to the MTV audience and manageable within the context of rock culture.[5] That admission having once been made, Run-DMC's production could affect as it would not only the black hip-hop communities that had previously constituted the primary audience for rap, but the young, white viewers presumedly glued to MTV who would now become familiar with what that production entailed.

It must immediately be acknowledged, however, that the Run-DMC production featured on MTV differs significantly from that promulgated through radio in that, by definition, it comprises a compelling visual component. Thus the crossover project in which Run-DMC participated entails as much a transformation in *modality* as it does a traversal of audience divisions. The ramifications of this fact are profound and wide-reaching, though the fact itself does not originate with Run-DMC. Indeed, it will be useful for the ensuing analysis to consider some exemplifications of it that predate the rap group's success.

Visions of Motown and Upward Mobility

A noteworthy forerunner to Run-DMC with respect to crossover success is veteran musician and recording artist Stevie Wonder, whose 1972 album *Talking Book,* interestingly enough, actually thematizes the modal interplay that I have noted at work in the later group's video production. Not only does the title of Wonder's album implicate the interrelation of aural and visual experiences—spoken word and printed matter (thereby firmly situating Wonder in a centuries-old African-American cultural tradition),[6] but a limited number of covers for the album present the blind musician's name, the album title, and an exclusive dedicatory message in the tactile medium of braille, thus underscoring the effective "multimedia" quality of Wonder's professional activity.

That quality, it probably goes without saying, did not derive from Wonder's production of music videos, since the latter did not emerge as an influential medium until well after Wonder had already achieved his pop-musical crossover, in 1972, the very year of *Talking Book*'s release. Nor was that crossover effected by the *Talking Book* recording per se, but through Wonder's work in a rather more old-fashioned mode than even the twelve-inch LP record—namely, live performance. Throughout 1972, Stevie Wonder toured in concert with what is arguably the most classic of classic rock bands, the Rolling Stones, thereby reaching an audience of young, white rock fans whose notice he had not previously gained in his by-then already decade-long career. The differences in applied media technologies aside, Wonder's 1972 efforts effectively anticipated those of Run-DMC in 1986, helping him break through the barriers constituted by the restrictive playlist policies of mainstream radio. As Wonder himself specifically said of the tour, "It wasn't a money-making thing, that wasn't the idea—exposure was the thing" (for quotation, see Slater, 1975, p. 18; also see Orth, 1974, p. 62; Waller, 1985, p. 198). That exposure apparently paid off: Soon after Wonder ended his 1972 road trip, the *Talking Book* single "Superstition" hit number 1 on *Billboard*'s "Hot 100," becoming his first chart-topper since 1963; and another cut from the album, "You Are the Sunshine of My Life," reached number 1 in the ensuing months (Whitburn, 1985, p. 341). Over the next two years there appeared a wave of articles in the popular press that remarked upon Wonder's enormously broadened appeal: The *New York Times* spoke of Wonder's "new audience of young and not-so-young whites" (Slater, 1975, p. 18); *The New Yorker* commented upon his "huge interracial audience" (Willis, 1974); a *Newsweek* cover story gushed that "Stevie is the favorite of young, old, black, white, the hip and the square" (Orth, 1974, p. 59); and *Time* said Wonder's records "transcend musical categories" ("Black, Blind," 1974, p. 51). By 1975, Wonder's popular appeal was so great—and, necessarily, so cross-racial—that he was able to renew his contract with the

Stevie Wonder playing to an enthusiastic New York City audience in 1974, at the height of his crossover success. Photos: J. P. Laffont/Sygma.

Motown Record Corporation at the then-unprecedented rate of $13 million (N. George, 1985, p. 183; "Wonderbucks," 1975).

It is neither surprising nor coincidental that Wonder should have achieved his market success under the auspices of Motown, since the company had banked on just such musical "transcendence" as Wonder putatively achieved since producing its first big hits in the early 1960s. Indeed, the tenure on *Billboard*'s "Top 40" of Wonder's own first number 1 hit single (and his *only* one prior to "Superstition")—1963's "Fingertips, Pt. 2"—ended just before the magazine began a fif-teen-month hiatus in the publishing of a specialized "rhythm-and-blues," or "R&B," chart (precursor to the "Black" music chart of the 1980s), arguably owing to the extensive degree of chart overlap that had been effected by the general pop-ularity of Motown's black acts (see Whitburn, 1985, p. 341; Shaw, 1986, p. 227; Waller, 1985, p. 22). Whatever Motown's role in *Billboard*'s alteration of its chart-ing policy, the alteration itself bespeaks some racial-categorical turmoil in the industry at the historical juncture in question. While the history of racial market-ing in the popular-music industry extends at least as far back as the "race" record-ings of the 1920s through 1940s (see Shaw, 1986, pp. 93–128), specifically cross-racial *influence* in pop-musical culture achieved unprecedented saliency with the emergence of rock-and-roll in the 1950s, and this in such a way as to problema-tize greatly the racial classifications that governed music-industry policy until that point. It is not possible, in this context, to consider comprehensively the import of that problematization, but we can glean its potential implications for pop-musical crossover by briefly reviewing the significances of the "pop" catego-rization itself.

My references to "pop" music in the foregoing pages—which fairly duplicate industry and media usage of the term—belie the complexity of the designation, which could stand to be decoded somewhat. Most generally, we can consider it as denoting recordings that receive airplay on chart-oriented radio stations and that sell well on the mass market, thus supposedly engaging the tastes of the widest segment of the public. In this sense, "pop" music is distinguished from seemingly more arcane musical traditions, such as classical or jazz, which enjoy neither the degree of airplay nor the high sales that characterize "pop." At the same time, how-ever, the existence of more-or-less black-oriented musical categories—classic rhythm-and-blues; disco, house, and other dance-club forms; hip-hop–based rap—that would clearly fall under this general "pop" rubric actually predicates the latter's relative instability. Thus, in addition to signifying in the way I have just outlined, "pop" is also used to refer less to a musical style than to contexts of play and distribution wherein African-American musical influence, however prevalent in the material at hand, is not acknowledged, and the audience to be engaged is conceived as racially generic, at best, if not absolutely white—if there indeed be any difference between the two. It is this fictive audience—which is both the justi-fication for and the product of such institutions as *Billboard*'s "Hot 100" chart—that is taken to be *the* "pop" or, more insidiously, "mainstream" market in which the producers of industry-defined "black" music hope to make a strong financial showing and thus establish themselves as examples of crossover success.

Given the marked dynamism not just of popular music in general, but of African-American forms in particular, "pop" in this latter sense is in a constant state of reconceptualization with respect to the specific instances of black musical production allowed under the rubric. Whether it is true that Motown music from the early 1960s unilaterally forced such an extensive reconceptualization as to render *Billboard*'s R&B chart temporarily redundant, it is certainly the case that the company was a "pop"-producing powerhouse throughout the period, managing acts and releasing product that enjoyed huge audiences and great market success.

According to at least one commentator, at the height of Motown's success company founder Berry Gordy, Jr., claimed that "when a Motown record sold a million, an estimated 70 percent of those copies were bought by whites" (Waller, 1985, p. 16). However this may be, it is well known that Gordy early on imagined that the music he produced—the vast majority of it by black artists—would have market appeal beyond a specifically African-American audience. In his autobiography, Gordy (1994) himself has recalled his plans for his 1951 composition, the first he ever completed, "You Are You": "Thinking of general audiences even then, I had written this song with Doris Day in mind. She was America's girl next door" (p. 53). Apparently unfazed by Day's lack of response to the copy of the song that he sent her, in 1959 Gordy based the name of his first record label, Tamla, on the title of her 1957 hit, "Tammy" (pp. 53–54, 111; see also N. George, 1985, p. 29; Morse, 1972, p. 30; and Waller, 1985, p. 29). Indeed, Gordy has made no bones about his desire for broad market success, remarking about the improvisatory inclinations of the jazz musicians he used in early Motown studio sessions: "I understood their instincts to turn things around to their liking, but I also knew what I wanted to hear—commercially. So when they went too far, I'd stop them . . ." (p. 125). And by way of indicating his attitudes about music-industry categorizations operative in the late 1950s, Gordy has published an observation on the racial politics of "pop" that approximates the critique I offer above:

> In the music business there had long been the distinction between black and white music, the assumption being that R & B was black and Pop was white. But with Rock 'n' Roll and the explosion of Elvis those clear distinctions began to get fuzzy. Elvis was a white artist who sang black music. What was it? (a) R & B, (b) Country, (c) Pop, (d) Rock 'n' Roll or (e) none of the above.
>
> If you picked C you were right, that is, if the record sold a million copies. "Pop" means popular and if that ain't, I don't know what is. I never gave a damn what else it was called. (pp. 95–96)

Various commentators have discerned Gordy's interest in such market "popularity" in a number of aspects of his work at Motown.[7] In her memoir of her career with the Supremes, for instance, singer Mary Wilson (1987) gives an account of Gordy's decision on a lead vocalist for the trio, quoting him as telling them in 1963, "I know everybody in the group sings lead, but Diane [Ross, later 'Diana'] has the more commercial voice, and I want to use her as the sole lead singer" (p. 170). Wilson identifies fellow-backup vocalist Florence Ballard as Ross's most serious rival for the lead position, and in doing so she verges on positing a more conventionally "authentic" black musical style for the group than it supposedly achieved with Ross in front, noting that Ballard led the group on its early "soulful" numbers, and that "[h]er sound and style were very similar to Aretha Franklin's," who—though passed over for a contract by Gordy in favor of her sister Erma, according to Wilson—would eventually be deemed the industry's First Lady of Soul (pp. 47, 88). Wilson is not the only commentator thus to imply Gordy's disassociation from African-American musical culture, being joined in this judgment by both Arnold Shaw (1986), who has suggested that Motown music actually represents a "white synthesis" of traditional black forms (pp. 223–36), and Don Waller (1985), who has flatly proclaimed that "Berry Gordy wasn't interested in making . . . soul records—Motown is a pop label" (pp. 71–72; see also N. George, 1985, p. 17). Not only do such pronouncements partake of the speciousness that I have already suggested characterizes the idea of objective pop-ular-musical categorization in the first place, but they also neglect the degree to which all styles of recorded musical product—and the notions of racial identifi-cation that attach to them—are inevitably shaped by the industry conditions under which they are produced, with such influence being manifest as much in "soul" music as in the Motown sound. The relevant question here, then, has to do not with what happens to the "authenticity" of black music once it is subjected to the demands of the mass market, but, rather, with how the very idea of "black-ness" itself is constructed and manipulated within the industry in such a way as both to produce and to meet those very demands.

In Berry Gordy's case, wide sales and the "crossover" success they implied entailed the construction and manipulation of one *particular* mode of black iden-tity over other, equally constructed and manipulated ones—for example, that associated with rhythm-and-blues. In the first years of the company's opera-tion—characterized both by officially sanctioned racial segregation throughout the country and by Motown's lack of national recognition—this manipulation took fairly crude forms, such as the decision not to include photographs of Motown artists Mary Wells and the Marvelettes on their albums so that white record store owners in the South would be more likely to stock the black singers' recordings (Waller, 1985, p. 20). Later, though, Gordy took careful steps to ensure the "mainstream" presentability of his acts when they *were* to be seen, either on-stage or off. The existence of Motown's in-house "charm school"—officially known as the department of Artist Development—is well documented by the various commentators on the Motown of the 1960s. Mary Wilson (1987) defensively asserts the gentility that Motown artists exhibited even before their grooming by the company and justifies the existence of the Artist Development department by insisting that most people, black or otherwise, "would not know how to . . . greet a president or a queen without some instruction" (pp. 180–81); but the point is precisely that, as Nelson George (1985, p. 88) tells us, Motown management preached that it was indeed training its artists "to perform in only two places: Buckingham Palace and the White House," for Gordy believed that "real longevity . . . lay in reaching crossover (i.e., white) audiences with stylish live shows" (parentheses in original).

Insofar as it implies that Motown's broad success was predicated on pandering to specifically "white" tastes, George's formulation here recalls the pronouncements previously cited, regarding Gordy's supposed lack of interest in "soul" music. Additionally, though, George's rhetoric indicates the centrality to Motown's project of another significant factor, which he nonetheless does not explicitly address in his discussion. George's reference to Gordy's vision of "stylish" live shows hints at the importance of certain class-status signifiers to the success of Motown's undertaking. Similarly, when he identifies the Supremes specifically as "the epitome of upwardly mobile, adult bourgeois charm" (p. 87), he has hit on class as a factor in crossover that is not accounted for in analyses that focus on racial politics alone.[8] Indeed, in the case of Motown, class signifiers played a particularly significant role, as can be seen from a brief consideration of the career of the Supremes themselves, who indisputably were most responsible for Motown's extensive crossover success during the 1960s.

Berry Gordy has acknowledged that, by 1965, when Motown had become known as a producer of Top 40 hits, he was looking ahead to "taking our people to the next level of show business—top nightclubs around the country. And I knew the Supremes could lead the way" (Gordy, 1994, pp. 208–9). While Gordy felt strongly that the Supremes' success in thus "leading" "our people" depended on their convincing delivery of show tunes and old standards, he was also sure that the best showcase for such a delivery was broadcast television, certain that "if I could get the Supremes to do a standard on national TV, millions of people would become believers like me" (p. 209). Consequently, while the trio's audio recordings were punctuated with such "mainstream"-oriented album releases as *A Bit of Liverpool* (on which they performed hits by the Beatles), *The Supremes Sing Country and Western and Pop,* and a tribute to Rodgers and Hart (see M. Wilson, 1987, p. 327), the drive to get them booked in upscale establishments like the Coconut Grove in Los Angeles and, especially, the Copacabana in New York entailed a strategic offensive in the emphatically audio*visual* medium of television. Beginning in December 1964, with an appearance on Ed Sullivan's Christmas program, the Supremes' television blitz lasted well after their summer 1965 debut at the Copa, comprising seven more performances on *The Ed Sullivan Show* and thirteen additional appearances on everything from *Hullabaloo* to *Hollywood Palace* to the Orange Bowl parade by the end of 1966 (Gordy, 1994, pp. 209, 216; N. George, 1985, pp. 143–44; Waller, 1985, pp. 236–37).

The televisual strategy by which the Supremes made their incursion into the "mainstream" music market entailed a noteworthy reversal of Motown's early policy of limiting the visual presentation of its artists for fear that the images of blacks would be wrongly "read" and incorporated into a record's audio message, negatively "coloring" that message. Now, with Motown a well-known black-owned company, the objective was to provide a sophisticated, upscale image that *could* be read back into the music, enhancing the overall impression made by a group that was simply "three colored girls from Detroit," as Ed Sullivan once introduced them, as if to remind everyone of the racial origins they had apparently transcended through their impressively urbane performance (recalled by Mary Wilson, in a television interview on *Hour Magazine,* 1986). Such "transcendence" was in keeping with Gordy's aim of making Motown a mainstream multimedia entertainment giant (partially realized with the company's eventual move to California and its forays into movie-making and other nonmusical projects) and of transforming Diana Ross into "the black Barbra Streisand," the epitome of cross-market success (N. George, 1985, p. 168). This latter objective was the engine for the second wave of television exposure that carried the rechristened "Diana Ross and the Supremes" through twenty-five network television appearances from January 1968 to December 1969, the primary import of which appearances, in terms of Gordy's plans for the company, was that the bourgeois orientation signaled by the group's sophisticated performances made the question of race irrelevant, since, according to the consumerist logic that drives the conception of the United States as a "classless" society in the late twentieth century, "everyone," "universally," could identify with the "stylish" visual presentation the group offered up. For Motown, then, such black identity as was represented in its top acts' televisual performances served primarily as a cipher, whose key function was to be rendered inconsequential by the artists' recognizably "professional" "style," itself the factor of paramount importance in their successful cultivation of a wide "pop" audience. This function would reach an apotheosis in the 1980s with the rapid career rise of the last major star to have been given early grooming by Motown, and whose own use of the televisual medium significantly bridges the crossover strategies of Stevie Wonder, on the one hand, and Run-DMC, on the other. At the same time, however, and paradoxically, that apotheosis would coincide with a dramatic heightening in the general cultural significance of blackness that has continued through the present, wrought in large part through precisely that televisual mode in which African-American culture had long been denied a place.

Michael Jackson, Music-Video Dance, and the Authenticity of the "Street"

At the end of 1969, Diana Ross left the Supremes (who, during their streak of mainstream popularity during the mid-1960s, did actually perform both for U.S. heads of state and for British royalty; see M. Wilson, 1987, pp. 246, 269) to embark on a solo career that entailed high-profile work in film and on the major nightclub circuit, as well as in the recording studio. For the sake of my analysis here, however, the significance of Ross's post-Supremes career lies specifically in the ulterior functions that it served. One of those, clearly, was the establishment of Motown as a major player in the multimedia entertainment industry, as I have already indicated; but a more pertinent one was the launching of the final major act to be produced by the company during its Detroit tenure. Though insiders were aware that the brothers known as the Jackson 5 were "discovered" by the leader of a lesser-known Motown group—Bobby Taylor of the Vancouvers—as Nelson George says, "the decision was made to use Ross to market the group" so it would share her access to television, and she officially "introduced" the Jackson 5 to the public in 1969, co-hosting (along with Sammy Davis, Jr.) the October 18 *Hollywood Palace* show on which they made their TV debut (N. George, 1985, p. 184; Gordy, 1994, pp. 279, 284; Waller, 1985, p. 46; M. Wilson, 1987, p. 278). The young family act did go on to make numerous television appearances, the bulk of which, like those of other Motown artists earlier in the decade, were timed to coincide with the release dates of singles the group had cut, so as to boost the songs' accession to "hit" status. In fact, in a move that presaged the cross-media marketing strategy that music videos presently constitute, the Jackson 5's appearance on Ross's 1971 television special was actually advertised on the label of a single cut by the group, effectively encouraging owners of the record to *see* (once again) the singers whom they had already *heard* on vinyl ("Never Can Say Goodbye"). Moreover, in addition to appearing on telecasts—including their own special—in the flesh, the Jackson 5 starred as animated drawings in a regularly featured Saturday morning cartoon series in the early 1970s, significantly blending visuals and recordings of hit songs to tap an even younger market than would eventually be targeted by MTV. Thus it was the Jackson 5, as Nelson George (1985, p. 187) asserts, who gave Motown "its most profound television success." Conversely, it was the group's lead singer, Michael, ten years old when Motown

The Jackson 5 (left to right: Tito, Marlon, Michael, Jackie, Jermaine) in an early television appearance. Photo courtesy of Photofest.

signed the act, who most benefited from television's ever-expanding capabilities to become the epitome of black crossover success in the 1980s. For just as Stevie Wonder used an association with a white classic-rock band to broaden his audience in 1972, thereby engaging a strategy that Run-DMC would later exploit, so too did Michael Jackson prefigure the rap group's notable televisual "breakthrough," initiating in 1983 a development that would culminate with and be transformed by Run-DMC's broad market success three years later.

However noteworthy was Run-DMC's appearance on MTV in 1986, it followed in some significant ways the path blazed by Michael Jackson, who was the indomitable icon of black crossover in the mid-1980s. Tracing Jackson's career during that period, "rock biographer" Albert Goldman (whose works include a life of Elvis Presley and, most notoriously, a biography of John Lennon) has pinpointed the time of the entertainer's ascendancy to the pinnacle of popularity: "When pop archivists page back to find the moment of Michael Jackson's epiphany as a superstar, they will pin the date as March 2, 1983. On that day, the first Michael Jackson video was telecast on MTV to 10 million American homes" (Goldman, 1984, p. 73). Goldman is right in asserting the momentousness of this occasion, for, as I have already indicated, MTV was generally devoid of video presentations by African-American artists throughout the early 1980s. Indeed, writing in October 1983, Roger Wolmuth noted the difficulty that Jackson himself had faced in gaining access to the station's cameras earlier in the year (p. 99), so the singer's debut on Music Television is notable in more ways than one, indicating both Jackson's official entry into a strategically defined "pop" bastion—an official "crossover"—and MTV's modification of its telecast policy, which would have wide-ranging long-term effects.

The effects on Jackson's career are well known. By October 1983 his album *Thriller*—music from which provided the material for the breakthrough videos— had sold over ten million copies in the United States alone; throughout 1983 the record sold at a rate of at least 200,000 copies per week (Wolmuth, 1983, p. 96); that rate jumped to 600,000 per week after the release of the video for the album's title track near the end of 1983 (Cocks, "Sing," p. 56); six of the nine songs on the album became hit singles (see Whitburn, 1985, p. 166); by the winter of 1983–1984 Jackson had garnered more than $66 million in royalties and a total of 140 gold and platinum awards for sales of music from the *Thriller* album; and by the end of that season, he had received recognition from the *Guinness Book of World Records* for having produced the biggest-selling record album of all time (R. Johnson, 1984, p. 164). Meanwhile, the popular media quickly translated Jackson's commercial triumph into his unassailable supremacy as a performer, fueling the mania that was evidenced by his huge financial take. Following the lead of CBS/Epic records, with whom Jackson signed on after leaving Motown, *Ebony* magazine proclaimed the singer "The World's Greatest Entertainer" (R. Johnson, 1984, p. 163); *Time* declared Jackson "the biggest star in the world" (Cocks, "Why," p. 54); and *People Weekly* published an entire special issue devoted to celebrating the performer's "superstar" status (*All about Michael*, 1984). That Jackson's fame and fortune were significantly boosted by the telecast of his videos on MTV cannot be in doubt, considering that, by August 1983, when his popularity was still on the rise, the entertainment industry publication *Daily Variety* had already conducted a survey whose results, as J. Hoberman (1983, p. 35) noted, indicated that "MTV viewers are more influenced by the cable music video channel than by radio, concerts or commercial [*sic*] TV when they buy records."[9] This statistic is not surprising since, as the *New York Times* noted in 1983, "a clip shown on MTV could be seen immediately in more than 12 million homes; a national tour might take six months and only reach 100,000 rock fans" (Levine, 1983, p. 58). As for the comparison with conventional TV, the sociopolitical suspiciousness of "narrowcasting" aside, MTV's exclusive, youth-oriented focus on pop-music culture undoubtedly draws interested viewers away from traditional stations, since it pretty much guarantees that they will see something to engage them whenever they tune in, whereas standard broadcast television has always framed its pop-music features as relatively "special" programming, not conducive to spontaneous viewing. Further, the general one-act focus and stage-performance format of traditional television's musical features would not allow for exposure of the vast multiplicity of acts that MTV—with its breakneck pace—can present within a comparable time span, and with substantially more visual stimulation than is allowed by the stage-performance framework. This latter point would also likely explain why MTV enjoys relatively greater market influence than radio, which, despite similarities between its play-format and that of MTV, is significantly less able than the latter to evoke the sort of "lifestyle" context that music videos' visual component helps to construct, and which itself has become a huge factor in the commercial success of pop-musical product.

Ironically, however, in almost barring Michael Jackson from telecast, MTV nearly failed to capitalize on that visual component in the way that has become characteristic of the station since the mid-1980s. Indeed, if MTV's ability to influence the pop-music market significantly boosted Jackson's career when his videos finally were aired, so too did one of the principal aspects of those videos eventually provide a shot in the arm to MTV, whose vitality came into doubt once *Thriller*'s tide of popularity subsided. By August 1986, there were reports of a decline in MTV's ratings by the A. C. Nielsen company, which surveys national viewing habits. MTV management both contested the accuracy of the Nielsen figures and denied that they would have been significant had they been correct (Farley and Vamos, 1986), but the slump continued into 1987 nonetheless (Zoglin, 1987). Assessments published in both years noted that MTV was still posting record revenues, but as early as 1986 *Business Week* magazine asserted that "[t]he channel was most popular when Michael Jackson mania swept the country, and it isn't likely to achieve similar ratings until another such phenomenon comes along" (Farley and Vamos, 1986). Apparently none had by the following June, however, when *Time* magazine declared that the videos showcased on the station "have settled into a yawn-provoking rut" (Zoglin, 1987). Yet by the summer of 1991, *New York Times* pop critic Jon Pareles was striking a significantly different note, marking the station's tenth anniversary by declaring: "Instead of reinforcing the mainstream of pop as it existed a decade ago, which might have been expected . . . , MTV has overseen 10 years of stylistic splintering and recombinations, united only by wild haircuts and a good beat" (p. 19). Moreover, Pareles noted specifically that the videos shown by the station had "sparked a resurgence of dance music" (p. 1); and *Rolling Stone* contemporaneously pointed out that the station's "Yo! MTV Raps" program was its top-rated show ("MTV Turns Ten," 1991, p. 74). Clearly, significant changes took place at MTV between 1987 and 1991, whereby not only did the "yawn-provoking" quality of the station's telecast give way to apparently intriguing stylistic innovation, but, more significantly, that innovation itself was linked specifically to *dance music* and *rap*—two distinctly African-American inflected forms—in a way that is hard to imagine characterizing such a bastion of white-oriented rock as MTV had once been. To trace MTV's renewed vitality to these two forms is to suggest a relation between Michael Jackson and Run-DMC that might seem unlikely at first, given that the slick productions of the former tend not to jibe with the relatively grittier sensibility taken to characterize rap. Yet there is strong justification for positing such a relation, as we will soon see, with that relation itself indicating much about the significance to contemporary pop-music culture not just of *blackness,* but specifically of *black masculinity.*

This is not to say that the import of black masculinity in music video is figured exclusively through the screen presentation of *black men.* I would argue, for instance, that that import is hinted at in Michael Hirschorn's October 1990 assertion—"These days only Madonna, Janet Jackson, and a handful of rappers release videos with imagination . . ."—where it attaches to the two female performers no less than to the stereotypically masculine associations of rap. That attachment derives from a key aspect of those performers' video productions that Albert Goldman had already noted in Michael Jackson's work seven years prior. Taking recourse in some eyebrow-raising invocations of racial stereotype, Goldman (1984, p. 73) attributes the lesser video success of "typical white rock star[s]" to the fact that "the klutzes can't move!"; on the other hand, Jackson, as a black performer, has natural rhythm—he's "got Bojangles in his bones." The frightful terms of his declaration notwithstanding, Goldman is onto a key element in the appeal of Jackson's videos—namely, the centrality to the productions of dance, which at the time of Jackson's ascent and of Goldman's writing, it will be useful to recall, figured most prominently in the public consciousness in the form of *breaking.* Now strikingly absent from popular-media discussion, breakdancing seemed ubiquitous by mid-1984, with a *Newsweek* cover headline proclaiming "Breaking Out!" as the preferred method of "dancing the summer away" (McGuigan, 1984), and the *Breakdancing* instruction book by Mr. Fresh and the Supreme Rockers at the top of the *New York Times* "Advice, How-To and Miscellaneous" bestseller list (see "Paperback Best Sellers," 1984). These two facts alone suggest the amount of mass-media coverage afforded breakdancing during 1983 and 1984, making for a cultural emergence to parallel that of rap, with which breaking shares roots in black urban street culture.

Indeed, as Tricia Rose has pointed out, breakdancing—the complex of highly acrobatic, syncopated movements originally performed by street dancers during the "breaks" of a DJ's musical mix—is a central element, along with rap and graffiti, in the larger hip-hop culture that came to full fruition in New York City in the late 1970s (see *Black Noise,* 1994, Chapter 2, esp. pp. 47–51).[10] Often enacted as a fierce competition between different dance "crews," breaking, like rap in its earliest incarnations, has been seen as a profoundly masculine endeavor, whose very moves, consequently, have connoted the virility and male bravado romantically associated with black urban street culture in the general popular consciousness. Albert Goldman (1984) exemplifies the romanticization of that culture even as he comments on it in his consideration of Michael Jackson's rise to popularity in 1983. Noting that "[d]uring this same period, the kids [by which he means *white* kids, specifically] got a new fix on black culture, the inspiration for both Elvis and the Beatles but long since relegated to the ghetto and black radio by the white rockers," Goldman concisely characterizes white youth's sense of black urban culture:

> The kids see the ghetto as a garishly colored, percussively accented
> cartoon world peopled by wildly animated break dancers, graffiti
> writers, rap masters and scritch-scratch deejays. It's a kid's world, just
> as break dancing and graffiti writing is kid's stuff. (p. 74)

It is impossible to tell from this passage the degree to which Goldman himself actually believes in the vision of "the ghetto" that he ascribes to "the kids," let alone how he has arrived at his conviction that it is the one to which they uniformly subscribe. What *is* clear, however, is Goldman's sense that this imagined ghetto itself constitutes the only legitimate repository of "black culture" per se, insofar as "white rockers'" supposed "relegation" of the culture specifically to that social-geographic site implies that it never has, does not now, and never *could* exist anywhere else. Having thus suggested the coextensiveness of the ghetto context and African-American culture, Goldman goes on to assert—albeit without actually explicating—Michael Jackson's import with respect to this black cultural complex, claiming that his function "is not so much to embody it as to transfigure it, lending it a glamour that is sorely lacking in the streets" (p. 74). Thus Jackson, according to Goldman's assessment, represents African-American street culture one step removed, almost literally *translating* it into the terms of pop-cultural consumption. The mode of that translation is precisely the dance performance that Jackson enacts and that Goldman himself has cited as the primary factor in the popularity of his music video. For as Tricia Rose has pointed out, that performance borrows liberally from and is largely continuous with the moves of early breakdancers, as are the dance routines performed on video by other artists who have risen to superstardom since Jackson's peak—artists such as Janet Jackson and Madonna (*Black Noise,* 1994, p. 51).[11]

I should at this point assert flat-out what will soon become clear enough anyway—that my discussion of Michael Jackson here does not touch on his cosmetic surgery, his skin lightening, his (allegedly illicit) interest in children, or his marriage to Lisa Marie Presley—or on these issues' supposed implications for his racial identification, sexuality, or gender identity, contrary to what might be expected from a study of contemporary black masculinity. I ignore these issues not because they are unimportant per se, but because I am interested less in the overall significance of Jackson as a specific public persona than in his relation to dominant conceptions of black masculinity that figure prominently in the shaping of contemporary U.S. popular culture. If, as I have already intimated, such conceptions inform the perceived significance of the street-cultural dance form of breaking—and if, as Goldman, Tricia Rose, and others suggest, that dance form constitutes the foundation of Jackson's own choreographic performance—then, all his personal-life issues aside, Jackson's dancing—as well as that of Janet Jackson, Madonna, and others—implicitly and inevitably *refers to* and thus *conjures up* those dominant conceptions of black masculinity through the elements of street movement that it incorporates.

Indeed, it is specifically the "street" elements of these artists' routines that have emerged as central to their on-screen moves. When, in 1984, Michael Jackson and his brothers called upon choreographer Paula Abdul to help them stage their "Victory" tour, Jermaine Jackson specifically extolled the fact that Abdul "is in tune with streetwise dancing" (Friedman, 1987, p. 101). And while Michael Jackson had his breakthrough "Thriller" and "Beat It" videos choreographed by Michael Peters (in a style no less "streetwise" than Abdul's), Abdul pretty much reigned over music-video choreography from 1986 through 1991, bearing primary responsibility for (among countless other video routines) the moves executed by Janet Jackson in the videos associated with her *Control* album—and this Jackson, too, has admiringly cited Abdul's emphasis on "street" moves (see Friedman, 1987, p. 101; Cohen, 1988, p. 86).

At the same time, however, the incorporation of "street" dance into the choreography of pop performance is nothing new. In a 1991 interview, dancer and choreographer Cholly Atkins indicated the currency of street dance in the high-precision routines he developed for Motown artists during the 1960s, when he worked in the company's Artist Development department. Explaining that much of the early work he did with the Temptations (whose steps were probably the most famous ones showcased by Motown artists) was based on routines devised by group member Paul Williams, Atkins pointed out that "most of the moves that Paul used were street moves. We just cleaned them up a little bit." Atkins then went on to explain that he himself adapted street moves in his work, his objective being "to make a happy marriage between the aural and the visual" ("Everybody Dance Now," 1991). However fortunate the union thus forged by Atkins, in terms of the pleasure experienced by audiences for his choreography,

The Temptations (left to right: David Ruffin, Melvin Franklin, Paul Williams, Otis Williams, Eddie Kendricks) show off their steps in a Motown publicity photo from the early 1960s. Photo courtesy of Photofest.

the happiest marriage yet achieved between the aural and the visual in terms of pop-cultural market success is the one presented in music video, which by 1991 typically was characterized not by the "scenes of the [featured] band in performance intercut with snippets of a fanciful 'story'" that Richard Zoglin found so tedious in 1987, but by just such street-based dancework as has been created by Abdul, Peters, and others. Indeed, as of MTV's tenth anniversary, Jon Pareles (1991, p. 1) identified dance as an eminently "popular video gambit," and PBS's 1991 documentary on music-video choreography posited dance as "the heartbeat of music videos," which it said featured moves deriving from "street dance of every description" ("Everybody Dance Now," 1991).

Thus, by the early 1990s, music video had become practically synonymous with popular dance, which by virtue of its own grounding in and evocation of idiomatic "street" movement came associatively to represent "street" culture— that is, Latino and, especially, African-American street culture—itself. Video choreographers have themselves referred to the mass-popularization of street dance effected through music video, with Barry Lather (who choreographed Janet

Jackson's 1987 "Pleasure Principle" video) affirming: "We try to get what's happening right on the street level or in clubs—you know, funky or street steps, or hip-hop steps. And if you can give them to an artist, then everybody gets to see it" ("Everybody Dance Now," 1991). Similarly, Vincent Paterson, who choreographed Michael Jackson's "Smooth Criminal" video and Madonna's rendition of "Vogue" at the 1990 MTV video music awards, has said that video "shows America what dance is about in America these days. It takes dance from the streets, from the clubs, and puts it in a visual medium where everyone across America—and the *world*—is exposed to what is happening . . ." ("Everybody Dance Now," 1991).

Thus, just as Cholly Atkins's routines for Motown constituted "cleaned-up" renditions of street movement, so too does contemporary video choreography generally constitute an adaptation of hip-hop–oriented street dance. Nonetheless, there is a crucial difference in the *significances* of Motown choreography and music-video dance, stemming largely from the differences in their presentational contexts. Because the former was performed in such upscale establishments as the Copacabana (to name a club where the Temptations, also, eventually appeared; see Gordy, 1994, p. 236), which context served to obscure the "street" origins of the dance steps, the "cleaning up" of those steps accrued to the artists' assumption of a bourgeois aspect that was the engine of their crossover success. By contrast, the televisual medium through which music-video dance is presented—and through which contemporary black-cultural crossover is effected—actually *thematizes* and thus *publicizes* the source function of street culture with respect to that dance, while its powerful spectacular logic figures the culture's conventionally masculine significance in highly masculin*ist* terms of public display. To be rather more concrete, because the format of MTV (to cite deliberately the most decisively "pop"-oriented example) allows for the typical juxtaposition of such videos as, say, Janet Jackson's broadly inclusive "Rhythm Nation"—with its stylized, didacto-realist, democratic-utopian staging—and Sir Mix-A-Lot's perversely Afrocentric "Baby Got Back"—depicting a "community" gathering whose central feature is a bevy of African-American women vigorously shaking their bikinied buttocks at extremely close camera range—it implicitly posits instances like the latter as representing the "authentic" locus of the black culture on which the former draws for its choreographic vocabulary, concomitantly establishing as common knowledge the lineal relation between the two.[12] Given this presentational mode, contemporary video dance not only inevitably *refers to* the masculine-oriented street-cultural forms from which it derives, it thereby actually helps to constitute as "authentic" the potently *masculinist* cultural presentations through which the street context is figured. By the same token and conversely, that masculinism itself functions as the seal of proof for any representation of the street context that aspires to the condition of cultural authenticity. The degree to which this is the case is best indicated not by the blatant (and by now *classic*) manifestations of misogyny and homophobia in many of those representations, but in the very presentational terms of some of the least obviously offensive examples.

A good illustration of this point is provided by an instance, not of music video per se, but of another key element in music video telecast—commercial advertisement, which is itself often posited as representing the authentic black street venue to which music videos themselves more obliquely refer.[13] The specific commercial I want to examine—which is extremely brief, running just fifteen seconds—enjoyed currency in the late fall of 1994. It opens with a medium-distance camera shot of a young African-American man—accessorized in ski cap, sunglasses, and hiking boots—seated in a reclining chair that is positioned outdoors, at the end of a long, narrow city block. While the camera swings quickly to show, from right to left, either side of the dilapidated building that rises up behind him, the man says to the camera, "Some people try to grab the bull by the horns"— which observation is followed by a fast cut to footage of a rodeo wherein a cowboy is indeed attempting to wrestle down a charging bull that he has grasped by the horns. Just as quickly, we cut back to the black man, who amends his first statement: ". . . or anything else they can get." Back again to the rodeo, where the cowboy now has one hand on the bull's horns and the other much further back on the animal's body, toward its hinder parts. Now the camera returns for good to the black man, who asserts: "But around my way"—and now he gestures with his right hand toward the tenement-like apartment buildings that the camera has swung to reveal looming in the background—"there's only one way to grab the bull . . ."; he reaches with his left hand into the ice bucket that sits on the sidewalk next to him and pulls out a forty-ounce bottle of Schlitz malt liquor: "by the neck." The commercial closes with his enjoining the audience to "chill," and with the printed slogan at the bottom of the screen: THE BULL IS TAKIN' CHARGE ("Bull Neck," 1994).

This slogan is interesting insofar as, by indicating the sovereignty of the Schlitz "bull" in the context conjured in the ad itself, it stands in tense relation to the man's own assertion of control *over* the bull—his having it "by the neck." In this way, the commercial seems to thematize cannily the very logic of advertising, whereby the featured commodity's purchase on a given market is actually figured in terms of the greater control and subjective power gained by the individual who consumes the product. In this specific instance, the "bull's" "taking charge" seems meant not only to signify the market dominance of Schlitz but, further, to indicate the properly masculine domination of the local context that has already been figured in the black man's taking the "bull" by the neck, by which he succeeds in subduing it as the white cowboy never does, even after resorting to the undignified strategy of grasping at the animal's rear-end. The cool control thus exhibited by what can only be termed the "homeboy" is posited, moreover, as a function of his absolutely perfect comprehension of life "around his way" (the essence of which seems to comprise an existence literally on the street), with his gesture toward the street suggesting his being completely *of* it no less than the location of his easy chair *in* the street suggests that it is indeed his "home." This ad, then, enacts a severe conceptual condensation whereby urban "street" life is figuratively encapsulated in the black male *denizen* of the street whose own authenticity *as* such a denizen is indicated simultaneously by his intimate knowledge of the demands that it makes and by his evidently having *met* those demands by appropriately mastering the terms of his environment, effectively becoming the "bull" through his masculine domination of it. Thus the authenticity of the street context figured in the ad derives from the more fundamental authenticity of the streetwise black man who functions as its primary symbol; and to the extent that this man's *own* authenticity with respect to the street context is predicated on the degree of masculine control over it that he implicitly exerts, then a masculinist orientation inevitably characterizes representational evocations of that context as the "norm" of contemporary African-American life.

The promulgation of such masculinism, then, is one of the several problems that arise from positing the "ghetto" (to continue using the term invoked by Albert Goldman) as the site of authentic African-American culture—or, in Paul Gilroy's (1994, p. 52) rendering, from positing street culture "not as one black culture among many but as the very *blackest* culture." We can deduce the general import of those problems by considering the specific connotations taken on by the "ghetto" and the "street" in the twentieth-century United States. Far from signifying merely the dense concentration of a socially or ethnically homogeneous collectivity within a specific urban geographic space, *ghetto* now generically connotes an implicitly nonwhite (most likely Latino or African-American), poor urban context uniformly characterized by danger and risk. Similarly the *street,* as Gilroy (1994, p. 58) has pointed out, no longer registers as merely "a privileged space for the elaboration of cultural authenticity" but also, definitionally, "as the location of violence, crime and social pathology." As a consequence of this *latter* significance of the street context, its continued apprehension in terms of the *former* ensures that "violence, crime and social pathology" will themselves become incorporated as fundamental elements in presiding conceptions of "authentic" African-American culture.

I am not concerned here to expound on the "pathological," largely because I am skeptical as to how it might be identified in African-American communities, by whom, and for what purposes. After all, as recently as May 1995, U.S. Senator Bob Dole engaged in the time-honored practice of racial-cultural scapegoating, positing "gangsta" rap as the emblem of everything that is wrong with U.S. popular culture (see Klein, 1995; Reibstein, 1995); given the logic of "authenticity" that I have suggested now characterizes influential conceptions of black life, it is easy to consider Dole as really suggesting that African-American culture per se comprises everything that is wrong with U.S. society—a suggestion to which the concept of "pathology" might be unscrupulously assimilated as a polemical buttress. At the same time, though, I am concerned to interrogate a masculinism in black culture that is evidently problematic and undesirable—detrimental to the well-being of African-American communities however variously they may be constituted. A prime mechanism of that detriment is the incorporation of masculinism—according to the logic sketched previously—into "authentically" black culture such that not only the offshoots of that "authentic" culture (music-video choreography, for example) but also its colineal counters (e.g., "pro-woman" or antisexist rap) will inevitably be positioned as aberrations with respect to the norm that it represents.[14]

So the key issue raised by this current, most extensive mode of black cultural crossover is neither of those classically associated with the phenomenon: control over the immense amount of capital that it generates, and the possible "selling out" of the race by artists involved in the exchange. Rather, it is the promulgation—through the very mechanisms that underwrite African-American culture's disproportionate influence in U.S. society—of one aspect of that culture as essentially authentic in such a way that deviations from it are seen as constituting not proof of the culture's necessary diversity, but fundamental failures of the will to blackness. This development is troublesome for the general reason that it largely disallows the variation and flux that have been prime attributes of African-American culture since its emergence, and that are necessary in any event to culture's crucial critical edge; and for the more specific reason that some of the characteristics thus solidified as "essentially" black deserve no quarter in a tradition to which the pursuit of individual, social, and political freedom has been so central as it has to African-American culture. Writing in 1985, Sally Banes proposed that "America . . . is fascinated by black and Latin kids' street life precisely because . . . it symbolizes hope for the future" (1994, p. 153), and this latter assertion may still hold true. The question, however, given the enormous changes that have taken place over the past decade in the way that life is represented in mass culture, is to whom and how many it still thus signifies. For if black street life now dominates the view proffered by a significant segment of the culture industry, it is being represented to African-Americans ourselves no less than to those outside our disparate communities. And for that industry, rather than the "street" per se, thus to shape the dominant sense of how black culture is to develop is for us all to be implicated in an electronic-media loop whose constraining effects we may not only dislike but find ever more difficult either to mitigate or to escape.

PART II

THE LIMITS
OF RACE
AND SOCIAL
REGULATION

$$\boxed{5}$$

GENDER POLITICS
AND THE "PASSING" FANCY

Black Masculinity as Societal Problem

Tragedy, Femininity, and the Literary Mulatto

One of the propositions implicit in Chapter 4 is that racial identity—in the fore-going instance, "authentic" African-American identity in particular—can be, or effectively *is*, gendered—coded specifically as *masculine* in the case of popular music. However jarring the suggestion may be, the fact itself is nothing new in African-American literary culture, a whole subtradition of which centers on the figuration of a specific racial type in decidedly *feminine* terms. I am referring to the "tragic mulatto," a stock figure in U.S. fiction by blacks and whites alike from the nineteenth through the early twentieth centuries. In asserting that the tragic mulatto has been conceived as a specifically feminine character, I in no way mean to imply that U.S. literature contains no male characters of mixed European and African "blood," for it certainly *does*—Tom Driscoll in Mark Twain's *Pudd'nhead Wilson* immediately comes to mind—and I examine one important instance of such a depiction at some length in this chapter. The mere existence of such depic-

103

tions, however, does not mitigate the fundamental feminine orientation that characterizes the genre; on the contrary, what I consider to be the most significant of those depictions actually underscores the fact of that orientation, as I make clear in the subsequent discussion.[1] That orientation itself, moreover, not only accrues in certain instances to the conservative reaffirmation of women's traditional social role, as I shall demonstrate, but it also figures a constraint on black masculinity that has long been a defining cultural feature in the U.S. context, substantially founding the black masculine anxiety that is my primary object of interrogation. Consequently, I want to consider carefully the feminine gendering of the literary mulatto, beginning with an inquiry into the precise character of her "tragic" condition, itself a function of her fundamental femininity.

A key aspect of the tragic mulatto figure familiar to us from U.S. fiction of the nineteenth century, especially, is that she stands in an ambiguous relation to the tragedy with which she is associated. On the one hand, and most notoriously, she functions as the object of any number of unfortunate occurrences—death foremost among them—all of which are generally taken to indicate the untenable position that she occupies in the larger society due to her mixed-race identity. In short, because she is generally too refined to live among the black population to which law and custom relegate her, but too inescapably identified as having some African ancestry to be accepted among the white society for which she is most properly suited, the mulatto usually has no recourse but extinction, which development is typically taken as indicating her fundamentally tragic status.

On the other hand, however, and simultaneously, the mulatto is routinely presented not only as the suffering victim of tragic circumstances, but also (and often in tandem with her presentation as victim) as the subjective agent of tragic developments that impinge not merely upon other individuals, but on the entire social structure that she inhabits, and this in such a way that her feminine identity itself is deeply implicated in the danger that she poses. Let us examine, by way of illustration, a short passage from Frances Ellen Watkins Harper's 1892 novel, *Iola Leroy*—a retrospective passage in which the title character's white, Southern aristocrat father, years before her birth, announces to his cousin his intention to marry the woman who will become her mother, a quadroon slave light-skinned enough to "pass" for white. The horrified cousin, Lorraine, tries to dissuade his kinsman from pursuing this foolish course, brushing aside the claims Eugene Leroy has made as to his fiancée's innocence and virtue:

> "Why, Eugene, what has come over you? Talking of the virtue of these quadroon girls! You have lived so long in the North and abroad, that you seem to have lost the cue of our Southern life. Don't you know

that these beautiful girls have been the curse of our homes? You have
no idea of the hearts which are wrung by their presence." (p. 70)

The tragedy invoked by Lorraine in this passage is clearly associated with
the quadroon figure (and it matters little, in such a context as this, whether the
character in question be identified as a mulatto, a quadroon, or an octoroon), but
it is not she who suffers it, in his formulation, but rather the "hearts" gathered in
the domestic enclaves of Southern white society, for which she functions as a
potent "curse."

Just as the mulatto woman is portrayed as both subject and object of psy-
chosocial tragedy, however, so too is the tragic threat that she poses itself twofold,
both its aspects inhering in her very "presence" in the social setting, as Lorraine
indicates. Again I turn for illustration to a nineteenth-century novel, this time
William Wells Brown's *Clotel; or, The President's Daughter* (1853), in which the
light-skinned quadroon title character finds herself abandoned by her white
"husband" (their marriage is not, of course, sanctioned by law), who legally takes
a white wife in order to further his political career. The tranquility of Horatio
Green's marriage to Gertrude is disrupted, however, when the latter discovers the
truth of her husband's attachment to Clotel, and that the "interracial" couple
actually already have a child, the young girl Mary. Arranging with the help of her
father to have Clotel sold into slavery, Gertrude seeks to humble Horatio further
by taking Mary into her household as the couple's own servant. Initially vexed by
the question of how the "white slave-girl" could be made to "look like other
Negroes," Gertrude finally puts a bare-headed Mary to work in a garden just off
the parlor. There, the narrative indicates, "[a] hot sun poured its broiling rays on
the naked face and neck of the girl, until she sank down in the corner of the garden, and was actually broiled to sleep" (p. 158).[2]

On the surface, Gertrude's determination to make manifest Mary's Negro
identity indicates merely her desire to obliterate the evidence of the girl's actual
mixed-race parentage, and of Horatio's implication in it; Mary herself serves as
the living reminder of the fact of interracial sexual relations, which pose a grave
threat to the stability of Gertrude's domestic life. Behind the symbol that Mary
constitutes, however—which could theoretically be constituted by any child, of
whatever gender—lurks another presence that wrings Gertrude's heart, that of
Clotel, who serves not merely as a *reminder* of the danger that Gertrude faces, but
as the danger itself, due precisely to her status not only as a quadroon, but as a
quadroon *woman*, who, as Lorraine indicates in *Iola Leroy*, is envisioned as an
irresistible sexual lure for any white man whom she happens to meet.[3]

Brown's narrator, like Lorraine in Harper's novel, suggests the degree to which the mulatto or quadroon woman is conceived as the deliberately active subject in white men's seduction in a highly overdetermined disquisition on the faulty morality of the antebellum South. The subtleties of this lengthy narratorial statement, which appears in the opening pages of *Clotel,* are such that a full quotation is in order:

> In all the large towns in the Southern States, there is a class of slaves
> who are permitted to hire their time of their owners, and for which
> they pay a high price. These are mulatto women, or quadroons, as
> they are familiarly known, and are distinguished for their fascinating
> beauty. The handsomest usually pays the highest price for her time.
> Many of these women are the favourites of persons who furnish them
> with the means of paying their owners, and not a few are dressed in
> the most extravagant manner. Reader, when you take into considera-
> tion the fact, that amongst the slave population no safeguard is
> thrown around virtue, and no inducement held out to slave women
> to be chaste, you will not be surprised when we tell you that
> immorality and vice pervade the cities of the Southern States in a
> manner unknown in the cities and towns of the Northern States.
> Indeed most of the slave women have no higher aspiration than that
> of becoming the finely-dressed mistress of some white man. And at
> Negro balls and parties, this class of women usually cut the greatest
> figure. (pp. 62–63)

While a number of features render this passage somewhat bemusing—for instance, the conflation of the mulatto and quadroon categories, and the implication that women in these categories are the only "class of slaves" allowed to hire their time—of primary interest for the current discussion is the passage's presentation of light-skinned black women as themselves the source of the moral degradation that is the object of the narrator's critique. It is, after all, specifically these women's failure to be chaste—however much that failure may derive from the corruption of the slave system—that apparently engenders the "immorality and vice" that plague Southern cities. This is emphasized through the depiction of these women as wilily conniving to establish liaisons with wealthy white men, in which endeavor they apparently cannot fail, since they are uniformly endowed with an essential, literally "fascinating," beauty.

Insofar as this fascinating quality *is* conceived as essential to mulatto or quadroon identity, the only way to quell it in any given individual woman (and thus neutralize the threat that she poses to the stability of the white familial entity) would be to undermine that identity itself—or at least to destroy all evidence of it, which effectively amounts to the same thing. As we have seen, this is precisely the strategy undertaken by Gertrude when she strives to darken Mary's skin, thereby effacing her octoroon status by rendering manifest her Negro parentage. A similar alteration in appearance is effected in the case of Clotel by the jealous Mrs. French, the woman who becomes Clotel's mistress after she is sold away from her daughter. Having posited by way of apparent explanation the judgment that "[e]very married woman in the far South looks upon her husband as unfaithful, and regards every quadroon servant as a rival," the narrative informs us that "Clotel had been with her new mistress but a few days, when she was ordered to cut off her long hair" (p. 150).

The exact relation of this hair-cutting episode to the skin-darkening one involving Mary might not be clear until we remark the coincidence of the two strategies in a single case, presented in Harriet Wilson's *Our Nig* (1859). The title character of that novel is a mulatto girl named Frado, who exists in a condition of nonslavery servitude to a white family in the North, the Bellmonts. By way of ensuring that Frado constitute a proper foil for her own daughter, Mary, the ruthless Mrs. Bellmont forbids the servant to cover herself when she is at work in the hot sun: "She was not many shades darker than Mary now; what a calamity it would be ever to hear the contrast spoken of. Mrs. Bellmont was determined the sun should have full power to darken the shade which nature had first bestowed upon her as best befitting" (p. 39). Subsequent to undertaking this strategy, however, Mrs. Bellmont also subjects Frado to the same sort of hair cutting suffered by Clotel at the hands of Mrs. French, "shav[ing] her glossy ringlets" so that she becomes "anything but an enticing object" (pp. 68, 69).

In Frado's case, the associative conjunction of skin darkening—whose objective to render Negro identity more manifest is unmistakable—with hair cutting suggests that this latter operation, too, is meant to emphasize the character's African lineage, especially insofar as long, flowing locks are conceived as a prime signifier of European beauty. At the same time, however, Wilson's explicit observation that the cutting of Frado's hair renders her less "enticing" reminds us that the mulatto's appearance signifies not only in terms of racialized standards of aesthetic appeal, but also in terms of gendered conceptions of sexual allure; the *enticement* that the mulatto figure is believed to embody corresponds largely to the erotic temptation that women, generally, have represented in Western culture.[4] Consequently, their mistresses' cutting of Clotel's and Frado's hair is an attempt not only to "Africanize" their appearance by divesting them of a sign of their European parentage, but also to undermine their femininity, which is equally figured in the long tresses they theretofore sport.

My objective in going over these points at such length is to indicate the degree to which the mulatto figure's tragic quality derives from (and thus indicates) her fundamental femininity, which itself contributes greatly to her economical connotation of illicit sexuality—always, I think, the mulatto's primary referent. Given this intricate interrelation of mixed-race identity, femininity, illicit sexuality, and tragic fate—which seems absolutely to *define* the significance of the literary mulatto—it is obvious that the literary depiction of the white-skinned Negro *man* must inevitably raise difficult questions regarding governing conceptions of black masculinity, perennially problematic in the U.S. culturohistorical context. A tentative beginning to a full consideration of these questions can be achieved through a brief examination of James Weldon Johnson's *Autobiography of an Ex-Colored Man* (1912).

The Feminine Function of the Ex-Colored Man

If there is any passage in Johnson's novel that indicates the degree to which mulatto identity implicates both the intermingling of African and European features and a feminized process of erotic "fascination," it is the one in which the white-identified title character first becomes aware of his Negro ancestry. At this point still a young boy, the nameless protagonist has had it indirectly indicated to him, by an administrator at school, that he is not really white, as he had always thought. Churning with anxiety about the ramifications of this fact, he hurries home after school and tries to settle the question for himself:

> I rushed up into my own little room, shut the door, and went quickly to where my looking-glass hung on the wall. For an instant I was afraid to look, but when I did, I looked long and earnestly. I had often heard people say to my mother: "What a pretty boy you have!" I was accustomed to hear remarks about my beauty; but now, for the first time, I became conscious of it and recognized it. I noticed the ivory whiteness of my skin, the beauty of my mouth, the size and liquid darkness of my eyes, and how the long, black lashes that fringed and shaded them produced an effect that was strangely fascinating even to me. I noticed the softness and glossiness of my dark hair that fell in waves over my temples, making my forehead appear whiter than it really was. How long I stood there gazing at my image I do not know. When I came out ... I ... rushed to where my mother was sitting. ... I buried my head in her lap and blurted out: "Mother, mother, tell me, am I a nigger?" (pp. 11–12)

Of greater interest, for my purposes, than the specific fear embodied in this question is the process by which it is engendered in the character, entailing not primarily his recognition of "Negroid" characteristics in his apparently European aspect, but rather his appreciation of his own beauty in specifically feminine terms, which latter occurrence functions as tantamount to the former. The "ivory whiteness" of his skin, the apparently full shape of his mouth, the limpidness of his eyes, the length and blackness of his lashes, and the soft glossiness of his hair collectively indicate the undeniable intermixture of white and Negro "blood" in the protagonist's "veins," but they do this not primarily by means of their specifically racialized qualities, but rather through the explicitly feminine terms in which he apprehends them, and which, as we have seen, have already been conceived as essential to mulatto identity. Thus, by the time the protagonist demands to know whether he is "a nigger," his anxiety seems based less on his recognition that the paleness of his skin is a sort of optical illusion resulting from its contrast with his dark hair than on his new realization of the "fascinating" feminine beauty that he possesses. Moreover, this feminine characterization is intensified through the clearly narcissistic nature of the protagonist's *own* fascination, which entails not only his obsession with his mirror reflection, but also his minutely detailed description of and rumination on his appearance in a way that seems to epitomize stereotypically feminine vanity. Thus the protagonist's mulatto identity is simultaneously figured through and grounded in those aspects of his persona that have been rendered as feminine in the cultural contexts from which the novel derives.

Soon after his self-discovery, the protagonist seems increasingly to develop in the feminized direction that is suggested in the looking-glass scene. This is indicated particularly by the emotional excess triggered in him during his boyhood musical performances, on account of which, he says, he suffered fits of "sentimental hysteria": "Often when playing I could not keep the tears which formed in my eyes from rolling down my cheeks. . . . I would jump from the piano, and throw myself sobbing into my mother's arms" (p. 18). For her part, the protagonist's mother was innocently unaware that he "should have been out playing ball or in swimming with other boys" (pp. 18–19), and thus unwittingly supported his suspiciously effete orientation:

> I lived between my music and books, on the whole a rather unwhole-
> some life for a boy to lead. I dwelt in a world of imagination, of
> dreams and air castles—the kind of atmosphere that sometimes
> nourishes a genius, more often men unfitted for the practical strug-
> gles of life. I never played a game of ball, never went fishing or
> learned to swim; in fact, the only outdoor exercise in which I took
> any interest was skating. (p. 32)

This feminized orientation itself potentially constitutes the protagonist's personal tragedy, indicating a gender identity that is anything but properly masculine, and verging dangerously on a sexual identity that is anything but hetero. Luckily for the protagonist, however, the relationship that he undertakes that most nearly approximates a homosexual coupling also functions as the means by which the narrative can exorcise this unwholesome element.

After his mother dies, forsaken by the white Southern gentleman who is his father, the protagonist gathers his meager savings and leaves his Connecticut home to attend college at Atlanta University. After a series of mishaps that leaves him destitute, however, he ends up first in Jacksonville, Florida, working in a cigar factory, and then in New York City, where he quickly becomes absorbed in a life of gambling and nightclubbing. He is rescued from this precarious existence by a mysterious gentleman who turns out to be a wealthy socialite. This man hires the protagonist as a high-paid personal musical entertainer and valet, taking him along on luxurious jaunts to various European locales in his quest, as the protagonist puts it, "to escape time" (p. 104).

By the point in the novel where these travels occur, this unnamed benefactor has already been characterized by his "languid" gestures (p. 84), unmistakably "cultured" demeanor (p. 84), and uniformly "blasé" associates (p. 86), all of which comport with his description as a "clean-cut, slender, but athletic-looking man" (p. 84) to conjure an aura of stereotypical homosexual identification. This sense is bolstered by the narrator's description of his relationship with his patron, which is presented in notably coded terms. Indeed, not only does the benefactor provide the protagonist with the "best" clothes, supply him with funds "far beyond what ordinary wages would have amounted to," and treat him so much "as an equal" as to make it doubtful that "anyone could have guessed" the true nature of their relationship, but, additionally, the two men are inseparable during their initial time in Europe: "For the first two weeks we were together almost constantly, seeing the sights, sights old to him, but from which he seemed to get new pleasure in showing them to me" (p. 95). In other words, between the protagonist's enjoyment of financial support and material luxury and the patron's pleasure in sharing his experience with a less worldly partner, the domesticized relationship that these men experience looks remarkably conjugal and, thus, evidently diverges from standard patterns of heterosexual masculinity.

Not only is this divergence indicated by the protagonist's forthright declaration of his and his benefactor's mutual love—"Between this peculiar man and me there had grown a very strong bond of affection . . ." (p. 104)—and his assertion of the deep impression his patron has made upon him—"My affection for him was so strong, my recollections of him are so distinct, he was such a peculiar and striking character, that I could easily fill several chapters with reminiscences of him" (p. 108); its specific import is suggested by the protagonist's characterization of his wealthy companion as "all in all, the best friend I ever had, except my mother, the man who exerted the greatest influence ever brought into my life, except that exerted by my mother" (p. 108).

The repeated invocation of the mother, here, connotes her dual function with respect to her son, in which she comprises, first, the object of his intense cathexis—she is his "best friend"—and, second, the object of his identification—she is his "greatest influence"—so as to approximate very closely to the function of the mother in Freud's (1922) notorious theorization of the genesis of male homosexuality (see pp. 50–51). According to the logic of that account (which, however etiologically void, nonetheless beautifully exemplifies prevailing conceptions of homosexuality's sociocultural significance), we could say that the protagonist's benefactor both assumes the mother's identificatory function and instantiates the protagonist's unorthodox object-choice, while the protagonist himself eventually accedes to the mother's social-subject position—but not before the threat of homosexuality is exorcised from the text with the suicide of the patron, who, by "leaping into eternity" (p. 104), simultaneously underscores the protagonist's implication in a tragic situation, assumes its burden, and salvages for the protagonist the possibility of a feminine identification without the male-directed sexual orientation that it regularly implies.

Indeed, the overdetermined significance of the patron's banishment from the narrative is suggested by the proleptic referencing of his suicide amid the narrator's account of his break from him, with the protagonist's determination to quit his benefactor in Europe outlined in one paragraph, the intensity of their relationship and the patron's eventual suicide ruminated on in the next, and the extended leavetaking detailed in the subsequent four pages (pp. 104–8). While the text indicates no specific diegetic relation between the protagonist's decision to depart and his benefactor's suicide, their narrative imbrication and the wholly unelaborated character of the patron's death suggest the classic, melodramatic possibility of one-to-one causation, with the patron's relative coldness at the moment of parting leading the protagonist himself to wonder "whether he was striving to hide deeper feelings" (p. 108). However this may be, the precipitation of the protagonist's decision to leave his "friend" by his sudden realization that he is in fact "a man, no longer a boy" (p. 104) implicates that decision in what the protagonist himself sees as his increasing approximation to perfected masculinity, the achievement of which condition he identifies with his successfully returning to the United States, reassuming his identity as an African American, and employing his talent and skill in composing a specifically "American" music based "on Negro themes" (p. 105). This resolution, though—whereby the protagonist would accede to healthful manliness precisely through his forthright acceptance of his Negro identity—is undermined when, while traveling in the South collecting musical materials, he witnesses the lynching of a black man by a mob of whites. He subsequently determines that he cannot be associated with a race that is so shamefully treated, and reembraces his ambiguous racial identity by deciding to "change my name, raise a mustache, and let the world take me for what it would" (p. 139).

It is precisely this "forsaking" of the race, as the protagonist calls it (p. 139), that permanently thwarts his progress toward normative masculinity, since it sets him on a course whereby his social subjectivity is forever fixed in conventionally feminine terms. Not that the question of sexual object-choice is ever again rendered problematic; indeed, under his new identity the protagonist eventually meets and falls in love with a white woman, actually confesses to her his mixed parentage (which she finally accepts after much struggle), and then embarks with her on a marriage that is "supremely happy" (pp. 144–53; p. 153 for the quotation). At the same time, however, the narrative exposition of that marriage is so brief and attenuated (filling less than fourteen lines) as to achieve practically no substance at all before the wife dies in giving birth to their second child, upon which occurrence the protagonist himself makes a decision with definitive consequences for his masculine identity:

> My children need a mother's care, but I shall never marry again. It is
> to my children that I have devoted my life. I no longer have the same
> fear for myself of my secret's being found out, for since my wife's
> death I have gradually dropped out of social life; but there is nothing
> I would not suffer to keep the brand from being placed upon them.
> (p. 153)

In other words, this passage implies, the children do *not* really "need a mother's care," for the complete self-sacrifice that the protagonist indicates he is willing to make for their benefit is precisely the central characteristic of maternal nurture as it is conventionally conceived in Western culture. Thus the protagonist, having been characterized as inappropriately feminine since boyhood and yet purged of the intimations of homoerotic desire generally attaching to such a characterization, finally reaches maturity by reprising the sort of selfless devotion enacted by his own mother, thus underscoring the fundamentally feminine significance of his mixed-race status and white skin.

My point here is not to suggest the ex-colored man's "emasculation," the very notion of which implicates the masculinism that is the object of my critique; it is, rather, to indicate the conceptual limits that govern the novel of racial "passing" such that it seems inevitably to support a conservative gender politics wherein black masculinity itself is conceived as fundamentally problematic. To the extent that such social conservatism instantiates the status anxiety associated with any group's enjoyment of increased upward mobility, it is logical that it should be evidenced quite strongly in the literature of black embourgeoisement from the Harlem Renaissance of the 1920s, which rendered the figure of the tragic mulatto nearly synonymous with the "passing" character, meanwhile repositing in the latter the practical essence of feminine subjectivity.

"Passing" and the Production of the Properly Feminine Subject

Not wanting to overstate the similarities among the three works that effectively define the "passing" novel of the Harlem Renaissance, I nonetheless would like to suggest that they all share in a recognizably modernist tendency to temper the emphasis on physicality that the genre demands with a simultaneous focus on psychic disposition such as is scarcely discernible in precursor works published before the turn of the century. Specifically, Walter White's *Flight* (1926), Jessie Redmon Fauset's *Plum Bun* (1928), and Nella Larsen's *Passing* (1929) all address the status of feminine identity as it is constituted at the troubled boundaries of racial identification, with the femininity of their passing characters resting not only on the peculiar physical manifestations of their mixed-race ancestry, but also on the subjective duplicity that those manifestations potentially underwrite.

To be sure, all three of the novels in question recur to the physical beauty of their passing characters as a primary signifier of their racially ambiguous status: White ascribes to Mimi Daquin such "startling beauty" that, even after the prime of her youth, "[m]en instinctively turned and looked at her again as they passed her on the street" (pp. 145, 224); Fauset notes Angela Murray's "extraordinary good looks" (p. 314); and Larsen's Irene Redfield is fixated on the beauty of the passing Clare Kendry, judging her to be "almost too good-looking" (p. 156), suggesting to her husband Brian that Clare is "extraordinarily beautiful" (p. 209), and spontaneously exclaiming to Clare herself, "Dear God! But aren't you lovely, Clare!" (p. 194). Nevertheless, this physical beauty seems to figure as the merely visible manifestation of a femininity that consists at least as much in an impulse to variation that is itself conceived as quintessentially feminine. For instance, White tells us that Mary Robertson, the dark-skinned woman from Chicago who marries Mimi Daquin's widowed father, Jean, is won over by the sense of "romance" that Jean seems to represent; this sense, the narrator of *Flight* explains, "had appealed to her feminine love of the unstable, the exotic, the unusual" (p. 26).

The suggestion of such a "feminine love" on the part of Mary, for whom Mimi's antipathy is quite pronounced throughout the bulk of the novel, renders all the more noteworthy the later ascription to Mimi herself of "a woman's love for the unusual, the unstable, the unforeseen" (p. 103). The primary *difference* between the two characters' relation to this trait, however—and this is precisely what I want to examine in some detail here—is that while Mary might indicate a "love for" the "unstable," or herself even be represented as unaccountably variable (though in general she is not), Mimi, by virtue of her extremely light skin and her eventual decision to pass as white in order to escape censure from the Negro community after giving birth out of wedlock, actually comes to *instantiate* onto-logical instability through her ambiguous racial identification itself, and in con-trast to a social order that, for all its incorporation of racial-categorical transgres-sion, nonetheless strictly prohibits the crossing of certain bounds of decorum.

Consider, for example, the section of *Flight* in which Mimi herself first becomes aware, not only of passing Negroes, but of the extensive interracial socialization that their existence implies. Having fled north from Jean's and Mary's Atlanta home after Jean's death and the birth of her son, *Petit* Jean, Mimi attends a Harlem dance with her sympathetic paternal aunt, Sophie, who points out to her various light-skinned members of the crowd known to be passing as white during the day. Emphasizing not just the racial, but also the class, barriers transgressed in the mêlée of the ball, Aunt Sophie tells Mimi, "You'll find all sorts of people here—it's a pay dance and anybody who's got the price can get in. There are women who are being kept and men who live the same way, doctors and lawyers, and about every class in the world represented here." Feeling a "thrill of adventure" at this information, Mimi wonders aloud, "Goodness, haven't they any lines they draw?" To which her aunt replies, "Strictest in the world—you've noticed that you've been asked to dance only by folks you know and who move with our set" (pp. 200–201). The full import of this observation soon becomes clear when, rumors of Mimi's illegitimate motherhood having gained ground in Harlem, she meets with coldness from people who had been her friends, which disappointment is figured as the crumbling of Mimi's own psychic framework: "Mimi could almost hear the tumbling down of the walls she had so confidently been building" (p. 205). This psychic instability manifests as the negotiation of racial ambiguity two pages later, when Mimi informs her aunt of her decision to leave Harlem and pass as white amid the lower regions of Manhattan, the better to support herself and to provide for *Petit* Jean.

Of course, such feminine "instability" as I am suggesting is assimilated here to the ambiguous implications of racial passing has long been conceived as con-stituting women's fundamentally sinister character—an enigmatic "nature" the fathomless interiority of which is registered as a profound self-absorption that can only be evil. It is to this influential conception of femininity that Nella Larsen's Clare Kendry approximates, exhibiting "no allegiance beyond her own immediate desire"; appearing "selfish, and cold, and hard" (p. 144); manifesting a "having" way (p. 153); "not at all considering anyone else's feelings" (p. 175); and admitting ominously to Irene, "Why, to get the things I want badly enough, I'd do anything, hurt anybody, throw anything away. Really, 'Rene, I'm not safe" (p. 210). Indeed, Judith Butler has suggested that Clare's figuration of danger derives precisely from her passing itself, a duplicitous keeping of one's own counsel that is by definition a violation of the governing racial/sexual order, and thus a threat to the bourgeois, masculinist, black nuclear family conceived as the *sine qua non* of racial uplift (Butler, 1993, pp. 177–79). Insofar as Irene, according to Butler, not only identifies with Clare's transgression but also locates her own sense of social security within that family construct—both of which facts fuel Irene's resentment of Clare—Clare's demise at the end of the novel might be considered as the expulsion of the disruptive, evilly feminine force from its normative realm. At the same time, however, that expulsion would not constitute an end to either feminine duplicity or essential femininity per se, since Irene herself still harbors an identification with Clare's transgression, and her suppression of that identification in favor of a more socially legitimated investment in the nuclear family actually represents the sublimation of her duplicity to a disposition of domestic devotion that, while more "acceptable" than Clare's sinister self-absorption, is registered as no less fundamentally feminine.

This latter fact is made strikingly clear in Jessie Fauset's *Plum Bun* (1928), which presents feminine inconstancy and its sublimation to a socially acceptable norm of femininity as characterizing two phases in the maturation of a single passing character, and this in such a way as to figure passing itself as constitutive of a socially unproblematic feminine identity. Fauset's protagonist, Angela Murray, learns to "pass" from the example set by her similarly light-skinned mother, Mattie, whose own excursions among Philadelphia's segregated fashionable settings Fauset posits as mere instances of the older woman's "harmless" sampling of such luxuries as her circumstances afford during her occasional breaks from domestic duty. "Mrs. Murray," the narrative tells us matter-of-factly,

> loved pretty clothes, she liked shops devoted to the service of women; she enjoyed being even on the fringe of a fashionable gathering. A satisfaction that was almost ecstatic seized her when she drank tea in the midst of modishly gowned women in a stylish tea-room. It pleased her to stand in the foyer of a great hotel or of the Academy of Music and to be part of the whirling, humming, palpitating gaiety. . . . To walk through Wanamaker's on Saturday, to stroll from Fifteenth to Ninth Street on Chestnut, to have her tea in the Bellevue Stratford, to stand in the lobby of the St. James' fitting on immaculate gloves; all

innocent, childish pleasures pursued without malice or envy con-
trived to cast a glamour over Monday's washing and Tuesday's ironing, the scrubbing of kitchen and bathroom and the fashioning of
children's clothes. . . .

Much of this pleasure, harmless and charming though it was,
would have been impossible with a dark skin. (pp. 15–16)

The "innocence" of Mrs. Murray's illicit sojourns derives, then, both from
their relatively inconsequential character and from their subordination to the
proper black bourgeois domesticity represented in her family life. Indeed, not
only do Mrs. Murray's individual adventures in passing fall short of constituting
her full passing *over* into white society, but they actually reinforce the black
domestic bond, since Mrs. Murray invariably relates them in detail to her dark-
skinned husband, Junius, who "had had . . . the sympathy to take them at their
face value"; indeed, the narrator assures us, Junius "preferred one of his wife's
sparkling accounts of a Saturday's adventure in 'passing' to all the tall stories told
by cronies at his lodge" (p. 16). And well he might, since the very frivolousness of
Mattie Murray's activities while passing indicates not only the innocently "childish" quality of her transgression, but also her own fundamental femininity, in
which that childishness itself is a component, and which ideally suits the masculinist interests that the bourgeois family is designed to further. Thus it is under-
standable that Junius Murray should find "perfectly harmless and rather charming" his wife's illicit indulgence of her luxurious tastes, since he considers those
tastes themselves an example of "the qualities known as 'essentially feminine,'" his
pronounced "weakness" for which is actually a manifestation of his investment in
a masculinist gender-political order (p. 15). That investment, coupled with
Junius's belief in the basically feminine character of the pleasures to be had in
passing, obviates his possible resentment at being excluded from the activity,
since that exclusion is based not only on his skin color, but on his highly valued
staunch masculinity, which itself precludes his enjoyment of passing's pleasures.
Thus, the Murrays' pursuit of separate Saturday afternoon entertainments—while
Mattie takes tea and goes shopping Junius engages in his "beloved . . . pastime of
exploring old Philadelphia" (p. 16)—is dictated as much by their gender difference as by the difference in their skin color, with the effect that "passing" itself
appears as a profoundly feminine undertaking.

This said, passing's feminine character does not always register in *Plum Bun*
as so socially innocent as it does in Mattie Murray's case. Angela Murray, whose
light skin coincides with an approximation to her mother's love of luxurious
excursions (while the dark skin of her sister Virginia, conveniently, does not),
assimilates the illicit adventures that she and Mattie share to a notably different

significance than does the older woman. Insofar as passing is for Mattie only "play-acting" (p. 19), it dissembles a more fundamental devotion to kith and kin that both fortifies her to suffer discriminatory treatment when in the company of darker-skinned friends and enables her to consider her passing itself as a strike for the race against segregationist practice. Indeed, far from "disclaiming her own" by sitting in "whites-only" theater seats, when out with her husband or other dark-skinned friends Mattie exemplifies racial solidarity, being "the first to announce that she liked to sit in the balcony or gallery, as indeed she did; her infrequent occupation of orchestra seats was due merely to a mischievous determination to flout a silly and unjust law" (p. 15).

Angela, on the other hand, while recognizing her mother's conception of passing as primarily "a lark" (p. 73), herself comes to see it as a means of acceding to the social status she covets, a detailed vision of which she entertains soon after commencing to pass as a white woman in New York City. Ruminating on the achievements she would like to realize in this new life, Angela acknowledges to herself the limitation presented by her gender while nonetheless reveling in her dawning sense of liberation:

> She remembered an expression, "free, white and twenty-one,"—this was what it meant then, this sense of owning the world, this realization that other things being equal, all things were possible. . . . Power, greatness, authority, these were fitting and proper for men; but there were sweeter, more beautiful gifts for women, and power of a certain kind too. Such a power she would like to exert in this glittering new world, so full of mysteries and promise. If she could afford it she would have a salon, a drawing-room where men and women . . . should come and pour themselves out to her sympathy and magnetism. To accomplish this she must have money and influence; indeed since she was so young she would need even protection; perhaps it would be better to marry . . . a white man. (p. 88, last ellipsis in original)

But Angela Murray (known among her New York friends as the indeterminably descended Angèle Mory) never does marry a white man—a fact that is central to the plot of *Plum Bun*, inasmuch as it is precisely the *refusal* of her wealthy white beau to marry her (he cannot claim his family's inheritance if he weds someone beneath his own social standing) and his suggestion that, alternatively, she become his kept mistress that eventually catapult Angela out of her masquerade and into the arms of Anthony Cross, a *non*-"passing" white-skinned Negro whose attentions she had formerly discouraged, due to his lack of money (p. 142). It little matters for my purposes here that, with Angela's return to

Anthony, the novel degenerates into a cliché romantic comedy incorporating not only such mistaken identity as is conveniently built in to the passing novel (since Anthony initially believes that Angela is actually white) but also the temporary mismatching of siblings with each other's rightful love (pp. 299–305, 355, 367), and finally ending with the happy restoration of the proper pairings (pp. 368–69, 378–79). Much more important is that that return itself not only underscores— precisely by contrasting with—Angela's quondam materialism and shallowness but also constitutes her accession to her mother's brand of stalwart devotion, in relation to which her ability to pass becomes a merely superficial circumstance that can be deployed in the basically inconsequential manner undertaken by Mattie herself. Thus Angela Murray's racial passing is actually constitutive of the normative femininity to which she eventually attains, insofar as the very duplicity and inconstancy comprised in that passing are part and parcel of an essentially feminine "nature" that, when properly channeled into a grounding affective attachment, is refigured as the inoffensive frivolity of proper bourgeois womanhood.

To the extent that such bourgeois feminine propriety as is achieved by Angela Murray and Irene Redfield represents the successful working through of racial passing's maleficent duplicity, it also constitutes an order of social activity different from that in which passing derives its primary effect. Successful passing, after all, requires not only the passer's possession of a white skin, but such social affirmation of her "white" identity as can only be achieved through some degree of public engagement, however minimal this may be and however implicitly it is enacted. Clare Kendry, for instance, is able to meet this necessity in a profoundly passive manner: Responding to Irene's incredulous query regarding the practicability of passing—"You mean that you didn't have to explain where you came from? It seems impossible"—Clare insists, "But it wasn't necessary. There were my aunts [who raised her after the death of her widowed father] . . . , respectable and authentic enough for anything and anybody." "I see," Irene replies. "They were 'passing' too." "No," Clare explains. "They weren't. They were white" (Larsen, 1929, p. 158).

In Angela Murray's case, legitimation comes through her enrollment in art classes in which her fellow students speculate that she is of Spanish descent (Fauset, 1928, p. 95). And Mimi Daquin purveys her assumed French ancestry among her co-workers at the New York fashion house, Francine's (White, 1926, pp. 212–19). Thus passing entails a degree of circulation in the public realm such as is not conventionally associated with the fundamentally *private* functions of feminine domesticity that triumph at the ends of *Plum Bun* and *Passing*. Indeed, even Mimi Daquin's final return to the black community, which doesn't involve her conjugal union, figures roughly as her recurrence to an extended-familial privacy that offers, in her own words "*Petit* Jean—my own people—and happiness!"

(p. 300). Given this, we could say that the social propriety represented in the resolutions of these novels inheres as much in the protagonists' return to the private realm conventionally posited as women's proper sphere as in their assumption of the racial identity that the law dictates is their own. Insofar as men's conventional relation to the private realm differs from women's—properly incorporating recognizable evidence of a successful *public* engagement whose achievement black men have historically been denied—so, too, will it be impossible not only for the narrative of the passing man to culminate in his accession to a socially acceptable masculine position, but for the African-American man's occupation of such a position even to be allowed by the terms of the conventional passing narrative. Of course, those terms themselves implicate social factors beyond the dictates of literary convention. Key among these is a general anxiety about black men's assumption of such masculinity as has been deemed socially proper and normative, evidence of its problems notwithstanding. Indeed, the degree to which this anxiety permeates U.S. culture is indicated by its manifestation in one of the most famous passing narratives of the late twentieth century, whose stated objective is to expose and condemn the sufferings of "the black man" under the regime of racism.

The Political Ambivalence of the White Passing Narrative

As of this writing, paperback copies of John Howard Griffin's *Black Like Me* on sale in stores represent the sixty-sixth printing of the book since its appearance in 1961. The enduring interest that it has for readers derives, no doubt, from the counterintuitiveness of the exploration it chronicles; for while it has been a truism of U.S. race relations that most blacks are, perforce, at least "passingly" familiar with the ways of white society, and so can negotiate it as necessary, it is also generally granted that whites' *lack* of familiarity with black society is not only a function of their not *needing* such, but an indication of their rightful lack of *desire* for it, since the benefits it offers are few, if any. Yet Griffin's fame rests almost entirely on his account of the six weeks he spent at the end of 1959 disguised as a black man in the deep South, convinced that only "by becoming a Negro could a white man hope to learn the truth" (p. 7). Basing this dubious claim (for it implies a curious dismissal of black people's own accounts of life in the segregated South) on his sense that "the Southern Negro" will not divulge "the truth" to a white journalist such as himself (pp. 7–8), Griffin seeks to discover that truth by darkening his skin and going among the Negro populations of Louisiana and Mississippi.

It is not my interest here to review the various degradations suffered by

Griffin during his experiment, since they are the standard ones visited upon any man perceived as black in the context in question, and since to do so would be implicitly to concur in Griffin's own judgment regarding his privileged access to the "truth" of black experience.[5] Rather, I want to consider the curious manner in which Griffin figures his experience of "blackness," and thereby registers not only the injustice of African Americans' "second-class citizenship" (Preface), but the impossibility of putative first-class manhood for black men relegated to that inferior status—seemingly the most deplorable consequence of 300 years of racist practice.

It is perhaps a measure of black men's thorough physicalization in "mainstream" U.S. consciousness that Griffin sees his Negro "identity" as almost entirely inherent in his bodily appearance. Recalling his first look in a mirror after completing his skin-darkening regimen, he notes that "a fierce, bald, very dark Negro . . . glared at me from the glass" (p. 15). While his "glare" might account for his apparently "fierce" aspect, the reason for the glare itself is unclear. Nonetheless, this stereotypically angry expression seems to work in concert with the dark skin to obliterate all trace of Griffin's personal history, in whose place is invoked a generic African-American experience that, however little it figures Griffin's own ancestral past, seems to ground his new sense of thoroughgoing Negro-ness:

> I looked into the mirror and saw reflected nothing of the white John Griffin's past. No, the reflections led back to Africa, back to the shanty and the ghetto, back to the fruitless struggles against the mark of blackness. . . . I knew now that there is no such thing as a disguised white man, when the black won't rub off. The black man is wholly a Negro, regardless of what he once may have been. I was a newly created Negro who must go out that door and live in a world unfamiliar to me.
>
> . . . I became two men, the observing one and the one who panicked, who felt Negroid even into the depths of his entrails. (p. 16)

However it may "feel" thus to register so deeply as "Negroid" in the absence of any actual lived experience to constitute one as such, that experience soon comes, and it is of two specific types, both of which serve to render Griffin not only as a *Negro* but, specifically and significantly, as a Negro *man*.

Having left the friend's house where his physical transformation takes place and checked into a Negro hotel on New Orleans's South Rampart Street, Griffin has his first intimate encounter with "other" black men after walking from his room "down the narrow, dim-lit hall to the door with a crudely lettered sign reading MEN" (p. 19). Meeting two "fellow" Negroes in this communal bathroom,

Griffin engages with them in such "courteous" and "respectful" conversation as affirms their common *humanity* at the same time that the incongruous fact of the other men's nudity implicitly affirms Griffin's sense of their shared *black maleness.* "One man," Griffin explains, "was in the shower. Another, a large, black-skinned man, sat naked on the floor awaiting his turn. . . ." Conveying "an air of dignity" in spite of his nakedness, this man constitutes an unavoidable physical presence, "lean[ing] back against the wall with his legs stretched out in from of him" (p. 19). Recognizing both Griffin's desire to wash his hands and the disrepair characterizing the bathroom sink, the man on the floor calls to the other one—"Hey, how about stepping back and letting this gentleman wash his hands?"—to which the showerer replies generously, "Sure—come on." As he tells it, Griffin's subsequent entrance into the stall is marked by his coy disavowal of the black male body, related in astonishingly stereotypical terms: "In the shower's obscurity, all I could see was a black shadow and gleaming white teeth." As he moves toward this vague figure, Griffin keeps an ostensibly respectful distance between himself and his black companions, "stepp[ing] over the other's outstretched legs and wash[ing] quickly, using the soap the man in the shower thrust into my hands" (p. 20).

This apparently unsettling initial encounter with black male physicality soon gives way, however, to Griffin's less anxious and more aesthetically fascinated experience of it, as he comes to a sense of kinship with the other men. Having offered the man on the floor a cigarette after he's finished washing his hands, Griffin carefully registers the other's response, noting that, as "[h]e leaned his heavy body forward to accept one[, h]is black flesh picked up dull highlights from the bare globe overhead" (pp. 20–21), and simultaneously making a significant realization: "I was having my first prolonged contact as a Negro with other Negroes . . ." (p. 20). When the other man finally steps out of the shower and the seated one rises so that they are both bodied forth in Griffin's presence, the latter finally takes his leave: "I told them good night and returned to my room, less lonely, and warmed by the brief contact with others like me . . ." (p. 21).[6]

The next day, two additional encounters impress upon Griffin the full significance of his newly felt black masculinity. The first takes place on a crowded city bus, when Griffin gazes appealingly at a white woman who, though obviously exhausted, declines to take an empty seat among the Negroes at the back of the bus. Thinking that he sees his "sympathy" for the woman reflected in her own look, Griffin sorely mistakes the meaning of their mutual glance: "The exchange blurred the barriers of race (so new to me) long enough for me to smile and vaguely indicate the empty seat beside me, letting her know she was welcome to accept it." He is soon corrected in his misapprehension when the woman's initially "pale" blue eyes "sharpen," and she demands, "What're you looking at me like *that* for?" (pp. 24–25).

The "barriers of race" to which Griffin refers—and his prior ignorance of which bespeaks the general lack of racial consciousness that even Southern whites such as himself are allowed in the U.S. context—are here manifested as a specifically *sexual* prohibition, as Griffin's glance at the white woman is assimilated to the threat of interracial rape that the black man is typically imagined to represent. Later in the afternoon, having settled in at the shoeshine stand of Sterling Williams, his "contact for . . . entry into the Negro community" (p. 14), Griffin quickly becomes implicated in the possibility of a more legitimate disposition of black male sexuality, attracting the attention of a "fine-looking middle-aged Negro woman, dressed in a white uniform." "You got that widow woman interested," Williams tells him, and, indeed, she visits the stand on each of the next two days, even suggesting to Williams that she might invite Griffin to her house for Sunday dinner before Griffin "gently" indicates to her that he is already married (pp. 28, 41).

If his engagement with the two black men in the bathroom affirms for Griffin his own "black manhood," these interactions with the two different women establish the contexts in which he afterward tries imaginatively to negotiate the social significances of that status, with notably frustrating results. Relocated from New Orleans to Hattiesburg, Mississippi, Griffin reprises his encounter with white womanhood by attempting to write a letter to his wife in Texas: "I needed to write to her, to give her my news[,] but I found I could tell her nothing. . . . She had nothing to do with this life, nothing to do with the room in Hattiesburg or with its Negro inhabitant" (p. 68). Subsequent sentences of the narrative indicate, however, that this "nothing" actually comprises the *everything* that the racist imagination believes the white woman represents to black male consciousness, as Griffin insists earnestly:

> My conditioning as a Negro, and the immense sexual implications
> with which the racists in our culture bombard us, cut me off, even in
> my most intimate self, from any connection with my wife.
>
> I stared at the letter and saw written: *Hattiesburg, November 14.*
> *My darling,* followed by a blank page.
>
> The visual barrier imposed itself. The observing self saw the
> Negro, surrounded by the sounds and smells of the ghetto, write
> "Darling" to a white woman. The chains of my blackness would not
> allow me to go on. Though I understood and could analyze what was
> happening, I could not break through.
>
> *Never look at a white woman—look down or the other way.*
>
> *What do you mean, calling a white woman "darling" like that, boy?*
> (pp. 68–69, italics in original)

Griffin's claim that it is specifically a "visual barrier" that he confronts suggests that his demurral is based less on the degree to which he feels himself a Negro than on the extent to which he shares in the stereotypical white revulsion at the idea of any interaction between a black man and a white woman. Indeed, it is specifically Griffin's "observing self"—which he has earlier carefully distinguished from the one "who fe[els] Negroid even into the depths of his entrails" (p. 16)—that recoils, and not at the notion that a man who really is white should address his white wife tenderly, but at the *vision* of tender rapport between black man and white woman that is underwritten by the white man's—*his own*—masquerade. By assimilating this fictive vision to a racist belief in the actual inevitability of the black man's sexual interest in the white woman, Griffin himself becomes the local instantiation of white racism that he presents himself as merely reacting to, as one "conditioned as a Negro." Thus autonomously prohibited from the social interaction that he implicitly posits as the black man's idealized objective, Griffin is left with the more "legitimate" alternative of intimate intercourse between the black man and the black woman, only to find that this, too, is no real option, so far as "proper" masculinity is concerned.

Having disposed of the respectable Negro "widow woman" within his first few days incognito, Griffin interrogates black male–female relations from a relatively detached perspective for the remainder of his sojourn. Early during his adventure, Griffin has already been apprised of the black man's difficulties in establishing proper domesticity; the elderly black proprietor of a YMCA café has affirmed for the newly minted "Negro" the black man's abiding awareness that "no matter how hard he works, he's never going to *quite* manage . . . taxes and prices eat up more than he can earn" (p. 42, ellipsis in original). Consequently, he continues, the Negro man "can't see how he'll ever have a wife and children. The economic structure just doesn't permit it unless he's prepared to live down in poverty and have his wife work too." In short, the social restrictions faced by the black man are such that "[a]ny kind of family life . . . seems impossible from the outset" (p. 42).

Thus the black man's debarment from full participation in the *public* arena of the labor market precludes as well his proper functioning in the *private* context of domestic life, since the latter requires a man's presentation of the economic spoils gained through public engagement. With Griffin himself denied employment despite continued searching during his weeks in disguise (see pp. 41, 47, and 97–98), he repeats this analysis to a white man who has given him a lift along the highways of Mississippi. Contrasting the fates of rural and urban Negroes, Griffin asserts that

[i]gnorance keeps them poor, and when a town-dwelling Negro is poor, he lives in the ghetto. His wife has to work usually, and this

leaves the children without parental companionship. In such places, where all of man's time is spent just surviving, he rarely knows what it means to read a great book. He has grown up and now sees his children grow up in squalor. His wife usually earns more than he. He is thwarted in his need to be father-of-the-household. When he looks at his children and his home, he feels the guilt of not having given them something better. His only salvation is not to give a damn finally, or else he will fall into despair. In despair a man's sense of virtue is dulled. He no longer cares. He will do anything to escape it—steal or commit acts of violence—or perhaps try to lose himself in sensuality. Most often the sex-king is just a poor devil trying to prove the manhood that his whole existence denies. (pp. 90–91)

Thus the black man's inability to function normatively in either public or private contexts predicates a turn to the antisocial behavior that implicitly defines him, as much in Griffin's account as in the national consciousness. For it must be emphasized that Griffin offers *no more than* a mere account, his journalistic disposition apparently allowing him to conceive the very publication of his experiences as substantive social intervention. Consequently, not only does Griffin, as might be expected, neglect to interrogate—thereby implicitly *endorsing*—the dominant sense of men's psychic "needs" invoked in the preceding citation; his book's status as journalistic document exempts him from having to outline a political program for redressing the racial inequalities that he supposedly wants to condemn, incorporating instead the indirect appeal for "justice" with which *Black Like Me* rather weakly ends (p. 157). This failure by Griffin either to indicate how black men might be admitted to normative masculinity or to critique the terms of the latter effectively posits as permanent the antisocial orientation into which black men understandably devolve, according to Griffin's analysis of the situation, and thus renders his book assimilable to the culture's overwhelming anxiety regarding black masculinity even as it purports to further the interests of the genericized "black man." In other words, the peculiar details of Griffin's situation ensure not only that *Black Like Me* will partake of the gender-political conservatism that traditionally characterizes the passing narrative, but that that conservatism will itself militate directly against the racial-political critique that the passing narrative is considered to represent.

Nor is the political ambiguity that marks *Black Like Me* unique to the masculine version of the white passing narrative; it characterizes as well Grace Halsell's example of the genre, *Soul Sister* (1969), an absolutely awe-inspiring jumble of humanist platitude, sexual prurience, homophobic panic, and pop sociology. In her book, Halsell not only manages to reprise the tenor of Griffin's conversation with the proprietor of the YMCA café, quoting Mississippi civil rights leader Charles Evers (brother of the slain Medgar) on Southern black men's "emasculation" and the need for the black man to "[s]tart being *a man*" (p. 164, emphasis in original), she also registers the racism to which blacks are subject in terms that reaffirm the gender- and sexual-political status quo. Working as a maid while living as a black woman in Mississippi, Halsell notes the laziness of her white employer—reflecting that "if Mrs. Dunlap loved her husband and child she could and would do the work I am doing"—and then slips into a nostalgic reverie on her own girlhood home, "always bright with sunshine, bright with flowers, a tea kettle humming on a stove, and mother always singing, never tired, up at five or six, cooking, cleaning, washing, ironing, making all my clothes, taking care of her big family" (pp. 147–48).

This unconsidered celebration of motherly sacrifice and devotion (of which Halsell herself has only ever been the receiving object, rather than dispensing subject, as far as her narrative indicates) is matched in *Soul Sister* by Halsell's rumination on the flawed masculinity of one Cliff Jones, a black man she meets in Harlem during the first half of her adventure in passing. Having related the details of Cliff's sexual impotency (which she herself has gotten secondhand) with notable thoroughness (pp. 100–101), Halsell ponders it so earnestly as to invest it with well-nigh metaphorical significance, wondering, "How . . . can a woman be a woman with him? And how, also, can he be a man without a woman, *a complete woman,* to give him all the assurance that he needs? . . . Tears well up in my eyes, moving the black contacts around" (p. 102, emphasis in original). The destabilization of Halsell's status as a "black" woman that is figured in the shifting of her colored contact lenses occurs in direct consequence of her realization of Cliff Jones's inability to be a "man," with Halsell thus figuring "black" femininity as dependent on a black *masculinity* whose very social import (deriving from a woman's "assurance") is itself rooted in the physical manifestation of sexual virility. Thus Halsell—who elsewhere is able to cite the speciously fictive quality of Euro-American phallic authority, referring to the Carthage, Mississippi, courthouse as "that cheap façade of manhood" (p. 157)—not only registers the degree to which black men have been prevented from attaining such problematic masculinity as functions as the social norm, but herself contrives to constrain black masculinity per se by conceiving it in precisely the essentializing physical terms that have long constituted its effective limit.

Griffin and Halsell claim to have received the same warning from well-meaning friends about the dangers of their passing: "You'll get yourself killed" (Griffin, p. 8; see also Halsell, p. 205). Reflecting on these words, Halsell asserts, "Getting killed is a remote abstraction to me and has never frightened me, anyhow" (p. 205), and perhaps rightly so. For if we *do* consider the matter in abstract terms, then neither Halsell nor Griffin would appear to be at risk, both of them emerging from their undercover experiences with their normative social subjectivities intact.[7] And this may not, after all, be very surprising, insofar as the passing narrative structurally demands the affirmation of the social bounds whose transgression it records: The passer returns to "the race"; she accedes to proper "femininity." Yet what the passing narrative seems to rule *out of bounds*—definitionally inassimilable to socially normative codes—is the very possibility of black *masculinity*, which is thus the real casualty of this cultural intervention. To the degree that this demise constitutes the oft-repeated story by which black men have been accounted for in the U.S. context, black masculine anxiety is largely intelligible, bespeaking a desperate urge to survival. On the other hand, insofar as that demise itself is both sign and symptom of a more generalized and socially fundamental anxiety about masculinity per se, the conceptualization of new, responsible black masculinities not only will accrue to the enhanced subjectivity of African-American men, but will position us at the forefront of progressive social transformation in a way that, the stridency of our political rhetoric notwithstanding, cannot be achieved under the current *gender*-political order.

6

THE REASSURING SHOCK
OF RECOGNITION

Blackness, Social Order,
and Crimes of Identity

The Blackness of O. J. Simpson

By October 1995, when actor and former pro football star O. J. Simpson was acquitted in the 1994 murders of his estranged wife, Nicole Brown Simpson, and Ronald Goldman, so much media coverage had been accorded to so many details of the case that one could well have forgotten a relatively small wrinkle from the earliest days of the reportage, involving a likeness of Simpson printed on the cover of one of the nation's leading weekly news magazines just after his arrest by the Los Angeles Police Department. Both *Time* and *Newsweek* based the covers for their 27 June 1994 issues on a mug shot of Simpson taken by the LAPD, running the portrait at full-page size along with headlines bristling with sensationalism—*Newsweek*'s "Trail of Blood"—and melodrama—*Time*'s "An American Tragedy" (see cover stories by Turque et al. and by Gibbs); but the fundamental identical-ness of the images was largely overridden by some distinguishing features that a *New York Times* reporter evidently found difficult to ascribe:

Covers from Newsweek *and* Time *magazines featuring O. J. Simpson's June 1994 mug shot.* Newsweek *cover: Copyright © 1994, Newsweek, Inc. All rights reserved. Reprinted by permission.* Time *cover: Copyright © 1994, Time Inc. Reprinted by permission.*

> . . . Time's cover was darker, blurrier and more sinister-looking than Newsweek's, and his case number, a 15-character jumble of numbers and letters, were smaller in Time than in Newsweek.
>
> Mr. Simpson's expression, his blazer and his open-at-the-collar shirt were the same from one cover to the other, and the two images were almost exactly the same size, positioned squarely in the center of each cover. But what appeared to be a 5 o'clock shadow in Newsweek looked like much heavier stubble in Time. His skin was also darker on the Time cover. (Barron, 1994)

It is plausible, I guess, to consider the confusion of pronominal antecedents that characterizes this passage as signaling merely the same editorial laxity that allowed for the number disagreement in the clause, "his case number . . . were smaller"; but, of course, it also seems to indicate something more: the faulty referencing of "Time's cover" by the possessive "his"—besides giving the passage a rather Anglo-Saxon cast—suggests that the "sinister" appearance of the magazine cover can also be attributed to "him" with the dauntingly long official case number. And if that sinister quality seems to issue, for the cover as a whole, from the relative "darkness" of the composition, so too might it derive, for Simpson himself, from *Time's* depiction of him as "darker"-skinned than he appears to be on

Newsweek. So ran the contemporaneous popular critique, which is nowhere mentioned in the *New York Times* article.[1] The terms engaged in the piece, however, raise the same questions addressed by that critique, in a manner whose very obliqueness suggests their potential volatility.

In explaining to the *Times* how her publication's presentation of Simpson's portrait differed from that of *Newsweek*—which, according to a spokeswoman, "ran [the photo] exactly as we received it"—*Time*'s Nancy Kearney (Barron, 1994) effectively denied what I have suggested is the fundamental similarity of the two images: "They're two completely different covers. Newsweek is a photo, ours is a photo-illustration"; and this fact, she suggested, would be clear to most readers, not only because the image "was clearly identified as a photo illustration," but because "[t]his was a photo most people would have seen" by the time of the magazine's publication and thus "would know was different" in *Time*'s cover presentation. Leaving aside Kearney's implicit acknowledgment here that the *Time* cover picture was at least *based on* the well-known Simpson photo—her protestations of the "complete difference" between the *Time* and *Newsweek* covers notwithstanding—we can note some degree of peculiarity in her assertion that the majority of observers would know that the *Time* image "wasn't the mug shot but was being used as an illustration." This use of *illustration* conflates at least two of the word's potential significances, one of which is at work in the term *photo-illustration* itself. Indeed, inasmuch as Kearney acknowledged that *Time* editors commissioned work for the magazine cover from artist Matt Mahurin because they "wanted to make it more artful, more compelling," it is clear that *photo-illustration* implicates such manual craft as is generally undertaken by professional "illustrators," who traditionally provide hand-drawn visual matter to supplement a printed text. Kearney seems also to be applying this sense of the term when she distinguishes between *Time*'s cover "illustration" and the "mug shot" that it most emphatically is not, according to her statement. At the same time, though, the sentence in which she insists on that distinction invokes "illustration" less as a *status* than as a *function:* Her explanation that the image "was being *used* as an illustration" implies not its having been hand-wrought by an artist, but rather its supposed illumination of references made in the text with which it is associated. Such a function could be served, of course, by a visual image of whatever technical origin: Witness *Newsweek*'s proclaimed deployment of the untouched Simpson mug shot to presumably the same text-enhancing effect as the *Time* editors apparently hoped to achieve—its *use* of the *photo* "as an illustration." Indeed, *Newsweek*'s acknowledged employment of the police photograph in this way raises the question of what, exactly, Nancy Kearney saw as being thus "used" on the cover of *Time*.

In citing Kearney's explanation here, I have given her the benefit of a clear grammatical subject where none exists in her statement to the *Times*, positing her as claiming that *Time*'s cover *image* "wasn't the mug shot." In fact, however, Kearney's actual formulation is rather less lucid than my rendering suggests, running in its unedited version as follows: "This was a photo most people would have seen and would know was different, that it wasn't the mug shot but was being used as an illustration." Like *Times* reporter James Barron's own prose, Kearney's statement manifests a great deal of pronoun-based confusion, with, first of all, the referent of "this" becoming increasingly problematic as the sentence progresses: While the syntax of the initial clause indicates that "this" refers to "photo," the subsequent characterization of the item in question as "different" undermines such a reading, since it is precisely the police "photo" or "mug shot" from which the item is being differentiated—based, as we know from another of Kearney's assertions, on the fact that it *isn't* a photo, but a "photo-illustration." Consequently, by the time "this" transmutes into "it"—whose referent grammar dictates must be the same as that of "this"—both pronouns appear to represent specifically the *photo-illustration* whose unique character Kearney seems at pains to emphasize. In this case, though, "photo-illustration" would be the implicit grammatical subject of the final clause of Kearney's statement, with the result that that clause could be rendered in the relatively inelegant and redundant form: "the photo-illustration was being used as an illustration." But since we have already established that the photo itself could just as easily be used to "illustrate" the magazine's article on Simpson, it seems clear that the *photo-illustration* must necessarily be "illustrating" *something else,* and this by virtue of its qualitative *difference* from the mug-shot photo. That difference inheres not in the precise character of the work wrought on the raw material that the police photo clearly constituted for the *Time* cover image—indeed, according to the *New York Times* account, artist Matt Mahurin "refused . . . to talk about what instructions, if any, that Time editors gave him or what he had done to alter Mr. Simpson's appearance"—but rather in the visual effects resulting therefrom. The primary such effect, as the *New York Times* article indicates, was the general darkening of Simpson's aspect such that, James Barron's subjective discernment of something "sinister" in the image aside, there was registered an association between that relative darkness and the criminality alleged in and through Simpson's arrest. It is precisely that link, in other words, that the *Time* cover seems to have illustrated, rather than a story about Simpson per se, the presentation of whose likeness would in that case have supposedly served merely to edify readers as to his general appearance. Thus the principal claim in the popular critique of the *Time* cover that I have mentioned—that the cover presentation is based on (and furthers) the idea that dark skin implies a criminal disposition—is apparently substantiated through the very statements by *Time* staff that were meant to exonerate the editors of malicious intent.

It is by no means novel, of course, to posit dark-skinned peoples as essentially disposed toward criminal behavior; at least as far back as the eighteenth century, after all, European commentators imputed a tendency toward both theft and violence to native Africans whose dark skin color itself was taken as the fundamental sign of their divergence from norms of white civilization (see W. Jordan, 1968, for instance pp. 26, 115). In O. J. Simpson's case, however, the darkening of Simpson's skin in *Time*'s "photo-illustration" seems to function not only as an indication of his alleged criminal orientation, but as a remedy for what has apparently been one of his primary transgressions—an unsettling approximation to a condition of whiteness. Indeed, as little as two months after Simpson's arrest, *Newsweek* (E. Thomas et al., 1994) ran a cover story on "The Double Life of O. J. Simpson"—tellingly titled "Day & Night"—that, while purporting to expose the "real" Simpson supposedly underlying the popular media image, seemed more pointedly concerned to show up as his most sinister dissemblance his pretenses to "white" styles of social behavior:

> His wife believed he was a cocaine addict; his friends, who saw him
> on the prowl at wild parties in Los Angeles, thought his real addiction
> was white women. The smooth talker took lessons to make his dic-
> tion more "white." . . . To many whites, he was not so much enviable
> as safe, and to some blacks, particularly his brothers in the sports and
> entertainment world, he was too white. (p. 43)

This last judgment, ascribed to Simpson's unnamed professional "brothers," would seem to be endorsed by the article itself, inasmuch as the quotation marks around *white* that are apparently meant to signal that condition's purely conventional quality work in concert with the snide description of Simpson as a "smooth talker" to suggest disdain for his supposed cross-racial aspirations. To the extent that those aspirations are socially suspect (scorned not only by blacks who understand them in terms of a faulty identification, but also by whites to whom they putatively signal Simpson's very "safeness"), *Time*'s cover illustration serves as a twofold corrective, disciplinarily reaffirming Simpson's "actual" blackness while underscoring the criminality inherent therein. For this positing of Simpson as constitutionally "wrong" to operate simultaneously as a crucial setting "right" of the social order suggests that even more rests on the congruency of skin color and racial identification than we already know from our daily experience; indeed, historical efforts to stabilize it may well carry an import beyond considerations of mere racial status as such, implicating a will to social regulation for which black masculine identity serves a notably instrumental function.

Racial Perceptibility in the Rhinelander Case

Before we consider the social-regulatory significance of black masculinity per se, it is important to note that O. J. Simpson is by no means the first African Ameri-can to be deemed "too white" in the court of media culture, and that black *women*, too, have been the objects of such a judgment. One of the novels of racial "passing" that I cite in Chapter 5 fleetingly refers to a historical instance in which perceptions of a black woman's inappropriately "white" identification became the focus of intense official concern. Indeed, as Mark Madigan (1990, p. 524) has pointed out, so "offhand" is Nella Larsen's mention in *Passing* (1929, p. 228) of "the Rhinelander case" that it suggests a contemporaneous readership's thorough familiarity with a proceeding of apparently crucial social import. If the amount of newspaper space given over to accounts of the case is any indication (Madigan counts eighty-eight articles published over a two-year period in the *New York Times* alone [525]), the Rhinelander suit likely was as familiar to the literate U.S. public throughout the late 1920s as the details of the O. J. Simpson case became to mass-media audiences in 1994 and 1995. The Rhinelander affair involved none of the brutal physical violence officially at issue in the more recent case, however, but instead centered on a specifically social transgression of the sort later com-mentators would discern in O. J. Simpson's supposed cross-racial identification.

The central facts of the Rhinelander case are fairly simple. In late November 1924, twenty-two-year-old Leonard Kip Rhinelander—scion of one of New York's wealthiest families—petitioned for the annulment of his marriage to Alice Beat-rice Jones, which had taken place just six weeks earlier, on the grounds that she had misrepresented herself to him as white when she in fact had "negro blood" ("Rhinelander Sues," p. 1). In settling the case a little over a year later, a New York Supreme Court jury found in favor of Alice Rhinelander, declaring that she had perpetrated no fraud as to her racial identity, and that Kip Rhinelander would have married her even had he known for certain that she was "of colored blood" ("Rhinelander Loses," p. 27). While the jury was not charged with determining whether Rhinelander *did* in fact know Alice Jones to be of Negro ancestry before he married her—and it did not officially rule on this question—the case of the defense rested on what can only be considered circumstantial evidence as to both Jones's Negro identity *and* Rhinelander's inevitable awareness of it, consisting in details of bodily appearance and linguistic practice that were brought before the court. Indeed, it seems to have been precisely the possibility of discerning the racial-identificatory import of such phenomena that was at stake in the court proceedings, with the jury foreman explaining the committee's reasoning by insisting: "Race prejudice didn't enter into the case at all. . . . We decided it merely as a case between a man and a woman, and in reaching our verdict considered

Rhinelander as a normal man *with normal sense of perception*" ("Rhinelander Loses," p. 27, emphasis added).

Rhinelander was prevailed upon to exercise this "sense of perception" at key points during the court proceedings, with some of the most critical moments occurring during his delivery of testimony on 17 November 1925. While the central legalistic development of that day was Rhinelander's admission that, contrary to his official claim of being "induced" into marriage by a duplicitous Alice Jones, he actively "pursued" her, both romantically and sexually ("Rhinelander Says"), the most sensorily charged aspects of the proceedings had to do with exactly how he *perceived* her whom he thus pursued. Intent on establishing the character of this perception for the court, Alice Rhinelander's attorney, Lee Parsons Davis, purposefully directed attention toward his client as he questioned Kip Rhinelander. As the *New York Times* related it: "Mrs. Rhinelander's counsel went around behind her, as she sat at the end of the counsel table in front of the jury box. She removed her hat, patted her black straight hair into place, and looked defiantly at her husband." Immediately following this account, in a passage introduced by the heading "Has to Look at His Wife," the *Times* retails Davis's interrogation:

> "Does your wife look the same now as when you met her?" Mr. Davis asked Rhinelander.
>
> "Yes," he said, looking at her for what was apparently the second time since the trial opened.
>
> "No inquiry arose in your mind as to her color until when?" demanded Mr. Davis. "When, when, when?" he reiterated as Rhinelander hesitated. Finally Rhinelander said it was after a letter from her in March of 1922.
>
> "That was the first time the question entered your mind as to the color of your wife."
>
> "Yes."
>
> "You never thought of it before?" asked Mr. Davis, and Rhinelander said he had not. Mr. Davis moved away and Mrs. Rhinelander put her hat on again, her face looking darker than ever under the shadow of the brim. ("Rhinelander Says")

Notably, Davis neither demanded that Rhinelander describe his wife's appearance nor himself suggested a characterization of it, but rather allowed her aspect effectively to "speak for itself," and thus to make clear both her approximation to whiteness (by means of her "straight hair") and—more important—the nonetheless easy perceptibility of her "negro blood"; indeed, the very form of the *Times*'s acknowledgment that Alice Rhinelander eventually came to look "darker than ever" suggests that the registration of that darkness derived not merely from the shadow of her hat brim, but—more crucially—from the training on her person of the courtroom audience's "normal sense of (visual) perception," effected through her attorney's interrogatory strategy. That registration having once been made, the additional physical evidence subsequently presented by Davis seems merely to have corroborated this primary apperception of Alice Rhinelander's negro identity, by appearing as its logical corollary; the *New York Times* described the presentation of that evidence thus:

> . . . Mr. Davis produced another of his dramatic effects when he asked Robert Brooks, the negro who married Emily, Alice's sister, to stand up.
> "That's Mr. Brooks, isn't it?" he asked [Rhinelander].
> "Yes."
> "When did you first meet him?"
> "In 1921." . . .
> "Do you know this lady," said Mr. Davis, pointing to Mrs. Brooks, who also stood up. She is undeniably of colored blood.
> "Yes."
> "When did you first meet Mrs. Brooks?"
> "In 1921."
> This was the first year he met his wife, three years before they were married.
> "So in 1921 you knew that Emily had married a colored man?"
> "Yes." ("Rhinelander Says")

In other words, Kip Rhinelander's sworn claim that he first learned of Emily Jones's marriage to a black man—and consequently suspected her own and her sister Alice's negro identities—in 1924 was shown to be false; and so too was Alice Rhinelander unequivocally shown to be commonly identifiable as a negro, by virtue of her sister's apparent negro identification, itself attested as much by that sister's marriage to an uncontestedly negro man as by her own "undeniably" "colored" appearance.

The corroborative effect served by the presentation of Alice Rhinelander's family before the court was augmented by Davis's reference—central to his case—to letters exchanged by Kip Rhinelander and Alice Jones before their marriage. Ostensibly presented by way of demonstrating to the court Rhinelander's independently formed intentions of, first, convincing Alice to become his kept mistress and, later, actually marrying her, the letters—and, specifically, the language comprised therein—served equally as evidence of Alice's negro identity, to the apparent detriment of Rhinelander's legal suit:

> Mr. Davis read several . . . letters, and then came to one in which Rhinelander referred to a "strutting party," as he said Alice called them.
>
> "Ever hear anybody say, 'I'm goin' to a struttin' pahty'?" asked Mr. Davis, rolling it out in the best negro dialect. "Ever hear Alice say it?"
>
> "I believe so, yes."
>
> "Ever hear the expression, 'You-all goin' to a struttin' pahty'?"
>
> "Yes."
>
> "When she used that expression early in the game you had no suspicion of her color?"
>
> "No," he said.
>
> "What was this 'struttin'?"
>
> "Strutting was dancing," explained Rhinelander.
>
> "Didn't you recognize that as being a typically negro expression?"
>
> "No, I can't say I did." ("Rhinelander Says")

Thus without Alice Rhinelander's ever uttering a word (she never took the stand to testify in the trial; see "Rhinelander Loses," p. 27), Davis imputed to her patterns of diction and intonation that clinched her negro identification, in much the same way that, earlier, he effectively conferred upon her a recognizably dark complexion under the gaze of courtroom observers. These effects, of course, were on one level merely the by-products of the attorney's strenuous effort to clear his client of the charges of fraud that had been leveled against her; strictly speaking, however, they were also unnecessary and gratuitous, inasmuch as they indicated not Alice Rhinelander's innocence of wilful misrepresentation, but rather the latter's practical impossibility, which is a significantly different thing. That Davis apparently *did* consider that demonstration necessary suggests not only that the deception with which Alice Rhinelander was charged was indeed practicable— her actual guilt or innocence aside—but also that that very practicability was a source of profound anxiety within the official culture whose representative—as much as Alice Rhinelander's—Davis effectively was.[2]

For how else, except by that anxiety, can we account for the anonymous *Times* reporters' apparent eagerness to concur in—indeed, to further—Davis's implicit positing of Alice Rhinelander as a manifestly negro woman? That eagerness is evident not only in the *Times*'s judgment of the defendant as perceptibly dark-skinned, but also—and in keeping with Davis's additional, idiomatic line of reasoning—in its careful attention, during the aftermath of the trial, to Alice Rhinelander's speech patterns, noted from remarks she made to reporters in the sanctuary of her lawyer's offices:

> "Do you still love your husband?" she was asked.
>
> She hesitated a long time, looking down at her hands in her lap, and finally said slowly:
>
> "I do and I don't."
>
> . . . It had been noticed during the trial that the engagement ring which figured in the testimony was never worn by Mrs. Rhinelander, and she was asked why this was.
>
> "I don't think I can answer that," she said, after a long pause. As to the verdict she said:
>
> "Naturally, I am happy over it, but I was not happy over the torture I went through." . . .
>
> Mrs. Rhinelander said she did not think the trial had lost her any friends, and that she thought she had gained a few.
>
> "Would you go back to your husband?" she was asked.
>
> She hesitated a moment and then said: "I can't answer that," and then quickly added, "No."
>
> "You two were very much in love, weren't you?"
>
> "We was, yes," she said, making her first grammatical slip.
>
> "It was a beautiful love affair," somebody said, and she answered quickly:
>
> "It certainly was." ("Rhinelander Loses," p. 27)

The pathos that characterizes this final exchange derives less from its implication that a perfect love has been spoiled (indeed, in light of the "filth" that Davis claimed characterized the proceedings, this very suggestion constitutes a properly *bathetic* turn; see "Rhinelander Loses," p. 27) than from the condescending attitude toward Alice Rhinelander that the proposition bespeaks. That condescension—and the relief I think informed it—was predicated on the confirmation of Alice Rhinelander's negro identity provided by her "grammatical slip" during the interview, so carefully noted by the reporting correspondent. While this slip also signaled Alice Rhinelander's class status (she was working as a chambermaid when Kip Rhinelander first met her; see "Rhinelander Says"), the centrality to the case of her racial identification (and its putative demonstration by Davis as discernible in her speech patterns) made it the salient issue in the posttrial interview, in which it grounded reporters' implicit conception of her as a stereotypically ignorant negro with laughably grandiose social aspirations.

In other words, the resolution of the Rhinelander affair—for all the financial reward it eventually brought to Alice Rhinelander[3]—functioned in much the same way as the "passing" novels of the contemporaneous Harlem Renaissance, reaffirming the viability of existing racialized social categories so as to quell anxiety about their possible collapse. At the same time, however, one of the elements in that reaffirmation rendered it tentative at best, predicating it on the establishment of facts that themselves unsettled key elements in the stability of the social status quo.

During his examination of Kip Rhinelander, attorney Lee Parsons Davis voiced a question that uncannily prefigured the one John Howard Griffin would later imagine being hurled at his "Negroid" self: "What do you mean, calling a white woman 'darling' like that, boy?" Intent on proving not only that Alice Jones had not deceived Kip Rhinelander as to her racial identity, but also that Kip harbored an affection for Alice to which that identity would have presented no impediment, Davis introduced to the court a letter of 28 September 1921 that Kip ended by writing to Alice, "Well, dearest, I must close and go down to mail this to you. Much love, LEONARD." "If you weren't in love with her," Davis demanded in response to Kip Rhinelander's claims to that effect, "what was the idea of writing 'dearest' and sending 'much love[']?" Getting an inconclusive response to this query, Davis later suggested that it was Kip, and not Alice, who had first practiced deception in the relationship, which Kip denied, "though," as the *Times* reminded its readers, "he said he loved her when he didn't really." "You don't call that deception?" Davis wanted to know. "I did—love her," Rhinelander hesitatingly admitted.

Davis then proposed to establish a logical progression whereby, if Kip did indeed love Alice, he must in truth have desired and intended to marry her, which fact alone, according to the already stretched social conventions governing the course of the trial, could have justified Kip's previously admitted objective of, in Davis's words, "trying to get into her mind the sex idea." Apparently incredulous at Kip's prior claim that he did not plan to marry Alice, Davis euphemistically invoked Kip's acknowledged sexual designs: "You had no thought of marriage at that time when you thought you could get her to like you?" Rhinelander replied, "No, I had not." Davis pursued this line of questioning from a slightly more oblique angle:

> "What is the worse deception, to lead a girl to believe you want to marry her and take that which is most precious to a woman, or for her to say she is white and not colored?"
>
> "The latter," said Rhinelander.
>
> "It's not worse for a man to deceive a girl to accomplish his desire?"

"I didn't deceive her," said Rhinelander. (All quotations taken from "Rhinelander Says")

Thus Kip Rhinelander was caught in a double bind: if he hadn't intended to marry Alice Jones, as he claimed was the case, then his admitted sexual pursuit of her, according to social convention, entailed a grave deception; if, on the other hand, he hadn't deceived her, as he also claimed was the case, then he must have intended to marry her. In the end, the jury evidently opted to believe in the "good faith" of Kip's manifested sexual interest, since, as I have already indicated, it ruled specifically that he would have married Alice even had he known her to be "of colored blood" ("Rhinelander Loses," p. 27). At the same time, however, that very finding verged on such official recognition of a miscegenational relationship as to make uncomfortable at least one juror, who told the *Times,* "If we had voted according to our hearts the verdict might have been different" ("Rhinelander Loses," p. 27).

Indeed, a similar discomfort on Davis's part might be discerned in his reference to the "filth" whose presentation before the court the trial necessarily entailed. Ostensibly, that characterization pertained to the description of the "intimate" encounter that took place between Kip Rhinelander and Alice Jones during a "pre-nuptial visit to the Hotel Marie Antoinette" in 1921 ("Rhinelander Says"); but insofar as the logic by which Davis demonstrated Kip's intention to marry Alice assimilated such intimacies to a condition of effective matrimony, the "filth" that they constitute must have tainted that marriage itself, making it, too, an object of Davis's disgust.

I have argued elsewhere that, however popularly discomfiting the idea of sexual relations between a white man and a black woman might have been during the heyday of the legal ban on miscegenation, it was the prospect of such persons' marriage per se that was the source of official alarm, since it constituted a threat to the regularized distribution of property that founds the normative social order (see Harper, May 1994, especially pp. 123–24). The Rhinelander case largely substantiates this claim, given that, as Mark Madigan (1990, p. 524) has pointed out, Kip Rhinelander and Alice Jones were married "just one week after the twenty-two year-old Rhinelander had received a share of his family's fortune in cash, jewels, real estate, and stocks," which timing likely contributed to the fact that, as the *New York Times* put it, "news of the marriage startled society" ("Rhinelander Sues," p. 16). Indeed, it is completely plausible that, had the couple never married, their ongoing sexual relationship could have enjoyed such tacit sanction as was stereotypically accorded wealthy white men's dalliances with working-class women of whatever racial identity. The actualization of the marriage, however, set at odds the societal needs for both regularized property distribution and the illusion of easily perceptible racial identification, since the buttressing of the latter that it demanded (and that Davis effectively provided) threatened the destabilization of the former by incorporating recognition of a connubial relation that confounded the conventions of inheritance.

Thus the importance of cultural strategies for managing apparent racial ambiguity—conventional "passing" novels, the alteration of O. J. Simpson's photograph—would seem to be a function of the threat that ambiguity poses, not merely in a generalized social realm, but in the specifically legal engagement whose thorough regulation it successfully evades. A look at a more recent instance of such engagement will further reveal the partialness of its regulatory success and, thus, the necessity of properly cultural negotiations to the maintenance of racialized social identities.

The Self-Defeating Logic of the "One-Drop" Rule

One noteworthy feature of the legal definition of black identity operative in the United States is that it is incredibly expansive—indeed, anomalously so—in comparison with those for other racial categorizations, a fact that Adrian Piper (1992) has traced to specifically economic concerns:

> A legally certifiable Native American is entitled to financial benefits from the government, so obtaining this certification is difficult. A legally certifiable black person is *disentitled* to financial, social, and inheritance benefits from his white family of origin, so obtaining this certification is not just easy but automatic. Racial classification in this country functions to restrict the distribution of goods, entitlements, and status as narrowly as possible to those whose power is already entrenched. (pp. 18–19)

This explanation, which is congruent with my prior claim regarding prohibitions on interracial marriage, renders intelligible the apparent logical contradiction whereby, as Piper points out, "an individual must have *at least* one-eighth Native American ancestry in order to identify legally as Native American," while "any proportion of African ancestry is sufficient to identify a person as black"—the "traceable amount" rule according to which as little as "one drop" of "black blood" constitutes a person's black identity (p. 18). (It also elucidates the by-now proverbial anger of some white men over affirmative action, which might be seen as making it actually advantageous, for once, to have "one drop" of "black blood"; for the founding exposition of the "angry white male" syndrome, see Estrich,

1994.) This "one-drop" rule, deriving from the customs of the slavery-era South, has been recognized by U.S. courts since at the least the 1896 case of *Plessy v. Ferguson,* and it was reaffirmed as recently as 1986, when the Supreme Court refused to hear an appeal by the plaintiff in a racial-designation case from Louisiana, where the "one-drop" criterion prevails (F. J. Davis, 1991, pp. 4–5, 8–11). The Louisiana case, however, while plainly indicating both the remarkable comprehensiveness of official black identification and the legal machinations through which it is achieved, demonstrates as well the degree to which that comprehensiveness itself predicates a practical limit to the manageability of blackness, thus making clear why the legal regulation of racial identity must be supplemented by strategies of cultural negotiation.

Technically speaking, the case of *Jane Doe v. State of Louisiana* (hereafter cited as *Jane Doe*) did not entail a direct challenge to Louisiana's rule of black identification per se; rather it addressed the issue of whether Susie Guillory Phipps (whose first name is sometimes cited as "Suzy" in court documentation) could legally change information recorded on her birth certificate, which proposed alteration potentially necessitated the adducement of that identificatory rule. By the time the stage for the case was set, in 1977, the Louisiana case law stipulating that any "traceable amount" of African ancestry constituted a person as black had been modified—the result of a 1970 legislative effort—to specify that

> [i]n signifying race, a person having one-thirty second or less of
> Negro blood shall not be deemed, described or designated by any
> public official in the state of Louisiana as "colored," a "mulatto," a
> "black," a "negro," a "griffe," an "Afro-American," a "quadroon," a
> "mestizo," a "colored person," or a "person of color." (Louisiana
> Revised Statute 42:267, cited in *Jane Doe,* p. 371 n. 1).

That Susie Phipps's parents *were* indeed listed as "Col."—for "colored"—on her 1934 birth certificate she claimed not to have known until she requested a copy of the document in the course of applying for a passport in 1977 (Finch, 1985, p. A29; Trillin, 1986, p. 62). Upon thus learning that, though she had allegedly lived all her life as a white person, she was not officially considered to be such, Phipps petitioned to have this recording of her parents' classification changed so as to remedy the discrepancy she discerned between legal designation and her felt experience (F. J. Davis, 1991, p. 10). As it turned out, Phipps was unsuccessful in her undertaking, with a New Orleans district court finding in 1983 that she and the relatives who had joined her suit had not presented evidence sufficient to warrant an alteration of the relevant documents, as the law clearly demanded, and Louisiana's fourth circuit appellate court affirming in 1985 the plaintiffs' failure "to prove by a preponderance of the evidence that their parents' racial designations are incorrect" (*Jane Doe*, p. 372); by refusing in 1986 to hear the case, the U.S. Supreme Court concurred in the lower court's ruling on the necessity of such proof, effectively killing Susie Phipps's chances of changing what she saw as her parents'—and, by extension, her own—faulty racial designation in the official record of Louisiana (F. J. Davis, 1991, p. 11).

Such evidence as Phipps was bound to provide, the court suggested, would counter received indications that her parents, Dominique and Simea Fretty Guillory—along with members of the community in which they lived—concurred in their designation as colored, the apparent lightness of their skin notwithstanding. Not only was Phipps unable to demonstrate the falsity of those indications, but depositions given by inhabitants of the Louisiana parish in which she grew up suggested that the Guillory family was widely recognized as colored—and Phipps herself told of being suspiciously distinguished both from whites and from recognizable blacks during her childhood years (Trillin, 1986, pp. 72–74). Thus it seems plausible that, Phipps's feelings on the matter aside, her parents actually acquiesced in (without, apparently, talking explicitly to their children *about*) Louisiana's notoriously intricate racial caste system, for "colored" was a common mixed-race designation that had different significances than "Negro" or "black" in 1934, possibly accounting for Phipps's own recollection of her peculiar positioning amid the other children lined up to take Communion in her childhood church: "always in the back of the white but ahead of the black" (quoted in Trillin, 1986, p. 74).

It was that apparent acquiescence that the appellate court seized on in its rejection of Phipps's claim, noting specifically that

> [t]here is no proof in the record that Simea or Dominique Guillory
> preferred to be designated as white. They might well have been proud
> to be described as colored. Indeed, we have no evidence that during
> their lifetimes they objected to the racial designations in dispute in
> this case. (*Jane Doe*, p. 372)

In addition to thus remarking the elder Guillorys' apparent concurrence in their designation as colored, the court cited the specifically social and cultural—as opposed to scientific—character of racial designation, identifying it as a function of "subjective perceptions" and concluding that such perceptions as were pertinent at the time of Susie Guillory's birth were accurately recorded on the birth certificate by the attending midwife (*Jane Doe*, p. 372). Finally, because it *was* indeed a midwife—possibly in consultation with the parents themselves—who recorded the data, the court ruled as irrelevant to the case "the infamous 'one-thirty second' statute," which specifically barred only "public officials" from designating as "colored" "a person having one-thirty second or less of Negro blood" (*Jane Doe*, p. 372).

Thus did the court indicate the at-best tangential pertinence to Phipps's case of Louisiana's rule of black identification, which had once again been altered by the time of the 1985 appellate court decision. It was, in fact, publicity surrounding the initial hearing of Phipps's case in the Orleans Parish Civil District Court that fueled the state legislature's repeal of the "one-thirty second" law in June 1983, and its concomitant granting to citizens the right to change information on a birth certificate if they can prove its incorrectness by "a preponderance of the evidence" (F. J. Davis, 1991, pp. 9–10; Trillin, 1986, p. 77). It was this standard that the appeals court invoked in affirming the lower court's ruling against Susie Phipps, finding that Phipps had not countered the evidence of her parents' "colored" identity inherent in the "subjective perceptions" of their home community, and thereby seeming to demur at the suspect scientism informing the "one-thirty second" rule, whose inapplicability was already clear. At the same time, however, what the court did not explicitly note is that such scientism itself—and the faulty science in which it is a factor—is a key element in the sociocultural complex in which racial categorization derives. After all, on what did the members of the Guillorys' home community base their notion of the family's "colored" identity but the common knowledge that their genealogy included some African ancestry, mistaken notions about the genetic significance of which largely underpin the conceptions of the "Negroid" race (just as misapprehensions about genetics in general underpin the concept of race per se) that have characterized both official and properly "popular" culture throughout U.S. history?[4] Indeed, in repealing the "one-thirty second" law, the Louisiana legislature did not abolish the state's reliance on problematic genealogical indications in assigning the "black" racial designation; rather, the standard for that designation merely reverted to the "traceable amount" criterion that had been in effect prior to 1970 (F. J. Davis, 1991, p. 10), though now a person could alter the racial designation given on a birth certificate by meeting the new "preponderance of the evidence" requirement, rather than the old stipulation demanding proof that left "no doubt at all" as to the need for the change (Trillin, 1986, p. 61).[5] Susie Guillory Phipps, we have already noted, failed to meet even this relatively relaxed criterion, and the U.S. Supreme Court's refusal to consider her appeal left standing her effective designation as "colored" according to the "one-drop rule" that applies in Louisiana.

In settling Phipps's case, the court demonstrated a remarkable elasticity that founds what I have noted as the capaciousness of legal black identification, ostensibly adhering to a sociocultural-constructionist theory of race while simultaneously—tacitly—admitting of the specious biologism that dominant social conceptions of race have long implicated. At the same time, though, the very elasticity of the legal system's definition of blackness predicates the limit to its practical regulatory effect. For if Susie Guillory Phipps is "colored" in the eyes of the law, she need not have been so in anyone else's eyes prior to taking her case into the spotlight of the public arena. In fact, technically speaking, Phipps was actually "passing" as white throughout her adult life, if her story is to be believed—at least until she stepped from behind the "Jane Doe" appellation through which she initially presented herself to the court. It is obvious that, to those who not only can but feel compelled to undertake it, such "passing" for white is necessitated by the existence of societal (if not, any longer, *legal*) constraints on those known to be black according to law; it may be less obvious, but it is equally true that, from a slightly different perspective, such passing is itself *made possible* by the existence of the very laws that, as Adrian Piper (1992) has pointed out, are designed to limit African Americans' access to material benefits, precisely by defining blackness in the most comprehensive terms possible. Because those terms extend beyond the bounds of visually discernible black identity, they allow for their own rejection by those who do not visibly appear as black, contrary to the hidden evidence of "blood." The difficulty of policing that border of black identification—the first line of which defense will always comprise merely visual inspection—is demonstrated by the Rhinelander case, which was characterized by intense anxiety over the possible invisibility of a negro identity that Alice Rhinelander claimed never to have attempted to hide in the first place.[6] If the law cannot fix black identity in such a way as to minimize the possibility of "illegitimate" upward social movement while simultaneously rendering potential transgressors identifiable at a glance, then it must obtain help from other quarters that are better equipped for the task at hand.

Policing the Color Line

My brief consideration of *Time*'s O. J. Simpson photograph has demonstrated the mass media's readiness to affirm the black identity of any African American perceived as disclaiming it, regardless of whether that person be judged guilty of any other transgression.[7] It would be a mistake, though, to consider the media an autonomous entity distinct from its consumers, who themselves have often been perfectly willing to prosecute such affirmations of blackness. Indeed, the U.S. populace has been so thoroughly conditioned to see African-American men, in particular, as the very embodiment of social transgression per se, that it has blithely accepted accounts of black men's alleged criminal behavior even in situations that offered no evidence of a black man's having been present. One of the most recent widely publicized such cases is that of Susan Smith, the white South

Carolina woman who confessed in November 1994 to the murder of her two young sons, having initially told authorities that they were kidnapped by a black male carjacker who accosted her at a stoplight (see Bragg, "An Agonizing Search" and "Mother . . . Held"). Smith's case recalled the one from October 1989, in which a white suburban Boston man reported that he and his pregnant wife had been shot by a black man who leaped into their stopped car as they were on their way home from a childbirthing class. Carol Stuart and her prematurely delivered baby died as a result of the attack, and over the next two months Boston police conducted an extensive sweep of the neighborhood in which it had occurred, vigorously pursuing black male suspects. Finally, just a week after Carol Stuart's husband, Charles, had identified the attacker as one William Bennett, picking him from among a group of African-American men presented in a police line-up, Charles Stuart himself was named as the prime suspect in the case. That same morning, Stuart apparently committed suicide by jumping off the Tobin Bridge into the Boston Harbor, from which his body was recovered during the afternoon; a note found in his car indicated that he had been unable to bear up under the allegations against him (see Hays, 1990).

The lesson of the Stuart case—coupled with criticisms of their handling of the Jeffrey Dahmer serial murders in 1991—apparently impelled Milwaukee police to be skeptical of a story similar to Charles Stuart's that was related to them by Jesse Anderson in 1992. It took only two days for Anderson to be charged in the stabbing death of his wife, Barbara, which he claimed had been perpetrated by two black men who assaulted the couple as they were leaving a Milwaukee restaurant. Still, Anderson's concocting of the tale in the first place bespeaks his awareness of its potential credibility within the community; and, indeed, the local press indicated a noteworthy readiness among some area residents to believe Anderson's story right after it was reported (Wilkerson, "Police Charge Man").

In addition to having grave effects on the material well-being of African-American men, the abiding popular association of black masculinity with criminality in U.S. culture confers particular symbolic significances upon black men's engagement with the legal system. Most important for the point I am making here, such legalistic negotiation of racial-identity confusion as was undertaken in the Rhinelander and Phipps cases registers in a distinctive way when the person whose identity is in question is male rather than female. For one thing, the official presumption of innocence notwithstanding, cases that implicate confusion of a *man's* racial identity seem to entail the a priori investment of blackness in individuals named as criminal suspects. Such investment suggests that, however the official charges are settled in a given case, racial indeterminacy itself constitutes a grave transgression of social rules, for which black masculinity is the perfect emblem.

This point is demonstrated, interestingly enough, by the infamous Tailhook "gantlet" case, in which Navy flier Lieutenant Paula Coughlin charged that she had been sexually assaulted by a group of male military officers gathered in a hotel hallway through which she passed during the 1991 convention of the Tailhook Association of Navy aviators in Las Vegas. While there seems to be no doubt that Lieutenant Coughlin was indeed molested—in fact, an official Navy investigation revealed that at least eighty women were sexually assaulted during the 1991 Tailhook symposium, of whom Lieutenant Coughlin was the first to make public charges (Dowd, 1993, p. A20)—it proved impossible to identify the man who was her primary attacker, so that no punishment was ever meted out in her case, the most high-profile one to come out of the mass incident. Not that no attempt was made to locate the guilty party in Lieutenant Coughlin's assault; indeed, the authorities were relatively successful in following up the description of him that Lieutenant Coughlin provided. Her assailant, Lieutenant Coughlin had reported, was remarkable for his "light-colored" eyes, characterized in news accounts as his "most prominent features," owing to the "strikingness" of their appearance in a man Coughlin said was "either light skinned black or Hispanic" (Dowd, 1993, p. A20; Lewis, 1993). By August 1993, the authorities had assembled a lineup of possible suspects, from among which Lieutenant Coughlin identified as her attacker Marine Captain Gregory Bonam, who was indeed "a light-skinned black man with blue eyes," according to the *Times* (Dowd, 1993, p. A20).

In October 1993, the Marine Corps determined that there was not sufficient evidence to warrant a court martial against Captain Bonam, who denied that he had ever even seen Lieutenant Coughlin or been at the scene of her assault (Lewis, 1993). The decision to dismiss the charges against Captain Bonam apparently issued largely from discrepancies between Lieutenant Coughlin's statements and visual evidence from the night of the assault (she said that her assailant had worn a burnt-orange-colored shirt, while photographs of Captain Bonam from the evening in question showed him wearing a green t-shirt with a camouflage pattern), but it also seems to have derived from uncertainties about her very identification of Captain Bonam as her attacker. In an account of the preliminary hearing held by the Marine Corps in August 1993, the *New York Times* noted that Captain Bonam's attorney, Patrick J. Mackrell, had

> forced Lieutenant Coughlin to admit that she had briefly considered implicating another light-skinned black man shown her in a photograph by Navy investigators, before settling on Captain Bonam. He repeated her remarks to the investigators: "That looks exactly like him. If it's not him, it's his brother." But then investigators told her that the picture was of a lance corporal assigned to the photo laboratory in Quantico who had not been at Tailhook.

... He also asked her about some lines he said she uttered, according to those present, when she picked out Captain Bonam in the
lineup: "What is bothering me is I am afraid I have this minor
shadow of a doubt. I think that is him. I recall him being larger. He
weighed more." (Dowd, 1993, p. A20)

In other words, the remarkableness of the assailant's "most prominent features" was apparently mitigated by the indeterminability of his less striking ones,
undermining the promise of identificatory certainty that racialized morphology
is generally considered to proffer. Or perhaps it is such morphology itself that was
pointed up as dubious in Captain Bonam's case. After all, to propose that anyone
appears "either black or Hispanic" is to beg the question of those identities' visually discernible character. Indeed, however he may appear in person, Gregory
Bonam does not register as necessarily other than white in the black-and-white
photo of him published in the *Times* (Dowd, 1993, p. A20). At the same time, if
he identifies as black, as the newspaper account makes clear that he does, then
that identification had to have been a matter of official military record when he
was chosen to appear in the police lineup, conceivably *predicating* his very inclusion in that lineup, since, taken in conjunction with his evidently light skin, it
made him conform to Lieutenant Coughlin's speculative characterization of her
attacker. That characterization having been made, Captain Bonam's arrest in the
assault not only conferred upon him alleged-criminal status, it also, willy-nilly,
served to reaffirm publicly his African-American identity, always potentially in
doubt due to the lightness of his skin color. Thus the terms through which the
case against Captain Bonam was rendered intelligible both in the military-court
context and in the larger arena, conjoined with the specificities of his physical
appearance, made for a situation in which the alleged perpetrator of a crime, who
never denied his African-American identification, was nonetheless forcibly re-
invested with it, irrespective of the intentions of the parties in the case. This effect
derived specifically from the inability of those operative terms to account for the
potential disjuncture between physical appearance and designated race—a disjuncture whose foregrounding in a criminal-court proceeding seems to suggest its
illicit character regardless of the suspect's official innocence.

That suggestion is even stronger in the converse situation where a suspect
eventually judged as guilty also apparently turned out to claim black parentage,
contrary to official published assessments. Not that there was not some evident
confusion as to whether it was a "white" or a "black" man who assaulted figure
skater Nancy Kerrigan just prior to the 1994 winter Olympics.[8] One day after the
6 January 1994 incident, in which Kerrigan was clubbed on her right knee by a
then-still-unidentified man during practice for the U.S. championship figure

U.S. Marine Captain
Gregory Bonam. Photo:
AP/Wide World Photos.

skating competition in Detroit, the *New York Times* characterized the attacker as "a white man about 6 feet 2 inches and 200 pounds" (Longman, "Kerrigan Attacked," p. B7). The next day, the paper reported that police had composed a sketch of the suspect, whom they officially described once more as "a white man, 6-feet tall, weighing 190 to 210 pounds and dressed in black," as though to lay to rest the divergent characterizations that had already begun to emerge. As the *Times* put it in this same article,

> There was some confusion over the description of the attacker. On Thursday [6 January, the day of the attack], witnesses said he was white. Today [Friday, 7 January], the police said the attacker might have been a black man with a light complexion, but later said the suspect was white. (Longman, "Attacked Figure Skater")

By 9 January, three days after the assault, Detroit police secured evidence that seemed to promise a less ambiguous description of the attacker—specifically, a videotape made by an ABC television staffer on assignment at the skating competition, in which the assailant's visage was momentarily perceptible: "You can see his face," deputy police chief Benny Napoleon asserted, according to the *Times;* and then, as if to render that face visually distinctive through the mere rehearsal of its generic features, he elaborated: "You can see his eyes. You can see his nose. You can see his mouth" ("Tape Shows Face").

The certainty connoted by these sharp declaratives—which themselves do nothing to indicate the exact appearance of the features they cite—belied the equivocation that still characterized the police account as little as one day before they were issued, when authorities followed up their initial drawing of the suspect—and their published assurances that he was indeed white—with the release of dual sketches, "one depicting a whi[t]e male and the other depicting a black male with a light complexion" (Longman, "Kerrigan May Be Back"; see also Longman, "F. B. I. Begins Own Search"). Two days after proclaiming the existence of the videotape, the *New York Times* reported that police were "positive" that the suspect was white, but in the context of the ongoing confusion—and certainly in retrospect, after *Time* magazine's publication of its O. J. Simpson "photo-illustration"—the announcement that police were "enhancing" the attacker's video image so as to make it more identifiable could be read cynically, as indicating a desire for that image to be rendered congruent with stereotyped notions of black male criminality, the police department's insistence on the suspect's whiteness notwithstanding (NPR News; see also Longman, "Kerrigan May Be Back" and "F.B.I. Begins Own Search"). In fact, as it turned out, the enlarged, digitally enhanced video image did not yield incontrovertible support for that "white" identification, apparently revealing that the attacker had "almond-shaped eyes, an oval face, long hair and a thin nose," the aggregation of which features does not necessarily bespeak a white identity (Longman, "F.B.I. Begins Own Search").

It was not until after the arrest of two presumedly white and white-identified men—Shawn Eric Eckardt, bodyguard to skater Tonya Harding, and Derrick B. Smith—in connection with the by-then one-week-distant attack that the mystery as to the assailant's racial identity was apparently solved. With the arrest of the attacker himself, which came a day after those of Eckardt and Smith, a degree of clarity finally settled on the features that had shown up only vaguely in the ABC videotape, and they were found to belong to a man identified by the *New York Times* as Shane M. Stant, who had been arrested once before and eventually served a short jail term for stealing automobiles in Idaho (Janofsky). Once Stant turned himself in, the *Times,* which had fairly diligently recorded the vacillations in police accounts of the suspected assailant's racial identity, dropped that aspect of its coverage; but the *Boston Globe*—the principal metropolitan daily in Nancy Kerrigan's home region—at least gestured toward resolving the issue in its "profile" of Stant, which cited a childhood friend as saying that Stant was "part black and part Polynesian," and consequently had "felt out of place" in the small, predominantly white, Washington town in which he attended high school (Adams and Grunwald, 1994, p. 6). Whether such a sense of displacement really did trou-

Shane Minoaka Stant being led to his arraignment on charges of assaulting skater Nancy Kerrigan. Photo: AP/Wide World Photos.

ble Stant (whose own characterization of his racial identity we never get), it is certainly figured in the confusion over his racial status that marked the police investigation of the Kerrigan attack from start to finish, and which seems, in retrospect, to have stemmed largely from the general unrecognizability of "Polynesian" identification in the U.S. racial order. Indeed, almost as though to render legible such an "exotically" indeterminate extraction, the *Globe* spelled out in full Stant's middle name—Minoaka—thereby emphasizing his Oceanian heritage (Adams and Grunwald, 1994, p. 1).

The fact that Stant reportedly does claim black parentage both ironizes Detroit police insistences that he had to be white and, from a more cynical perspective, seems to "justify" authorities' evident simultaneous following through on the supposition that he could have been black. To rest at thus observing the ramifications of investigators' having played it "both ways" would be to miss the point, though, since, as the foregoing account makes clear, Stant's racial identity is apparently inassimilable to the binaristic logic that still governs the U.S. racial order.[9] According to the one-drop rule of black identification through which that binarism operates, mixed-heritage individuals such as Stant are de facto African Americans, with the local result that the resolution of the Kerrigan assault case entailed the criminalization of yet another "black" man.[10] At the same time, that man's "failure" to manifest visually as one race or "the" other itself appears as an effective transgression of the received "rules" of racial identity; and the intolerability of that transgression, paradoxically enough, seems quite easily registered through the examples of those who are actually unable to commit the violation, which brings us back to *Time*'s portrait of O. J. Simpson. For if the mug shot of Simpson itself seems merely to confirm the criminal disposition stereotypically associated with black masculinity in the first place, then the "enhancement" of Simpson's blackness (which is already apparent) in that confirmatory visual depiction implies the seriousness, not of the offense with which Simpson is technically charged, but of the insidious undoing of racial identity at disparate unrelated social and cultural sites, which threatens to render him officially unintelligible. Thus this emphatically black O. J. Simpson not only serves as the corroborative evidence of his own alleged criminality; he also functions as the poster boy in a campaign against such destabilization of racial categories as he is physically unable to forward in his own person.[11]

For all the official anxiety that it occasions, though, that destabilization is far from having been fully accomplished. Were it already achieved, it would render impossible not only the use of O. J. Simpson's darkened aspect in the manner I have outlined, but also the authoritatively issued account whereby, his physical "blackness" notwithstanding, Simpson is inappropriately white-identified. Simpson's deployment in both of the functions that I have elaborated indicates not only the continued dominance of the traditional U.S. racial order, but its remarkable ability to adopt and adapt new bulwarks against its possible dismantling—in this case both the person and the image of the black man himself, one of the primary potential beneficiaries of the system's demise. And that ability, in turn, underwrites the ongoing constraint on just *who* it is possible to be in this country; for, more than making alternatives merely difficult to realize, it renders them, quite literally, nearly impossible to envision.

PART III

NEGOTIATING DIFFERENCE IN AFRICAN-AMERICAN CULTURE

EXTRA-SPECIAL EFFECTS

Televisual Representation
and the Undoing
of "The Black Experience"

The Complex Effects of Televisual Representation

Contrary to what the foregoing chapters might suggest, U.S. popular culture has, I think, often negotiated difference among African Americans in ways that, while not perfect, are at least potentially expansive, rather than limiting. Before I consider one instance of such negotiation from the notoriously pervasive medium of network television, let me offer two propositions that I think can serve as generally acceptable premises for my analysis: The first is that the representation of black people on U.S. network TV has been a highly contested phenomenon since at least the days of *Amos 'n' Andy;* the second, which has ramifications for the significance of the first, is that "representation" is an extremely complex affair whose intricacies we have only begun to theorize in the context of African-American cultural studies.[1]

It is, I think, safe to say that one of the reasons the televisual representation of black people has served for so long as a focus of debate is that it is seen as having effects that extend beyond the domain of signs as such and into the realm of African Americans' material well-being, which comprises, among other factors, the social relations through which black people's status in this country is conditioned. The standard of simulacral realism that has informed popular demands for greater representation of blacks on TV is rooted in the assumption that such representation would have a meliorative effect on the objective conditions that characterize daily life for the mass of African Americans living within the scope of television's influence.

For anyone engaged in critical cultural studies, the suggestion that representation conditions or shapes "reality" is hardly novel. We cannot hope, however, to construct an effective critique of the racial politics of popular culture until this rather elementary proposition is more fully elaborated to account for some of the specific *ways* that such conditioning occurs, which, since representation is itself a complex phenomenon, will most likely be complex as well, often counterintuitive at the least, and very possibly contradictory. Those contradictions are apt to emerge, not just as we consider various televisual productions either across different historical periods or within the same time frame, but even in the context of a single production; and they are likely to indicate not merely the complexity of any given show or series per se, but also the highly overdetermined nature of the historical context in which that show or series is produced. In order to get just a slight sense of such contextual overdetermination for the 1960s and early 1970s— on which period I want to focus in particular—let us examine not a television show itself, but some commentary *about* television that will illuminate a few of the claims that I have already made.

Throughout the period I am considering, one of the most consistent critics of television's treatment of blacks was the media commentator Robert Lewis Shayon, whose regular column on the broadcasting industry was featured in the *Saturday Review*. The general tenor of Shayon's remarks can be discerned through reference to a February 1963 piece in which he proposed that

> [i]f Negroes were seen more frequently on television—and in featured roles comparable to those played by white actors—their real-life employment picture might be favorably affected. Television's power to change mass habits and attitudes appears to be significant. An improvement in the Negro image on television might be a very important step toward real integration. ("Living Color—2")

An October 1966 column is similarly indicative, suggesting that "a sharing of power in the real world can flow from entertainment images of mutual accommodation . . . ," and that "[t]elevision's fantasy world does more than provide entertainment: It structures a belief in what is possible in the real world" ("Can TV Overcome?"). Both of these excerpts are characterized by the conviction to which I have referred—that television can have a substantive effect on the social context in which it operates, and that, as regards black people specifically, an improvement in social status can result from "the communication of the Negro image to millions of homes," as Shayon put it in November 1962 ("Living Color").

Whatever impact televisual images of "mutual accommodation" might have on lived social relations between blacks and whites in the United States, however (and it is by no means certain that these images will bring about the result that Shayon proposed),[2] it would not, according to Shayon, be the only effect of increased representation of black people on the small screen. Indeed, Shayon's commentary of 24 November 1962 touches on another potential implication of such representation in a way that indicates its profound complexity.

The piece to which I refer was occasioned by the contemporaneous findings of the Committee on Integration of the New York Society for Ethical Culture. Having monitored the programming of the three major TV networks from 8:00 A.M. to midnight over a two-week period, the committee found that only about 22 percent of it featured any appearances by blacks at all, and that a plurality of that 22 percent presented blacks only as singers, dancers, or musicians. While this data is clearly pertinent to a consideration of the broad social significance of blacks' televisual representation, Shayon also deployed it in order to address a more specific concern—the "employment of Negro actors" and blacks' general potential for material success within the industry ("Living Color").

Indeed, after reporting the committee's findings regarding the preponderance of musical acts among black television performers, Shayon immediately raised the topic of these performers' financial welfare, noting that

> it would be instructive to know how many performers had permanency of employment. The Negro singer or dancer on television is a transient, an itinerant, with no chance of earning his living exclusively in either the black and white or the color tube.

Shayon went on to remark that "people appearing as themselves" on news broadcasts, informational programs, and educational documentaries—which constituted the category of programming with the second highest frequency of appearances by blacks, according to the committee's study—"are again merely passing through—usually without benefit of any fee."

This observation is cogent and suggestive. It is absolutely true, for one thing, that a primary, though often elided, stake in televisual representation—as much in 1962 as today—is money, and, particularly, the financial interests of those corporate entities with monetary investment in the programming. These interests, it almost goes without saying, are only rarely, if ever, congruent with the concerns about "image" that we normally associate with the critique of the treatment of blacks in television. Thus, for Shayon to raise the question of the *performer's* financial position (leaving aside the historically, socially, and culturally fraught issue of pay *rate*, the astronomic scale of which for post-1960s entertainment "superstars" is a topic for a whole other extensive discussion) is for him to enact a crucial shift in analytical perspective whereby not only is financial interest granted its proper position in the discussion of industry politics, but the status of the "exploited worker"—to use that crude and evidently problematic term—is granted its proper centrality with respect to that interest. Shayon's sophisticated understanding of the complex issue of equity in the business is indicated in his continued discussion in the column I am citing, which considers the effect on black television performers' financial success of various rapid developments in the burgeoning field—among them the advent of corporate sponsorship for programs and the establishment of talent unions and with them regularized pay scales.

More pertinent for our consideration here, however—indicating as it does the potentially complex effect of televisual representation—is the link Shayon draws between the relatively small financial take for blacks in television and their relatively frequent TV appearances "as themselves," since this link suggests a similar and converse connection between blacks' financial *success* and their television appearances specifically as persons *other than* themselves. In other words, while Shayon's advocacy for "[a]n improvement in the Negro image on television" implies that such an improvement would bring about certain presumably positive social developments—racial integration, for instance, and the erosion of stereotypes about black people among whites who would otherwise not become familiar with them—his rhetoric here indicates that more immediate material gain by blacks in the field depends not upon the televisual dissemination of an exemplary image of singular black integrity, but rather on black performers' projection of *multiplicitous* images that do not coincide with their "real-life" identities.

This fact is readily explicable, of course: It is a function of the difference in the incomes earned by actors in regular fictional series, on the one hand, and musicians, dancers, and persons appearing on "factual programs," on the other, whereby the former make significantly more money than the latter. My concern here, however, is not the objective intelligibility of this income differential, but rather its association specifically with acting in regular fictional series, which activity seems actually to *implicate* it as a factor in social stratification within a segment of the black populace. Televisual representation of African Americans thus potentially has at least a dual effect, according to Shayon's logic: The mere appearance of black performers on television can further the *integration* of blacks generally throughout the society as a whole; on the other hand, their *acting* in fictional series also specifically entails a process of social *differentiation* within the black populace per se. This dual effect of blacks' televisual representation may help to explain the vexed nature of discussion about it among African Americans themselves during the period under consideration.

The Dual Interests of the Black Performer

A particularly economical way of discerning this complexity is to consider comments made not by journalistic observers or "average people"—though I will turn to such comments shortly—but rather by actual black performers, whose remarks often indicate what we might call the divided interest that they experience with respect to the representation of blacks on TV. A prime personage with whom to begin our consideration is Bill Cosby, not only because of the "superstardom" he achieved during the 1980s and early 1990s through the success of his NBC series, *The Cosby Show,* but also because of his "pioneer" status in the television industry—he was, after all, the first African American to star in a dramatic series on network television, appearing alongside Robert Culp in the show *I Spy,*

Bill Cosby and Robert Culp in I Spy. *Photo courtesy of Photofest.*

which debuted on NBC in 1965. Among the spate of print publicity that accompanied that debut was a feature in *Ebony* magazine in which Cosby made a statement that indicated simultaneously his belief in the unique contribution that the show could make to improved U.S. race relations and his sense of solidarity with other blacks involved in the civil rights struggle:

> Negroes like Martin Luther King and Dick Gregory; Negro groups
> like the Deacons and the Muslims—all are dedicated to the cause of
> civil rights, . . . but they do their jobs in their own way. My way is to
> show white people that Negroes are human beings with the same
> aspirations and abilities that whites have. ("I Spy," p. 66)

At the same time, however, the unabashed statements Cosby made about his primary career objective suggest the possible mitigation of that solidarity by means of the very status with which he was conferred in the industry context. A 1965 *Saturday Evening Post* profile summarized the work Cosby had done in stand-up comedy before being hired for *I Spy,* and indicated his plans for the future:

> If he clicks in the show [which, at the time of the article's publication,
> was just beginning its first season], Cosby hopes to phase perma-
> nently out of nightclub humor into TV heroics, for one simple rea-
> son—money. And he plans to retire from all strenuous activity
> within 10 years, when he expects to have saved a cool million dollars.
> "That doesn't mean I don't care about the show," he says. "I'd be
> upset if I looked like a dodo on that TV screen. But I've got no great
> artistic ambitions. What show business mainly means to me is
> cash. . . ." (Karnow, 1965, p. 88)

This sentiment was repeated in a *TV Guide* interview the following month, in which Cosby bluntly asserted, "Money is of the utmost importance to me," and he mused further, "If this series goes five years, I will be only 33 and rich" (de Roos, 1965, p. 15).

Similar dual references to the capacity of African Americans' televisual representation to improve U.S. social conditions generally and to the specific benefit enjoyed by the performers engaged in such representation were manifested in the press reports attending the emergence, three years after *I Spy,* of *Julia,* the notorious NBC series starring Diahann Carroll as a young black war widow raising her son in a racially integrated setting.[3] In one of numerous pieces in which Carroll angrily defended the series against charges that it did not deal realistically with the

Diahann Carroll and Marc Copage in a publicity still from Julia. *Photo courtesy of Photofest.*

exigencies of contemporary black life, she invoked the socially constitutive—as opposed to socially mimetic—function that television could serve, asserting that

> [t]he plusses for *Julia* are so obvious that they almost don't bear discussion. Those who are liberal—who already have Negro friends—are in the minority. TV reaches the whole country, offering everybody constant contact with this woman and her child. ("Wonderful World of Color")

Two paragraphs later, however, having noted this suggestion that *Julia* could further—precisely by *depicting*—blacks' integration into what show producer Hal Kanter recognized as the putative "mainstream of American life," the same article observes that

> Diahann has made a life for herself that is considerably better than the mainstream. She rents a handsome three-bedroom furnished

house in Beverly Hills; it came complete with gardens, swimming
pool and a grey Bentley. That is in keeping with Diahann's tastes. . . .
. . . Diahann's clothes are by Donald Brooks and Scaasi. In restau-
rants she asks the wine steward for Lafite-Rothschild '55. . . .

The text is accompanied by a photograph of Carroll posed in front of her Bentley
on the lot of the 20th Century-Fox studios.

Despite the clear dualism of their relation to the medium, there is no
duplicity at work in Cosby's and Carroll's characterizations of their activities
within the television industry; on the contrary, in a 1970 interview with *TV Guide*
that Shayon quoted in his *Saturday Review* column, Carroll stated forthrightly
that she was doing *Julia* "for money and power, because money *is* power in this
country, and power means freedom . . . to do what *I want to do*" (See, 1970, p. 27,
emphasis in original; cited in Shayon, "Changes"). What is clear, however, is that
the power to which Carroll refers, and, particularly, the financial success through
which it is achieved, set her apart from the majority of U.S. citizens generally—
and of African Americans, certainly—as the beneficiary of a process of social differentiation that can only be conceived in terms of class, in both its socioeconomic and stylistic connotations. And it is precisely intraracial distinctions of
class that became particularly problematic in considerations of the televisual representation of black people as both the medium and debate about it developed
through the 1960s and early 1970s.

Two Kinds of Realism and Their Social Implications

I have already suggested that criticism of television's treatment of blacks on the
screen such as that by Robert Lewis Shayon implicates a standard of what I call
"simulacral realism," whereby television programming is conceived as propound-
ing scenarios that might subsequently (and consequently) be realized throughout
the larger social field, regardless of whether they actually preexist there.[4] At the
same time, however, many of the critiques issued by the late 1960s and early
1970s implied a demand, not for this "simulacral" realism, but rather for a properly "mimetic" realism—typically referenced in terms of "relevance" in the pertinent discussions[5]—whereby television would "reflect" the social reality on which
it was implicitly modeled. Insofar as they diverge, these differing demands for
simulacral and mimetic realism might be taken to indicate distinct concerns with
the soundness of society generally, in the case of the former, and the psychological well-being of blacks specifically, in the case of the latter. The degree to which
televisual mimetic "reflection" has been conceived as a prime factor in black peo-

ple's sense of psychic identity is indicated in the rhetoric of a 1970 commentary by African-American writer John Oliver Killens, in which he noted that, through the mid-1960s, a black person could

> stare at television and go to an occasional movie, and go through this
> routine from day to day, month to month, and year to year, and
> hardly (if ever) see himself reflected in the "cultural" media. It was as
> if he had no real existence, as if he were a figment of his own imagi-
> nation, or, at best, if he had an existence it wasn't worth reflecting or
> reflection. (p. 6)

Killens goes on to admit that, at the time of his writing, "progress *has* been made, in that there are more actors employed in the medium" (p. 8). This development, however, which represents the industry's progress toward meeting Shayon's 1962 demand on behalf of black performers' financial interests, is not sufficient in Killens's view, in which a preliminary demand for television's fair treatment of individual black subjectivity—measured in the mere *quantity* of images of African Americans appearing on TV—must give way to a call for its presentation of authentic African-American social experience, evidenced in the specific *quality* of the images presented on the screen.

By the time Killens's article appeared, *Julia* had been joined on the tube by a notable few other programs that featured black performers, including *The Bill Cosby Show* (in which Cosby, in a transition from the by-then defunct *I Spy,* portrayed a high school basketball coach), *The Leslie Uggams Show* (an hour-long variety program), and *Room 222* (a classroom "comedy-drama" to which I want to give sustained attention shortly). The problem with all of these programs, according to popular critiques, was that they weren't really "Black shows." As one black man interviewed by Killens put it, "They're just shows with Black people acting like they White" or, to cite another of Killens's interviewees, "White folks masquerading in Black skin" (pp. 7, 8). In his own summation, Killens indicated his allegiance to the principle of mimetic realism that I have already outlined, charging that

> the television establishment is attempting to give to the world the
> image of an integrated society in all facets of American life . . . , which
> is all well and good except that it is a colossal lie, because America is
> not an integrated society. It is a segregated society. (p. 8)

And, while in this formulation Killens associates television's failure to mirror faithfully the conditions in which black people live their daily lives with its presentation of an integrated society that has no basis in "fact," later on in his piece he offers a slightly different account of what, really, is wrong with the televisual picture. Commenting specifically on *Room 222,* Killens asserts:

> The Black folk here are full of understanding and wisdom, sympathetic all the way. No basic problems between the races. All men are brothers. Right? An undramatic, middle-classish situation that hardly has anything to do with the Black experience. (p. 9)

In this rendering, the inauthenticity of televisual representation of black life is expressly identified with its presentation of a specifically "middle-class" situation in which "the Black experience" apparently cannot inhere, by definition. (Indeed, this suggestion approximates the one made contemporaneously by the Black Arts poets and that made by John Baugh in his later advocacy of the term *African-American.* See Chapters 2 and 3 of this book.) This fact indicates an interesting feature of Killens's critical position regarding television's treatment of blacks, whereby, on the one hand, concern for black performers' financial success and professional advancement—we might call it their social mobility—is simultaneously registered and bracketed (through Killens's fleeting recognition that "progress *has* been made[;] . . . there are more actors employed in the medium"), while, on the other hand, the call for authenticity is manifested precisely in the demand that the black characters *portrayed* in the medium demonstrate no such socioeconomic advantage.

Paradoxically, therefore, the insistence that television faithfully represent a set of social conditions conceived by Killens and others as composing a singular and unitary phenomenon known as "*the* Black experience" runs smack up against a simultaneous demand that it both recognize and help constitute the diversity of African-American society. The tension inherent in this situation was vividly expressed in the debut of *The Leslie Uggams Show,* in which Uggams exhorted her presumedly white audience to recognize that "not all black people look alike. I'm not Diahann Carroll. I'm not Julia." At that moment, Marc Copage, the young boy who played Corey, Julia's son in Diahann Carroll's series, ran onto the stage toward Uggams, calling "Mama, mama!" (broadcast of 28 September 1969; cited in Garabedian, 1969, pp. 113–14). The shock of this gag inheres, I think, in its simultaneous chastisement about the conceptualization of black people in a monolithic stereotype, and its exposure of profound anxieties about the political ramifications of actually instantiating difference among African-American subjects. Thus, if *Room 222* upset John Killens, I would suggest that, the ostensible import of his protest notwithstanding, this is because it showed up—precisely by working to negotiate—an intraracial social difference that is seen as potentially disruptive to the political solidarity of the African-American community.

Room 222 and the Differentiation of African-American Society

Room 222 ran on ABC-TV from 17 September 1969 through 11 January 1974 (Eisner and Krinsky, 1984, p. 711). Generally a critical success, it won the Emmy Award for Outstanding New Series of the 1969–1970 season. In that same season, Karen Valentine and Michael Constantine won Emmys for their supporting performances in the series (Norback, 1980, pp. 303–4). But neither of these white

The cast of Room 222. *Clockwise from top left: Denise Nicholas, Karen Valentine, Lloyd Haynes, Michael Constantine. Photo copyright © 1995* CAPITAL CITIES/ABC, INC.

actors was the primary focus of *Room 222*. As Vincent Terrace's *Encyclopedia of Television* (1986, p. 377) indicates, the series was conceived as a "comedy-drama" presenting "[l]ife at integrated Walt Whitman High School in Los Angeles, as seen through the eyes of Pete Dixon, a black American history instructor whose classes are held in Room 222." Pete was played by Lloyd Haynes, and his "love interest," to use the industry terminology, was black guidance counselor Liz McIntyre, played by Denise Nicholas. It was these two characters, and especially that of Pete, who provided *Room 222* with its unique focus and allowed it to serve its particular function in the construction of an African-American social collectivity.

In his criticism of the show, John Killens implies that it did not satisfactorily present or otherwise address race-based dissension among the characters who populated the halls of fictional Walt Whitman High School, where the action took place. While it is true that few of the story lines from *Room 222*'s five-year run (all of which are summarized in Eisner and Krinsky, 1984, pp. 711–19) treated race relations directly or explicitly, the series was characterized from the beginning by drily oblique statements about racial politics, whose ambiguity I think actually evidences the producers' canny awareness that it would have been impossible for the show otherwise to speak to the issue except through platitudes and well-meaning clichés. This ambiguity on racial issues became clear in the first episode, in which Karen Valentine's character, student teacher Alice Johnson, apologetically introduced herself to Pete Dixon, saying, "I know I have a lot of the middle-class hangups. I went to a segregated school." Pete replied evenly, "It's OK—so did I" (from "Richie's Story," quoted in Amory, 1969). A similar exchange takes place in the episode that I want to examine now. First broadcast on 2 November 1973, during *Room 222*'s final season on the air, "Pete's Protégé" depicts the trials of another young white student teacher, a man this time, whose eagerness to be friends with the students actually hinders his effectiveness as an instructor. The initial exchange between Arthur (Todd Susman) and Pete again manifests a refined ambiguity on issues of race relations. The scene opens on Pete's classroom, with Arthur busily distributing papers to the students, gathered for class at the start of the school day. Pete, equipped with a very professional-looking briefcase, enters the room and greets Arthur:

> PETE: Good morning, Arthur.
> ARTHUR: Hi, Pete. I already passed out the test papers so you wouldn't have to take up class time.
> PETE: Well, that's no way to get the students to love you.
> ARTHUR (*with a slight chuckle of hopeful anticipation*): If I get along with all my classes the way I do with this one . . . (*The bell rings, signaling the beginning of the class period.*)

PETE: Well, we'd better get started. I wouldn't want to waste that time
    you saved me.
ARTHUR: I'll go sit in the back of the bus. (*Starts to walk to the rear of
    the classroom, then realizes what he's said. Pete eyes him with
    mock wariness. He turns back to address Pete again.*) Hey, uh . . .
    I didn't mean, uh. . . .
PETE (*flatly*): Arthur, you've been student-teaching with me long
    enough to know better.
ARTHUR (*hesitantly, as he bemusedly ponders this remark*): Thanks,
    Pete. (*He ambles awkwardly away from Pete's desk as Pete looks
    on in smirking amusement.*) [transcribed from videotape]

Now, I have claimed that such scenes evidence the show's canniness about
the dubious project of making definitive statements about racial politics on prime-
time television. I can certainly see, however, that the noncommittal quips by Pete
Dixon might be interpreted as ineffectual efforts to gloss over the profound difficulty of race relations—and, especially, of racial integration—during the era in
question. Even if we read the statements in this way, however, we would have to
recognize that such "glossing over" can really only constitute the show's repression
of racial concerns into a sort of "political unconscious" that will necessarily inform
the working through of the surface-level plot for any given episode.[6] In other
words, I am suggesting that the cool shrugging off of raciopolitical concerns that
the show regularly enacts actually signals its profound engagement with racially
inflected social difference at a subtextual level, but also that its containment of
such concerns within conceptual parameters subjectively constituted by Pete
Dixon indicates that their import will become manifest specifically with respect to
intra- rather than interracial considerations. Thus I propose that, contrary to what
its superficial aspect might suggest, *Room 222* was not primarily about racial *integration* at all; rather it always represented an allegorical narrative about social *differentiation* among black subjects, and, in particular, thematized the articulation of
different black subjects into various socioeconomic class positions.[7]

Let me approach the matter from a different direction for a moment, in
order to buttress my claim that *Room 222* was not first and foremost about integration. In doing this, it will be helpful to consider a bit of advance ad copy for
another ABC series that premiered in the same season as *Room 222*. The premise
of *The Brady Bunch* involved a man and a woman, each widowed and raising
three children—he boys, she girls—who marry and thus consolidate their frag-
mented households into one big, happy family, weekly overcoming the obstacles
to that consolidation inherent in their children's gender difference. Thus, as the
network put it in its preseason publicity campaign, *The Brady Bunch* dealt with

"the most difficult integration of them all, that of the sexes" (quoted in "Premières," p. 84).

If we conceive of integration in this unusual way—in terms of the nuclear family that on U.S. network television has always epitomized the amalgamation of disparate elements into a harmonious social entity—then we must recognize *Room 222*'s singular disengagement from the networks' integrative mission. That singularity is emphasized if we refer to the programming schedules from the time of *Room 222*'s run, which evidence a contrast between *Room 222*'s function and that of the other ABC shows receiving prime-time airplay. Throughout its broadcast history, *Room 222* was juxtaposed in ABC's schedule with programs that depicted variations on the consolidated nuclear family within a specifically domestic context. The show was always preceded in the schedule, depending on the season, by one or a combination of the following programs: *The Courtship of Eddie's Father*, with Bill Bixby; *Make Room for Granddaddy*, with Danny Thomas; *The Partridge Family*, with Shirley Jones, David Cassidy, and Susan Dey; *The Odd Couple*, with Tony Randall and Jack Klugman; and the aforementioned *Brady Bunch*, with Florence Henderson and Robert Reed. The classroom series was followed in the schedule, most notably, by *The Odd Couple*, and *Adam's Rib*, an adaptation of the Hepburn and Tracy movie that again depicted the difficult reconciliation of the genders within the domestic context, with Ken Howard and Blythe Danner in the starring roles (Gianakos, 1978, pp. 42–55).

Unlike all of these shows, *Room 222* was emphatically not set in the domestic context of the traditional nuclear family. (Indeed, to my knowledge, it never depicted a single functional nuclear family in all of its five-year run.) While this does not necessarily mean that aspects of a familial dynamic cannot be identified as operative in the show, it does suggest a difference between the functions of such aspects in *Room 222* and in standard televisual representations of the domestic nuclear family. As the *Brady Bunch* ad copy indicated through its reference to "integration," the standard televisual depiction of the normative nuclear family generally symbolizes unproblematically stable social *synthesis*, socially "relevant" programs such as *All in the Family* still being the exceptions that prove the rule; on the other hand, *Room 222*, by using Pete Dixon as its central consciousness, implicated as its primary object of interrogation an African-American populace for whom a pressing challenge during the late twentieth century has been how to negotiate (rather than *resolve*) internal social *division*. Given this, not only did the classroom venue—with its inherent power differentials and social stratification—provide the ideal setting for the show's comic drama, but to the degree that the relations among the show's characters could be conceived along the familial model, Pete Dixon's understated patriarchalism served less to figure the satisfactory consolidation of disparate personages into a benign social unit than to signal the hierarchization of the differences characterizing the community in question.[8]

While Pete—and Liz McIntyre, too—was a solidly middle-class professional figure, there was also, as Cleveland Amory put it in a 1969 review, "menace in *Room 222*": "student Jason Allen (Heshimu) for example, could have stepped out of 'The Blackboard Jungle.'" Indeed, particularly in the early seasons, Jason presented a strong antidote to Pete's and Liz's upright middle-classness: a product of the Los Angeles slums, he was portrayed as an angry outsider, deeply suspicious and given to thievery. Over the years, Jason's character mellowed quite a bit, but he still provided the perfect foil to Pete's professionalism by clearly representing socioeconomic disadvantage. The means of this representation was partially explained by John Wasserman, in his 1969 profile of Denise Nicholas titled "The Girl in 'Room 222'":

> Black people, like whites, have different vocabularies and speaking
> styles for different situations. There are accents, phrasing and sounds
> for one's peers and friends. There are other noises for outsiders. . . . It
> is a subtle point, and one which is generally ignored in integrated
> theater. (p. 26)

Wasserman implicitly praises *Room 222* specifically for *not* ignoring this point, but he might have gone even further since, even *within* a given racial group there exist different modes of speech corresponding to, among other things, differences in socioeconomic class, and these, also, were represented in the series. Thus, even as Jason Allen became a respectable member of the Walt Whitman High School community, his dialectal speech (which, like that of the other students, was also marked by the youth slang of the period) set him apart from the professional class represented by Mr. Dixon and Miss McIntyre. In the episode I am considering here, this is evidenced in Jason's brief commentary (the notably drawn-out dialectal cadences of which I can only imperfectly suggest in print) regarding the erection of a statue of Walt Whitman in front of the school: "Man, it must be a real groove to have you a statue put up in front of a big buildin.'"

Thus, rather than figuring an African-American population distinct from the dominant white society, as Alice Rhinelander was taken to do through specific aspects of her speech pattern, Jason implicitly represented one of the various social classes into which the black community can be differentiated, in contrast to that represented by the black faculty at the school. With the difference between professionals like Pete and less advantaged students like Jason always operative as a subtext to the main action of *Room 222*, the explicit differentiation of the black community into various subcategories could be played out as the division between teacher and student that was regularly the ostensible subject of series episodes. In "Pete's Protégé," Pete has to correct student teacher Arthur Billings's too-close bonding with his students, thus reinforcing the necessary division upon which the community is founded. Having to take over Pete's class when Pete is out sick, Arthur finds himself overwhelmed by a roomful of unruly students whose respect he cannot gain precisely because he has identified with them too closely as a "friend," rather than as an authority figure. In response, he harshly criticizes the work of a slow—and, notably, white—student whom Pete has been tutoring privately, undermining what little self-confidence the boy had begun to achieve. Upon learning of this development after returning to school, Pete confronts Arthur with his error:

> PETE (*angry and exasperated*): A teacher can make mistakes. He can have his good days and he can have his bad days. But the one thing that he's *got* to do is stimulate his students! The one thing he *cannot* do is discourage them.
>
> ARTHUR (*dejectedly*): I know that.
>
> PETE: Then why did you tell Leo what you did? Now he wants to quit his tutoring; he doesn't think it makes any difference anymore.
>
> ARTHUR: I didn't think it was a good report.
>
> PETE: It wasn't the best report I've seen, but it's the best report that Leo's done. You know, I think that you took it out on him because of what the kids did to you, and you knew he would take it from you.
>
> ARTHUR (*defensively*): You weren't here Friday.
>
> PETE: Yeah, but I can guess what happened.
>
> ARTHUR: I've been nothing but a friend to those kids, all of them—a real friend! I've played ball with them, I've eaten with them. . . .
>
> PETE: That's fine! Don't stop doing that; but you're not a student anymore!
>
> ARTHUR (*subdued*): I know that.
>
> PETE: You can't be one of the class and in charge of it at the same time, it's too confusing.

Pete's invocation of "confusion" is apt, of course, but it serves just as well in relation to an undifferentiated black collectivity as it does with respect to an undisciplined high school classroom, suggesting the show's interest in distinguishing Pete's subject position from that of his black students, on more levels than one. And the engine of that distinction, as I have already hinted, was precisely the cool patriarchalism that Pete regularly manifested, the benevolent character of which thus extended beyond the practical assistance enjoyed by his students at Walt Whitman High to entail, as well, the rational disposition of the black population into diverse segments such that its social character more or less met the demands of the public realm operative in the contemporary U.S. context.

Those demands themselves, of course, are not necessarily anything to cheer about, with social-class differentiation implicating, for one thing, structures and practices of repression well worthy of resistance. At the same time, though, the enactment of such resistance itself likely depends upon the prior recognition of the various interest blocs that characterize the general social field, which it seems to me *Room 222* largely worked to effect, and this among a black population that could especially benefit from it. Similarly, the siting of the show's action and its assimilation to the particular needs of African-American society condition the meaning of Pete's patriarchalism in a noteworthy way. While the social management achieved through Pete's benevolent-patriarchal function might call to mind that enacted by the generically white father figure in traditional nuclear family–oriented television sitcoms, its operation in a specifically *public* context set it apart from the prototype, and usefully figured African Americans' necessary engagement in the expanded arena of U.S. culture and society. Moreover, by implicitly but emphatically recognizing the existence of significant social difference among the African-American population at a time of strident demands for televisual fidelity to a unitary "black experience," the show cannily pointed up the illusoriness of this latter phenomenon and made notable strides toward engaging the increasingly—and potentially *richly*—*dis*-integrated condition of contemporary African-American life.

The show even, I think, generally avoided succumbing to the black-bourgeois social conservatism that it obviously verged on reprising from the "passing" novel of the Harlem Renaissance, largely because its routine implicit engagement of intense social divisions militated against its achieving synthetic stability even at the surface level of plot development. Indeed, *Room 222* typically featured episodes that presented no conventional "resolution": it is never determined whether a promising black art student really did forge the signature of her middle-aged white English teacher on a scholarship application, as he says she did ("How about That Cherry Tree," summarized in Eisner and Krinsky, 1984, p. 714); Pete is stymied in his attempts to revive a student's interest in school when he learns that the boy is dying of leukemia ("You Don't Know Me, He Said," Eisner and Krinsky, 1984, p. 717); the explicitly homophobic harassment of a "sensitive" and "artistic" male student culminates in problematizing, rather than settling, the definition of masculinity ("What Is a Man?" Eisner and Krinsky, 1984, p. 715); and, as a quick examination of the story lines summarized by Eisner and

Krinsky makes clear, a full 10 percent of the episodes figured the disruption of the domestic-family relations through which network series generally register social stability, obliquely pointing up the central characters' apparent lack of such idealized domesticity—Pete and Liz, after all, never *do* get married.[9]

That irresolution should, I think, suggest the impossibility of any mass-cultural development's perfectly conforming to the interests of the African-American population, owing precisely to their phenomenally varied character. Such conformity aside, though, the variedness of African-American society remains almost entirely *unacknowledged* by commercial television even at this late date, except in instances where it manifests as the broadest possible caricature: witness the immensely overdrawn class "conflict" featured on NBC's hit show, *The Fresh Prince of Bel-Air*. Similarly, the notedly aggressive bids for black viewers made by the fledgling Fox and Warner Bros. networks (in the early and mid-1990s, respectively) were grounded in a stereotyped conception of generic "urban" life that doesn't allow for geographic specificity even, let alone more subtle distinctions in African-American experience. The producers of Fox's *Martin*, for instance, have never bothered to key the show to the topography of its putative Detroit setting— never mind getting the actors to drop the East Coast inflection that passes as *the* "recognizably" African-American speech pattern in favor of an accent that rings true to the ears of this native. (See Zook, "Blackout" and "Warner Bruthas," for accounts of the difficulties faced by black creative personnel at both Fox and WB.)

By *not* resting at such genericism, *Room 222*—like the ill-fated *Frank's Place* of the 1980s—while not performing the impossible task of perfectly representing the complexity of African-American society, *did* accomplish the next-best practicable thing: to exhibit an awareness of the limitations to its undertaking, even as it sometimes, inevitably, figured them in unproductive ways. The manifestation of such an awareness, conjoined with a social-politically conscious and technically savvy thematization of its very terms, can itself be considered effective and important cultural work, which is exactly what I think *Room 222* represented. That it did so without at the same time anxiously closing down possibilities for African-American subjectivity not only constitutes one of its most admirable achievements, it indicates that such an achievement *can* be realized—even in a mass-cultural context of which African Americans have rightly been wary; this, if nothing else, should give us cause for optimism as we negotiate black society's increasing complexity in the cultural work of the coming years and into the next millennium.

8

BACKING UP, CROSSING OVER, BREAKING OUT

Social Significances
of Pop-Musical Form

Absence, Presence, and Technologies of Culture

Not only do the analyses presented in Part II of this book indicate that black masculinity is a source of great anxiety throughout U.S. culture and society, but Chapter 6, in particular, suggests that that anxiety is so intense as to characterize even sites from which African-American men are notably *absent*. Even such absence itself, however, can obviously *signal* the anxiety with which I am concerned, resulting from the multiform subtle but nonetheless effective modes of discriminatory practice that still generally prevent black men from entering the bastions of, say, corporate capitalism. And yet, absence as such generally indicates more than simply a discriminatory boundary that bars black men from a given, relatively discrete, social realm; it also suggests that realm's extensive implication in the defining problematics of the larger culture.

Take, for instance, the profoundly white context of "high art" as represented in the museum or the gallery. While there is no denying the existence either of

African-American artists or of African Americans among the audience for "high art," the pertinent issue here is not that existence per se, but the extent to which blacks in general and black men in particular are still considered anomalous in the sites of high-artistic production and exhibition alike—a point brought home by the *Black Male* exhibition mounted at the Whitney Museum of American Art in 1994 and 1995. That very anomalousness founds the impact of artist Fred Wilson's contribution to the Whitney show, the 1991 installation *Guarded View,* which consists of four black-skinned, headless "male" mannequins dressed in security-guard uniforms, and which, when displayed in the museum gallery, strongly shows up the anonymous, functionary status that black men most frequently occupy in the exhibition site. This effect would seem to corroborate the claim of artist and philosopher Adrian Piper (1993) that the contemporary museum and gallery constitute an optimum locale in which the "cognitive failures" that underlie black men's discriminatory social positioning might be addressed and challenged, especially given the continued influence of the conceptualist ethic since the late 1960s and early 1970s (pp. 63–65).[1] At the same time, however, the fact that the "cognitive failures" interrogated by Wilson's piece are those of the art world itself indicates that that context enacts the same processes of discriminatory marginalization that characterize the broader culture. Piper herself thematizes those processes in her striking *Vanilla Nightmares* series, particularly number 20, in which charcoal drawings of monstrous black men emerge from amid the newsprint of the *New York Times,* suggesting African-American men's simultaneous suppression by and undergirding of the dominant discourses of U.S. society, effects that register in the gallery milieu as black men's general exclusion from the scene.

Fred Wilson, Guarded View, *1991. Courtesy Metro Pictures and the artist.*

Adrian Piper, Vanilla Nightmares #20, *1989. Courtesy
John Weber Gallery, New York.*

If such exclusion, however, is feasible only within contexts whose elite character itself (largely an effect of the amounts and modes of financial and educational capital that underwrite their operation) serves to regulate the admission
thereto of both groups and individuals, it must necessarily give way when the work
fostered in those contexts veers from such elitism and toward the condition of the
popular. In that event the significance to the work of black masculinity (along with
other previously discounted social formations) inevitably becomes increasingly
salient and the work itself evidently subject to raciopolitical critique. This is precisely what occurred in the case of Laurie Anderson—arguably the most widely
recognized conceptualist-influenced artist in the United States—around 1986. For
in that year Anderson, formally trained in classical violin and in sculpture, took a
definitive turn to popular media that predicated her expanded success in the late
1980s. The position of black men *within* those media makes Anderson's work,
however unexpectedly, central to the pop-cultural conception of black masculinity
that I am interrogating here. Thus the subsequent analysis, far from constituting a
topical detour, actually helps elucidate both the significance of that conception and
black men's own activities in the realm of popular culture.

The "turn" that I have suggested Laurie Anderson took in 1986 did not so much represent a new direction for her work as it culminated the aesthetic governing her practice since at least the late 1970s. We can divine the character of that aesthetic by considering a criticism of Anderson's pivotal 1986 piece, the feature-length film *Home of the Brave*. In a review of the movie, which is basically a standard concert film comprising a selection of the performance pieces Anderson showcased in live contexts during 1984 and 1985, Rosemary Passantino (1986) lamented that the "two-dimensional" cinematic format itself generally mitigated the "immediacy" characteristic of Anderson's live shows (p. 75). While Passantino's invocation of "immediacy" derives its significance from the critical context of performance art in which Anderson has participated since the late 1960s, it also crucially mischaracterizes Anderson's specific position within that context throughout the 1980s, with the result that Passantino's review itself misconstrues the place of the film among Anderson's larger artistic output.

It is certainly true that, at least until the end of the 1970s, performance theory and practice were dominated by precisely the ethic of immediacy that Passantino invokes. Identifying performance as the artistic "mode that was to become exemplary during the seventies," Douglas Crimp conceived of it in 1979 as comprising

> not only that narrowly defined activity called performance art, but all those works that were constituted *in a situation* and *for a duration* by the artist or the spectator or both together. It can be said quite literally of the art of the seventies that "you had to be there." For example, certain of the video installations of Peter Campus, Dan Graham, and Bruce Nauman, and more recently the sound installations of Laurie Anderson not only required the presence of the spectator to become activated, but were fundamentally concerned with that registration of presence as a means toward establishing meaning. (pp. 176–77, emphasis in original)

Notably, the 1970s productions to which Crimp refers were all "installations," whose immediacy was indeed predicated on "presence," but the presence specifically of the *spectator,* which was a prerequisite to experiencing the "meaning" generated through the electronic apparatuses comprised in the works. As little as two years after the publication of Crimp's reflections, however, Craig Owens (1981) considered the implications of artists' use of such apparatuses in contexts where their *own* subjective "presence" was at issue. Specifically remarking Anderson's increased reliance on electronic technology in her live performances, Owens noted that "the only access to herself that [Anderson] allows is through all kinds of technological filters which amplify, distort and multiply her actual voice in such a way that it can no longer be identified as hers." Consequently, Owens concluded, Anderson's contemporaneous work "mark[ed] a radical shift in the direction of . . . performance art, a shift away from the esthetics of presence which has dominated that mode since its inception" (p. 122); that shift would culminate in *Home of the Brave*'s apparently distancing filmic effect.

Indeed, it is precisely in such distancing that Owens has identified the social-critical element of Anderson's work, which by the early 1980s increasingly incorporated such electronic devices as the Vocoder (capable of synthesizing the spoken voice into a musical chord), the synclavier (used to articulate speech into its discrete constituent pitches), and the pillow speaker (small enough to fit inside the mouth so that the movement of the lips regulates the sound emitted by the audio system). These pieces, along with an array of additional such equipment, provided Anderson with a wealth of modes through which to produce the monologues and songs that constituted the core of her 1980s performances. Thus, in place of the unmediated "presence" of the human subject, Anderson visibly and explicitly substituted the media technology through which that subject is represented and refracted in the contemporary context; and the foregrounding of that technology, according to Owens, allowed Anderson to register a cogent social-philosophical critique. Citing Walter Benjamin, Owens (1981) notes that conventional manifestations of communications media unself-critically

> present an "equipment-free" . . . view of reality . . . which permits the
> fantasy of presence . . . to flourish. Anderson, by exposing rather than
> concealing the equipment through which she represents herself,
> destroys that fantasy. In its place, she shows us a world denatured by
> technology, and a self fragmented, pluralized. . . . (p. 123)

It is in this "pluralization" of the self that critics have identified the primary political import of Anderson's work, characterizing it particularly as a feminist strategy "to decenter the masculine subject" (Foster, 1985, p. 132), and thus as an indication of her concern with the representation of social Others.[2]

That concern was manifested in a number of ways in the work Anderson produced during the first fifteen years or so of her career. Indeed, some pieces from the late 1960s and early 1970s were explicitly polemical, including statements on the Vietnam war (see Marincola, 1983, p. 63) and on women's sexual objectification (see Owens, "Sex and Language," pp. 49–53). By the mid-1980s, however, not only had Anderson proclaimed her fear of appearing "dogmatic and didactic" (see Wood, 1983, p. 102), but her increasingly dazzling use of electronic media allowed for her social commentary to be disavowed by the growing audience for her work. As early as 1979, Mark Stevens had noted the "fleeting" quality of Anderson's messages, and later commentators often acknowledged the work's critical import only to remark the ease with which it could "slip by unnoticed" (Novak, 1986; see also Larson, 1984, p. 48). Even critics who admitted the power of Anderson's critique tended to disregard its full social implications, construing Anderson's electronic interventions either as a call for purely "personal" empowerment (Coe, 1982, p. 85), or as simply transcendent "vehicles" for her ideas (Goldberg, 1984, p. 86). And most popular-media notices were entirely unengaged, merely remarking Anderson's "playful" use of "electronic gadgetry" (F. Rose, 1984, p. 185) or characterizing her work as a collection of entertaining "on-stage antics" (Small, 1983, p. 108). Thus, while Rosemary Passantino suggested in 1986 that Anderson had "found the best way to get a message across: Pretend that there isn't one" (p. 88), it was also clear by then that a number of observers shared Ralph Novak's (1986) relatively unreflective assessment of the work—"[t]hinking about it just gets in the way of enjoying it"—which suggests that the electronic media through which Anderson increasingly lodged her critique actually deflected audience attention away from it.[3]

Granting the increased subtlety of Anderson's social commentary, however, its existence is still fairly discernible even in work from as late as 1986, with the *Home of the Brave* version of "Language Is a Virus," for instance, skewering the social myopia fostered by contemporary television culture:

> Well I dreamed there was an island
> That rose up from the sea.
> And everybody on the island
> Was somebody from TV.
> And there was a beautiful view
> But nobody could see.
> Cause everybody on the island
> Was saying: Look at me! Look at me!
> > Look at me! Look at me!

Consequently, while reviewers' inclination to disregard Anderson's critique might be attributed in part to her relatively oblique articulation, it seems that it likely derives from other factors as well, in particular from precisely the same formalistic developments that helped Anderson dramatically broaden her audience throughout the 1980s.

Art into Pop: Laurie Anderson and the
Racial Politics of Mass-Cultural Form

These developments include not only Anderson's use of electronic technology per se, but, more crucially, her engagement *via* that technology with modes of distribution not usually accessible to "high-art" practitioners. That engagement began long before the exemplary *Home of the Brave* was produced, being evidenced as early as 1977, when Anderson incorporated 45-rpm recordings of her songs into her "Juke Box" exhibition at New York's Holly Solomon gallery (see Lifson, 1983, pp. 34–42; P. Stewart, 1979, p. 112; L. Anderson, 1994, pp. 55–61). The "reconciliation" of high art and popular culture that in 1979 Patricia Stewart imagined Anderson might achieve (p. 110) did not occur, however, until 1981, when Anderson's recording of the song "O Superman" hit number 2 on the British pop charts (Small, 1983, p. 107; L. Anderson, 1994, p. 285), creating a ready-made audience for the 1982 album *Big Science* on which the song appeared, and for *United States*, the large-scale performance "epic" in which all the *Big Science* material was featured and which Anderson first presented in its entirety in 1983. Produced for $400, "O Superman" had by 1983 generated gross returns of $1 million (Small, 1983, p. 107), marking what Roxanne Snider (1986) described as Anderson's emergence "from avant-garde obscurity to mainstream success."

Obviously, Anderson's "crossover" from "high"-art contexts into the "mainstream" music market—from downtown New York galleries and small performance spaces into the broader realm of pop-cultural entertainment—was facilitated by the modes of distribution to which her use of recording technology gave her access. Additionally, though, some specifically musical-formal elements in Anderson's work also contributed to her appeal. Among the aspects of "mainstream American music" (Flood, 1981, p. 81) that helped make Anderson's material "accessible" (F. Rose, 1984, p. 185), critics cited especially "the current techniques of rock concerts" (Brustein, 1984, p. 25), implying that Anderson's marketability derived from her use of cultural forms—primarily pop-musical ones—already familiar to mass audiences in the contemporary United States. Anderson's use of these forms took on a characteristically self-ironic aspect in the work she produced after *United States*, implicating a wry commentary on her own crossover status.[4] At the same time, though, it also problematized the political critique imputed to her by such critics as Owens, Foster, and McClary, complicating in particular the interrogation of social "Other"-ness for which she had been cited. For if a fear of pedanticism motivated Anderson to avoid verbalizing explicitly the social and political critique comprised in her work, the pop-musical modes to which she increasingly turned after *United States* are so cultural-historically sedimented as themselves to speak volumes, the artist's will to tacitness notwithstanding.

A key instance of Anderson's borrowing from the performance vocabulary of popular music is referenced in Kathy Burkett's (1986) review of *Home of the Brave*, which notes that, in the film, Anderson "shares performance space with numbers of people, notably backup singers Janice Pendarvis and Dolette McDonald" (p. 17). Backup singers have, of course, long been a staple in pop-musical performance, and if the degree to which they are relegated to the back*ground* has always varied widely, Anderson's constituted a notably strong visual presence. Reviewer Tracy Young (1986) found them quite striking in "leotards that make [them] look like space-age Supremes" (p. 64). This passage communicates more than is explicitly stated in any reference to Anderson's supporting singers that I have found: specifically, Pendarvis and McDonald look "space-age" because they are dressed in unconventional leotards; they look like "Supremes" because they are visually identifiable as black women. This fact brings to the forefront another crucial difference that is implicated in Anderson's "pluralization of the social subject," but not, I think, adequately addressed in her performance—that of racial identity. This is not to suggest that Anderson's mere use of black backup singers cannot itself constitute an intelligible cultural critique. Indeed, it can easily be considered as just such an ironic commentary on white artists' appropriation of black "hipness" as Andrew Ross has discerned in Frank O'Hara's poem, "The Day Lady Died" (see Ross, 1989, pp. 65–67), with the objects of that commentary ranging all the way from Lou Reed's invocation of "the colored girls" doo-wopping in "Walk on the Wild Side" (itself fairly ironic) to the contemporaneous use of Dolette McDonald and Janice Pendarvis themselves by other white rock artists such as Sting and, in McDonald's case, Talking Heads.[5] Even in this event, though, the characteristically allusive (and *elusive*) quality of Anderson's racio-political commentary implicates it in the problematization of the specifically *gender*-political critique that she has been credited with achieving.

To attend to Anderson's choice of backup vocalists is not to deny the existence or the import of the numerous other aspects of her production, which themselves vary noticeably over different performance contexts. Rather, it is to recognize the distinct significance within the performance of vocal personnel as opposed to both the "materiel" utilized in the work and the individuals who operate it. This significance is suggested by Craig Owens's focus on the disorienting effect of Anderson's own electronically manipulated speaking voice, which indicates both the extent of our investment in discerning a human subjectivity amid the disparate elements comprised in the performance and our tendency to identify such subjectivity, if not specifically in verbal articulation, then at least in perceptible vocalization; indeed, Anderson's undertaking of such manipulation in

Laurie Anderson (center), along with Janice Pendarvis and Dolette McDonald, in Home of the Brave. *Photo courtesy of Photofest.*

the first place indicates her recognition of these facts.[6] At the same time, though, it is precisely my point here that various factors condition Anderson's performance in such a way as to mitigate not only the degree to which vocalization itself structures her backup singers' subjectivity, but the degree to which those singers actually register as subjects at all.

For, their specific musical function notwithstanding, Dolette McDonald and Janice Pendarvis do not even primarily register as *vocalists,* but rather elicit the sort of specifically visual attention that Tracy Young manifested in her *Home of the Brave* review. Such attention, however, is largely demanded by the context in which the performers appear—the live concert or concert film—whose inherently spectacular orientation is enhanced, not only by the singers' extraordinary costumes, but by their visually discernible racial identity, which, moreover, unmistakably contrasts with that of Anderson's own, itself a factor in the extent to which she is recognized as the production's *auteur.* I invoke *auteurism* here not by way of suggesting Anderson's perfect authorial control over the "meaning" of her performance text; indeed, the point I am interested in making is predicated precisely on her actual *lack* of such control. Rather, I invoke it to emphasize the degree to which the realms of both high art and popular culture remain permeated by a perceptual ethic that posits the individual artist as active *producer* of meaning (however that meaning might be understood), and thus as agential subject *par excellence.*[7] Given this, in the context of performance, any constituent *aside from* the recognized *auteur,* whether human or otherwise, will tend to figure primarily as an element in the artistic production that the *auteur* is seen as purposefully composing from a position of subjective centrality. And, in the instance at hand, the already strong tendency for that centrality to connote *neutrality* is augmented by Anderson's whiteness (on which see Dyer, 1988, especially pp. 44–47) and, paradoxically, by the signature androgynizing effects—unisex clothing and haircut, electronically degendered voice—by which in other performance contexts she foregrounds problematics of gender and thus lodges a powerful feminist critique. Hence, for all their vocalistic function, McDonald and Pendarvis appear not as the generative subjects of meaningful enunciations, but rather as ciphers whose significance in the production, however it is engineered and interpreted, must inevitably reside in their emphatically visual presentation, the abiding dominant feature of which is their African-American identity.

Given this, it is all the more noteworthy that McDonald and Pendarvis are not the only backup duo that Anderson has employed. On her 1986 "Natural History" tour, Anderson was supported by another pair of vocalists who, like McDonald and Pendarvis, were black, but were also male. Despite this, Phillip Bellon and Bennie Diggs sang many of the same songs their predecessors had in *Home of the Brave,* often in high falsetto voices that, I would suggest, not only locate them squarely within a tradition of male pop-musical vocalization (by, for instance, Frankie Valli of the Four Seasons, or the Temptations' Eddie Kendricks), but also underscore the problematic connotations of Anderson's pop-cultural citation.[8] For if a societally governing racial politics accrues to the emphasis of the backing vocalists' black identity as the primary factor in the specifically visual presentation that the live-performance context itself already foregrounds, then Bellon's and Diggs's falsetto singing serves less to highlight the fictive character of apparently natural gender markers (as it otherwise might) than to underscore the singers' similarity to those for whom they effectively substitute in terms of the performance's dominant visual logic. In other words, because visuality takes precedence over other orders of perception in determining the significance of Anderson's supporting personnel, Bellon's and Diggs's assumption of McDonald's and Pendarvis's "place"—right down to even the registers in which they sing—works to affirm their common racial identity, so powerfully figured in their black skin, rather than to point up differences between them that are less strikingly manifested in purely visual terms.

I have already suggested that Anderson's use of Pendarvis and McDonald might constitute an ironic commentary on white artists' continued recourse to

Laurie Anderson (center), in performance with Bennie Diggs and Phillip Bellon.

the authenticating "hipness" of African-American culture; and it seems just as likely (indeed, I would argue *inevitable*) that it also functions as an *instance* of such recourse, the hipness of irony itself necessarily implicating the raciocultural formation that Anderson parodically cites. The use of Bellon and Diggs in place of McDonald and Pendarvis extends these significances, but in such a way, as I have suggested, as to suppress the gender difference between the two duos, thus implying that such difference is not crucial to African-American experience or to the constitution of African-American identity, and thereby eliding a key aspect of the threat presented to U.S. culture and society by the very concept of "blackness."[9] This effect derives largely, as I have indicated, from the subordination of the backup vocalists' subjectivity to Anderson's *auteurist* function; but such simple subordination need not be an inevitable effect of the backup-vocalist construct. Indeed, some examination of uses of the form in African-American popular music will help us to see not only how complex can be the interplay between backup ensemble and the ostensibly dominant "lead" performer, but also how that interplay can be utilized in the sometimes surprisingly progressive negotiation of racialized gender identities already shown up as sources of anxiety both within African-American culture and in U.S. society in general.

Subjectivity and Pop-Group Vocalization

The subordination that I have suggested Laurie Anderson's backup vocalists suffer is seemingly bespoken in the oft-used formula for naming pop-musical acts—and particularly vocal groups—"A and the Bs," where "A" designates the group "leader" and "B" each of the remaining group members, the lack of differentiation among whom sets them off from the leader as a definitively collective entity. "Frankie Lymon and the Teenagers," "Diana Ross and the Supremes," "Gladys Knight and the Pips," and "Harold Melvin and the Blue Notes" all exemplify this form, which has the effect of connoting an act's division of vocal labors along an individual-versus-collective split, regardless of whether the designated leader is actually the group's *lead vocalist,* as Harold Melvin, for instance, is not. While the cultural valorization of individual *auteurism* that I have noted and the premium placed on "solo stardom" in the contemporary pop-music industry both encourage the elevation of the "lead" vocalist over the backing ensemble, however, the formal relation between lead and backing vocals can actually work to mitigate that tendency, thus substantially complicating the subjective significances of the lead/backup configuration in some of its classic manifestations.

If we often consider the backup vocalists' position to be *inherently* subordinate to that of the lead singer in any given pop-music production, this is probably due to our underestimation of the formal complexity of the backing-vocal function. By way of correcting this, it is necessary first to recognize at least the basic versions of the backing-vocal form manifested in many rhythm-and-blues-derived pop arrangements. In fact, we might usefully note Arnold Shaw's (1986) point that "[i]n its initial stage, R & B singing tended to be a group rather than a solo phenomenon" (p. 182), since this suggests the centrality of choral vocalization to the semantics of R & B production—a centrality that is obscured by the apparently merely supporting role of the backing chorus in relation to the lead singer.[10] That role seems evidenced in cases where the backing-vocal ensemble repeats a portion of the lyric that has already been articulated by the lead singer. The relatively little-known "In and Out of Love," by Diana Ross and the Supremes, presents a clear example when Ross laments her tendency to "keep fallin' in and out of love"—which is immediately followed by Mary Wilson's and Cindy Birdsong's exact repetition of the phrase—and then explains that she is "still searchin' for that special one," which phrase is also repeated verbatim. This backing-vocal form might be understood as a variation of "lining out"—the protestant-church practice whereby the church precentor chants, one by one, the lines of a given psalm, after each instance of which the congregation sings the same line, more fully elaborating the designated tune (Southern, 1983, pp. 30–31).

Often, however, the backing vocalists forgo such direct following of the "lead" line, articulating a distinct lyric in alternation with the solo vocalization, as when the Four Tops' "Duke" Fakir, Lawrence Payton, and "Obie" Benson offer the modifying refrain "right now" immediately after lead singer Levi Stubbs's verse line—"When I feel that old hurt comin' on, I stop and cry like I'm cryin'"—in the song "Without the One You Love." This form, of course, can be understood in terms of the "call-and-response" pattern characteristic of oral verse in general and particularly associated with African-derived forms (see Southern, 1983, pp. 17, 188), and the chorus's conditioning of the lead line that it entails clearly complicates whatever subjective dominance is otherwise registered by the lead vocal. Frequently, moreover, the solo subject appears absorbed in the larger collectivity through the use of unison singing, especially in instances where the lead vocalist joins with the backup ensemble to repeat the choral refrain, as in the Temptations' "Please Return Your Love to Me," which features Eddie Kendricks as the putative "front."

Of course, rarely does any of these three modes (my presentation of which as primary should be taken as merely anecdotal) manifest *exclusively* in a given production; much more typically a song will offer some combination of these formats, as in Smokey Robinson and the Miracles' "The Love I Saw in You Was Just a Mirage," which features not only a lining-out-style backup mode, but also a refrain whose general call-and-response character is modified by Robinson's occasional singing of the "response" line in unison with the backup singers. Further, the backup line of this song, like those of so many others, is regularly punctuated by phrases that carry no properly semantic import, comprising rather such nonreferential phonemes as extended "ohs" and "ahs" that, while they may be devoid of literal *sense*, are not at all without *meaning*. The combination of these various backing modes in a single piece clearly conditions the song's registration of subjectivity, since, for instance, the dominance of the solo figure suggested in lining out is mitigated by such varying choral articulation as is implied by call-and-response. And, given the preceding point about the potential significance of nonlinguistic vocalization, it is clear that, even within the context of lining out per se, the chorus's verbatim repetition of the lead line need not be understood as merely buttressing the subjectivity of the solo persona, since not only does the context of a repetition—and, thus, potentially its meaning—differ from that of an initial iteration, due precisely to the registration of the latter, but such factors as difference in vocal timbre will condition the connotations of various invocations of the same lyric. This point, as John Shepherd (1991) indicates in his very useful elaboration of it, has highly significant gender-political implications, largely accounting for my adducement of it here (in Shepherd, see especially the section on "Timbre and Gender," pp. 164–71). For if gender—and, specifically, gender among African Americans—seems to be precisely what is suppressed in

Laurie Anderson's "sampling" of the pop-musical form of the backup vocal, it emerges in classic uses of the form as a primary social fact to be registered and negotiated. The extent and character of such negotiation will, of course, vary from instance to instance, but its very manifestation in the first place suggests that the *primacy* of gender need not imply its fundamental immutability. Indeed, the degree to which it might be experienced as a contingent function of complex social factors is indicated in Aretha Franklin's insistence that a "do right woman" emerges only in relation to a "do right man," where not only sexual propriety but, by extension, proper gender identity itself is understood as issuing from the partners' mutually respectful behavior ("Do Right Woman"). Given this, it will be useful to begin our consideration by examining some instances wherein the very "natural"-ness of gender seems to be strongly asserted, with the aim of determining how many changes are actually worked upon it through such structures of group vocalization as I have outlined above.

"You Make Me Feel 'Unnatural'": Social Normativity and the Pop-Musical Challenge

Given our concern here with the musical registration of subjectivity, it seems appropriate to begin by examining Lou Rawls's 1971 single, "A Natural Man," whose primary conceptual element is the subjective sovereignty that, interestingly enough, is initially figured less in the "manhood" than in the "naturalness" referenced in the title. Indeed, the song begins with a spoken monologue in which Rawls contrasts the general respect for authority characteristic of yesteryear with a contemporary push for individual self-determination. Soon after thus casting such sovereignty as a universally desired trait, however, the recording identifies it as a specifically masculine attribute. Having indicated in the opening verse his aversion to working "nine to five" for the benefit of a luxuriating "boss," Rawls registers in the refrain his contrary desire to "be happy and free, livin' and lovin' . . . , like a natural man," after which he is joined for the first time by a female backing ensemble that repeats "like a natural man," lining-out style, such that the backing vocalists seem to enact a stereotypically feminine buttressing of male subjectivity. This sense is enhanced by the highness of the register in which the backing vocalists sing, and by their notably mellifluous tone, the smoothness of which suggests their perfect accordance with and support for the lead singer's stated desire. Things soon change slightly, however, in that Rawls immediately modifies his statement, repeating at a slightly lower pitch (in his already quite deep, faintly gravelly bass voice) just the words "a natural man," to which the backup singers now more or less *respond* rather than merely *assent* by repeating exactly their first line, "like a natural man." This choral reiteration emphasizes what Rawls's own variation obscures—namely, the fundamentally simulacral nature of "manhood," which consists in the never-perfect approximation to an imagined standard that is no less exacting for all its illusory character. Indeed, throughout the remainder of the song, Rawls, as lead, seems engaged in an attempt to transmute the *approximation* to manhood into manhood per se, inasmuch as every rendition of the chorus entails his first articulating a desire to be "like a natural man," and then merely invoking "a natural man" as a sort of autonomous, self-evident entity; each of these articulations, however, is followed by the backing vocalists' iteration of "like a natural man," or sometimes even "*just* like a natural man," as if to insist that manhood exists *only* as approximation, and thereby to correct Rawls's misapprehension of the matter. Thus, on the one hand, not only does Rawls seemingly attempt to achieve "natural manhood," but he appears to be supported in this endeavor by the backing vocalists, who join in unison with his assertion "I want to be happy and free" right on the word *be*, effectively rendering the infinitive as an encouraging imperative, and who during the vocal bridge seem to boost Rawls's assertion of his radical individuality with a swelling chorus of "oohs" and "ahhs." On the other hand, the backup ensemble seems to point up the impossibility of such achievement by its insistence that one can only ever be *like* a natural man, which it repeats in unvarying response to the improvised lead "call" lines that Rawls intones as the song fades out. The female backing vocalists' supporting function, then, while clearly registered through the abstract form of their line and the timbrel quality of their vocalization, is mitigated by both the syntax and the semantics of their utterance, with the result that the masculine subjectivity that the song potentially posits as "natural" and normative is troubled and problematized through the end of the production.

Judith Butler has noted such problematization of "natural" gender in Aretha Franklin's recording of "(You Make Me Feel Like) A Natural Woman," which also, as Butler further points out, presumes the existence of a "defining Other" in much the same way as Franklin's "Do Right Woman—Do Right Man" (see Butler, 1990, pp. 22 and 154–55 n. 34). The difference, of course, is that "A Natural Woman" doesn't implicate the mutuality that I have discerned in the other production, with the result that it seems to subscribe absolutely to the stereotypic conception of femininity as a condition achieved through one's legitimating recognition by an implicitly masculine subject. Even without examining the significance of the song's backing-vocal line, however, we can consider the feminine passivity suggested in the title lyric as significantly mitigated by the force of Franklin's lead delivery, which joins the sense of subjective control implied by extremely precise oral articulation and what Shepherd (1991, p. 167) calls the vocal "sheen" of throat-produced tones with the stereotypical connotations of maternal nurture that attach to fuller, chest-originating vocalization, especially as Franklin rides from top to bottom of the title-refrain line, her tone becoming increasingly round and resonant: "You-make-me-feel-like-a-na-tu-ral woman." In other words, the timbre of Franklin's delivery suggests that she autonomously produces herself as "a natural woman" even as the semantics of the lyric indicate otherwise. This vocalistic connotation of powerful subjectivity is buttressed, moreover, through the emphasizing function served by the assertively voiced backing "uh-ooh"s that follow each lead verse line. Because these are devoid of semantic import, they serve principally to underscore the assertions that they accompany, with the attendant effect of reinforcing the subjectivity implied by the vocal force of the lead. Indeed, because both that subjectivity and its reinforcement are qualitatively connoted rather than linguistically denoted, the lead persona is protected against such ironic undercutting as is effected through the semantics of the backing vocal in "A Natural Man." Further, when the backing line *does* incorporate properly linguistic articulation—in the unison singing of the "You make me feel like a natural woman" refrain—it not only reinforces the subjective implications of the solo line, but also, in a rich paradox, simultaneously supports and diffuses its individual character by, first, amplifying the putatively first-person-singular vocalization and, second, effectively collectivizing the implied "I" who is articulating the lines. Thus the backing vocalists' repetition of "woman" after the completion of the full unison chorus registers less as an individualistic, personalized articulation than as the invocation of a fully subjectivized feminine collectivity—a sort of inverse, we might say, of Helen Reddy's universalizingly singular "I Am Woman." Finally, what I call the staggered, or imperfect, unison singing that characterizes the final repetitions of the refrain (the lead and backing vocals are not fully synchronized in these ultimate iterations) suggests the complex relation that obtains between this newly articulated collective feminine subject and the individual woman through whose consciousness it is articulated but to whom it is clearly not identical. Thus the troubling of stereotypic gender formation that this recording effects derives both from the tension between semantics and timbre that characterizes the lead vocal and from the collectivization of the agential feminine subject whose existence that tension implies.

Neither Franklin's nor Rawls's production elides gender as a socially significant category, as I have suggested that Laurie Anderson's use of the backing-vocal form does; but nor do they posit its putative "naturalness" as immune to interrogation and reconceptualization. We can speculate on the possible cultural-political ramifications of this fact by briefly considering what happens to the "natural" in African-American pop-musical productions that subject it to even greater pressure; for it is those productions, in particular, that will likely indicate the

potential of African-American musical culture to negotiate progressively a notoriously potent social difference.

Such negotiation need not entail the explicit *invocation* of gender difference,
as is made evident in another pop-musical engagement of the "natural," the 1972
single "Natural High" by the male vocal group Bloodstone. This production—a
daydreamily mellow elaboration of the singer's love for someone he knows only
by sight—features a lead line attended almost throughout by a harmonizing vocal,
with both of these parts varying from high tenor to falsetto for the duration of the
song. A baritone-register backing vocal punctuates the production at low volume,
centering on the repetition of the phrase "I don't know you," a variant of the lead-
verse refrain line "I don't even know you." Semantically, the song presents a
repeated progression from the lead singer's verse rumination on his devotion to
his beloved (comprising his reference to "thinking about you every day" and a
promise to "do all the things you want me to") to the refrain's assertion that his
love sends the singer "to the sky on a natural high"; the devotion, in other words,
predicates the ecstasy that the singer experiences, which is itself mitigated by the
grounding undertone of the repeated "I don't know you" backing vocal. That
ecstasy, moreover, is specifically precipitated by the singer's idealized romantic
interactions with his love—"take me in your arms, thrill me with all of your
charms"; "when I see you on the street my heart skips a beat"—which are presented in a sort of bridging vocal (the only portion of the production in which the
lead line manifests as a true solo performance) that culminates the devotional
verses and introduces the refrain: "and I'll take to the sky on a natural high, loving
you more till the day I die." In that refrain, the high-tenor harmony that generally
characterizes the lead line is attended by a contrapuntal, semi-improvisatory vocal
commentary sung entirely in a proper falsetto, thereby apparently figuring the
"high" semantically referenced in the lyric. And yet, not exactly, since the primary
feature of that high, according to the refrain, is its fundamentally "natural" quality,
while the defining feature of the falsetto voice is its evidently *artificial* character,
the showcasing of which here accrues to the destabilization of gender implied by
the semantics of the lyric, since the latter never once specifies the gender identity
of the singer's love. At the same time, however, because falsetto singing constitutes
a recognizably masculine pop-vocal tradition, its use in "Natural High" unmistakably fixes the vocalist's own masculinity even as it shows up the loved one's gen-
der-indeterminacy. Thus the production expands the scope of legitimate black
male desire in such a way as to undercut the heterosexist assumptions that are
generally considered to define all manner of popular love songs, thereby dismantling a primary constraint on effective black masculine subjectivity.

The ramifications of that dismantling are more explicitly suggested in a roughly contemporaneous recording by another male vocal group, the Stylistics. On their 1973 single, "You Make Me Feel Brand New," lead vocal duties are shared by Airrion Love and Russell Thompkins, Jr., with the former rendering the opening portions of the verse in a low baritone and the latter singing the closing verse sections and the refrain in a characteristically piercing falsetto. The production achieves a distinct love-ballad quality by combining a slow tempo with a piano-based orchestral instrumentation that incorporates gently swelling strings during the refrain. At the same time, the dual character of the lead vocals is emphasized by the absolute lack of a backing line in the verse sections (a tenor chorus joins in unison with the falsetto lead only in the refrain), and by the almost perfectly symmetrical alternation between the two solo parts, each of which consists exclusively of direct-address pronouncements wherein the singer describes to his love the latter's profound effect on him. Consequently, not only does the recording bespeak a recognizably pop-romantic orientation, but as a seventh-grade classmate of mine noted with disgust at the time of the song's release, it seems to present the two male leads as singing *to each other.* This effect is produced not only by the alternating avowals to "you," but also by the falsetto's conjuration (owing to the engagement of a characteristically feminine vocal range) of a typically feminine love object to whom the baritone might well be singing; its capacity to *disturb*, on the other hand—or at least to disturb my classmate—issues from the falsetto's simultaneous registration (thanks both to the conventions of pop-music vocalization and to our presumed prior knowledge of Russell Thompkins's gender) as a specifically masculine subject. Thus, "You Make Me Feel Brand New" takes to a new conceptual level the gender nonspecificity of the loved one that it reprises from "Natural High," not only worrying the constraint comprised in heterosexist presumption, but connotatively figuring the possibility of positively regenerative homosexual attachment: after all, "you make me feel brand new."

Classic R & B–derived uses of the backing vocal form, then, need not buttress the normative social formations that the songs in which they appear seem lyrically to endorse, but rather can actually figure a coherent challenge to the constraint those formations represent. Indeed, not only might backing-vocal arrangements unsettle such naturalized categories as gender-identity, for instance, as in "A Natural Man," but that unsettling itself can be taken up by and extended through other traditional aspects of pop-musical production, like those at work in the recordings by Bloodstone and the Stylistics. Thus for all the anxiety potentially engendered by highly charged instantiations of social difference, anxious suppression need not be the primary mode in which they are negotiated. This fact founds the promise that is at least as inherent in popular culture as the social threat so commonly discerned there. Because the promise and the danger are often imbricated with one another, however, a careful critical eye must be trained on those forms of culture that register as most "popular" in the contemporary context, with particular consideration given to those of African-American derivation, inasmuch as such derivation itself seems almost to *define* the popular in the cultural moment now at hand.

Needless to say, when it comes to the productive negotiation of social difference, singing songs is not nearly enough. At the same time, though, if we take seriously not only the interrelation between cultural event and social formation, but the status of culture as itself social fact, we can see that popular music, television programming, music video, popular dance—indeed, the whole range of cultural practice that characterizes the contemporary era—not only comment on current social conditions, but are a fundamental factor in how they are experienced. Given this, musical production, while by no means the end of the story, is as good a place as any to begin crucial critical work. Precisely because cultural negotiations *are* so critical, however, they cannot be undertaken lightly or without careful thought. Which is to say, in production—material, social, or cultural—begins responsibility of a most profound sort; and if where it ends nobody can tell, this is only because there is no end in sight.

EPILOGUE

The more things change, the more they stay the same. Just as Michael Jackson was implicitly reaffirming masculinist definitions of proud black identity, drag performer RuPaul was achieving remarkable commercial success by putting forth a rather different version of black cultural pride in his 1993 album, *Supermodel of the World*. First represented over the airwaves by the brilliantly self-promoting camp title cut "Supermodel (You Better Work)," the album eventually issued in the communalistically nostalgic single "Back to My Roots," an unequivocal affirmation of African-American heritage whose metaphoric vehicle—a reminiscent meditation on the culture of black hair care—is both gynocentric and gay-inflected.

If RuPaul's ensuing crossover success—entailing, among other things, appearances on MTV, a duet recording with Elton John, and a role in the much-touted *Brady Bunch Movie*—has fed African Americans' old suspicions regarding white audiences' appetite for black caricature, it has also provoked a crucially important reassessment of what constitutes "proper" racial and gender identities in the contemporary context. The extent to which this is true is attested by a major development in RuPaul's career that took place in the winter of 1995.

On March 1, Toronto-based Make-up Art Cosmetics Ltd. (or M·A·C) announced that it had chosen RuPaul to be the "spokesmodel" for the various charity fundraising campaigns that it sponsors. This fact might seem insignificant, given M·A·C's relatively low profile (it runs no advertising, sponsors no promotions, and offers modestly plain product packaging), until one realizes that the ten-year old company projected sales of $107 million in 1995, its phenomenal

A M·A·C Cosmetics charity fundraising promotional featuring RuPaul. Photo: Albert Sanchez. Courtesy of M·A·C Cosmetics.

success—and corresponding industry influence—deriving chiefly from its reputed status as the favorite brand of fashion and beauty professionals (see Ono, 1995). Asserting the drag queen's "perfectness" for the job, company co-owner Frank Toskan proclaimed that "MAC is about all races, all sexes, all ages"—a universalism he claimed is "embodied" by no one better than RuPaul (see Kaminer, 1995). Evidently, though, it was just this indeterminacy and comprehensiveness that perturbed two critics of the M·A·C decision.

Writing in response to rumors of the hire that circulated prior to the official announcement, *New York Daily News* gossip columnists A. J. Benza and Michael Lewittes (1995) lamented M·A·C's choice of RuPaul, asking, "Aren't there plenty of beautiful women who were *biologically* born that way who could move their product equally well?" (emphasis in original). The question is odd, to say the least, since by implicitly granting RuPaul's ability to "move product," it suggests that the point of corporate publicity campaigns is actually to promote select "beautiful women," whom it conceives as inherently entitled to lucrative modeling contracts. Because Benza and Lewittes don't name names, we might surmise that they would gladly accept as M·A·C representatives any number of candidates who share RuPaul's racial identification but who are recognized as "beautiful" "biological" women—black "supermodels" Tyra Banks, Veronica Webb, and Roshumba Williams, for instance—but another peculiar aspect of their critique hints otherwise.

Asserting that RuPaul's landing of the M·A·C contract signals an "advertising world gone completely haywire," Benza and Lewittes compare the development to Marlene Dietrich's "donn[ing] a tuxedo" and Katharine Hepburn's "wearing man-tailored clothing," which they posit as similarly outrageous occurrences. What did these earlier instances of celebrity cross-dressing constitute, though, but the female stars' usurpation of an authoritative masculine aspect and, simultaneously, the corruption of an idealized feminine beauty that they were otherwise supposed to represent? That ideal, of course, is necessarily white, no less so now than when Dietrich and Hepburn profaned it, in Benza's and Lewittes's view. So the offense the writers see RuPaul as embodying is not just the affront of the drag queen to generic femininity, but the assault of the black man on white womanhood—that ages-old threat with a postmodern twist. The more things change, the more they stay the same.

Not that we should forsake efforts at change, the relative success of which is, after all, measurable in the backlash those efforts provoke. RuPaul, for one, has not been deterred, vowing in his 1995 autobiography to "be the man that I am, . . . the woman that I am, the everything that I am" (p. 220). This promise is fairly made good in the book, itself disallowed from being all things. An account of a specifically African-American experience, it cannot, after Gertrude Stein's example, purport to be "everybody's autobiography." An extensive instruction manual in the logistics of drag, it cannot serve as a comprehensive autobiography of "the race," as James Weldon Johnson's novel has been judged to do (Van Vechten, 1979, p. 115). Still, RuPaul's effort is not merely personal. A manifest challenge to the bounds of identity, it sketches a collective life *that might be,* as we re-think the limits of black masculinity in light of the *limitations* they pose. If RuPaul insists that *he* is up to this task, he seems also to assume that we must be, too. And in the face of his formidably powerful appeal, who would we be to say we are not?

APPENDIX

Imamu Amiri Baraka/LeRoi Jones

Poem for Half White College Students

Who are you, listening to me, who are you
listening to yourself? Are you white or
black, or does that have anything to do
with it? Can you pop your fingers to no
music, except those wild monkies go on
in your head, can you jerk, to no melody,
except finger poppers get it together
when you turn from starchecking to checking
yourself. How do you sound, your words, are they
yours? The ghost you see in the mirror, is it really
you, can you swear you are not an imitation greyboy,
can you look right next to you in that chair, and swear,
that the sister you have your hand on is not really
so full of Elizabeth Taylor, Richard Burton is
coming out of her ears. You may even have to be Richard
with a white shirt and face, and four million negroes
think you cute, you may have to be Elizabeth Taylor, old lady,
if you want to sit up in your crazy spot dreaming about dresses,
and the sway of certain porters' hips. Check yourself, learn who it is
speaking, when you make some ultrasophisticated point, check your-
    self,

when you find yourself gesturing like Steve McQueen, check it out,
    ask
in your black heart who it is you are, and is that image black or white,

you might be surprised right out the window, whistling dixie on the
    way in

Nikki Giovanni

The True Import of Present Dialogue: Black vs. Negro

Nigger
Can you kill
Can you kill
Can a nigger kill
Can a nigger kill a honkie
Can a nigger kill the Man
Can you kill nigger
Huh? nigger can you
kill
Do you know how to draw blood
Can you poison
Can you stab-a-jew
Can you kill huh? nigger
Can you kill
Can you run a protestant down with your
'68 El Dorado
(that's all they're good for anyway)
Can you kill
Can you piss on a blond head
Can you cut it off
Can you kill
A nigger can die
We ain't got to prove we can die
We got to prove we can kill
They sent us to kill
Japan and Africa
We policed europe
Can you kill
Can you kill a white man

Can you kill the nigger
in you
Can you make your nigger mind
die
Can you kill your nigger mind
And free your black hands to
strangle
Can you kill
Can a nigger kill
Can you shoot straight and
Fire for good measure
Can you splatter their brains in the street
Can you kill them
Can you lure them to bed to kill them
We kill in Viet Nam
for them
We kill for UN & NATO & SEATO & US
And everywhere for all alphabet but
BLACK
Can we learn to kill WHITE for BLACK
Learn to kill niggers
Learn to be Black men

Haki Madhubuti (Don L. Lee)

Move Un-Noticed to Be Noticed: A Nationhood Poem

move, into our own, not theirs
into our.
they own it (for the moment) : the unclean world, the
                                    polluted space, the un-censor-
                                    ed air, yr/foot steps as they
                                    run wildly in the wrong
                                    direction.
move, into our own, not theirs
into our.
move, you can't buy own.
own is like yr/hair (if u let it live); a natural extension of ownself.
own is yr/reflection, yr/total-being; the way u walk, talk,
                dress and relate to each other is *own*.

own is you,
cannot be bought or sold

> can u buy yr/writing hand
> yr/dancing feet, yr/speech,
> yr/woman (if she's real),
> yr/manhood?

own is ours.
all we have to do is   take it
take it the way u take from one another.

> the way u take artur rubinstein over thelonious monk
> the way u take eugene genovese over lerone bennett,
> the way u take robert bly over imamu baraka,
> the way u take picasso over charles white,
> the way u take marianne moore over gwendolyn brooks,
> the way u take *inaction* over *action.*

move.   move to act   act.
act into thinking and think into action.
try to think. think.   try to think think think.
try to think. think (like i said, into yr/own) think.
try to think. don't hurt yourself, i know it's new.
try to act,
act into thinking and think into action.
can u do it, hunh? i say hunh, can u stop moving like a drunk gorilla?

> ha ha   che che
> ha ha   che che
> ha ha   che che
> ha ha   che che

move
what is u anyhow: a professional car watcher, a billboard for nothing-
      ness, a sane madman, a reincarnated clark gable?
either you is or you ain't!

the deadliving
are the worldmakers,
the image breakers,
the rule takers: blackman can you stop a hurricane?

"I remember back in 1954 or '55, in Chicago, when we had
13 days without a murder, that was before them colored
people started calling themselves *black.*"

move.
move,
move to be moved,
move into yr/ownself, Clean.
Clean, u is the first black hippy i've ever met.
why u bes dressen so funny, anyhow hunh?
i mean, is that u, Clean?
why u bes dressen like an airplane, can u fly,
i mean,
will yr/blue jim-shoes fly u,
& what about yr/tailor made bell bottoms, Clean?
can they lift u above madness,
turn u into the right direction.
& that red & pink scarf around yr/neck what's that for,
    Clean,
hunh? will it help u fly, yeah, swing, swing ing swing
      swinging high above telephone wires with dreams
      of this & that and illusions of trying to take bar-b-q
      ice cream away from hon minded niggers who
      didn't event know that *polish* is more than a
      sausage.
"clean as a tack,
rusty as a nail,
haven't had a bath
sence columbus sail."

when u going be something real, Clean?
like yr/own, yeah, when u going be yr/ownself?

the deadliving
are the worldmakers,
the image breakers,
the rule takers: blackman can u stop a hurricane, mississippi couldn't
blackman if u can't stop what mississippi couldn't, *be it, be it.*
blackman be the wind, be the win, the win, the win, win win:

     wooooooooooowe boom boom   wooooooooooowe bah
     wooooooooooowe boom boom   wooooooooooowe bah
if u can't stop a hurricane, be one.
     wooooooooooowe boom boom   wooooooooooowe bah

      woooooooooowe boom boom   woooooooooowe bah
be the baddddest hurricane that ever came. a black hurricane.
      woooooooooowe boom boom   woooooooooowe bah
      woooooooooowe boom boom   woooooooooowe bah
the badddest black hurricane that ever came, a black
          hurricane named Beulah,
go head Beulah, do the hurricane.
      woooooooooowe boom boom   woooooooooowe bah
      woooooooooowe boom boom   woooooooooowe bah
move
move to be moved from the un-moveable,
into our own, yr/self is own, yrself is own, own yourself.
go where you/we go, hear the unheard and do,
do the undone, do it, do it, do it *now,* Clean
and tomorrow your sons will
be alive to praise
you.

Sonia Sanchez

a chant for young / brothas

& sistuhs

yall

    out there.   looooken so coool

in yo / highs.

       yeah yall

         rat there

    listen to me

screeaamen this song.

       did u know i've

seen yo / high

        on every blk / st in

wite / amurica

        i've seen yo/self/

imposed/quarantined/hipness

              on every

slum/

    bar/   revolutionary / st

& there yall be sitten.

          u brotha.

u sistuh.

    listen to this drummen.

this sad / chant.

      listen to the tears

flowen down my blk / face

           listen to a

death/song being sung on thick/lips

by a blk/woman

    once i had a maaan
    who loved me so he sed
    we lived togetha, loved togetha

and i followed wherever he led

now this maaan of mine
got tired of this slooow pace
started gitten high a lot
to stay on top of the race.

saw him begin to die
screeaamed. held him so tight
but he got so thin so very thin
slipped thru these fingers of might

last time i heard from him
he was bangen on a woman's door
callen for his daily high
didn't even care bout the score.

once i loooved a man
still do looove that man
want to looove that man again
wish he'd come on home again

need to be with that maaannn
need to love that maaaannnn
who went out one day & died
who went out one day & died.

yall

      out there   looooken so cooool

in yo / highs.

                      yeah.   yall

                                  rat there

c'mon down from yo / wite / highs

      and live.

June Jordan

Okay "Negroes"

Okay "Negroes"
American Negroes
looking for milk
crying out loud
in the nursery of freedomland:
the rides are rough.
Tell me where you got that image
of a male white mammy.
God is vague and he don't take no sides.
You think clean fingernails crossed legs a smile
shined shoes
a crucifix around your neck
good manners
no more noise
you think who's gonna give you something?

Come a little closer.
Where you from?

NOTES

Chapter 1

Eloquence and Epitaph: AIDS, Homophobia,
and Problematics of Black Masculinity

1. Centers for Disease Control, *HIV/AIDS Surveillance Report*, July 1991, p. 10, Table 5.

2. This situation is ongoing despite not only Johnson's announcement but also (a) the 1988 death of former ABC news anchor, Max Robinson, discussed in this chapter; (b) tennis champion Arthur Ashe's publication of his AIDS diagnosis in April 1992 and his death in February 1993 (see Finn, 1993; Rhoden, 1992); and (c) the announcement by black, openly gay former baseball player Glenn Burke that he was diagnosed as having AIDS in January 1994 (see Frey, 1994), and Burke's own death in May 1995 (see "Glenn Burke," 1995).

3. National Center for Health Statistics, *Health, United States, 1989*, 1990, p. 151, Table 3.

4. For an overview of the various black nationalist movements that have emerged in the United States since the late eighteenth century, see Bracey, Meier, and Rudwick (1970). It should be noted here that the different nationalisms (cultural, revolutionary, and economic, for instance) are not always considered as sharing a common objective; see, for example, Linda Harrison's (1970) commentary on the inadequacy of cultural nationalism with respect to a black revolutionary agenda. Nevertheless, it seems to me that a generalized cultural nationalism, more than any other form, has been a pervasive influence in African-American life since the 1960s, and it is to this brand of nationalism that I allude repeatedly both in this chapter and elsewhere in the book.

5. This dichotomy corresponds, of course, to that described by W. E. B. Du Bois in his classic discussion of blacks' "double-consciousness"—the effect of their inability to reconcile their blackness and their "American" identity. See *Souls* (1903), especially Chapter 1, "Of Our Spiritual Strivings."

6. An additional instance of the networks' explicit suppression of African-American identity involved black newsman Ed Bradley, a correspondent on the CBS News program, *60 Minutes*. According to an account by *60 Minutes* producer Don Hewitt, Bradley sent the

latter into a panic when he decided to change his name to "Shaheeb Sha Hab," thereby reflecting his allegiance with Islamic black nationalism. By convincing Bradley not to take this step, as he claims to have done, Hewitt succeeded in keeping black nationalist politics out of the scope of the *60 Minutes* cameras. See Hewitt (1985, p. 170).

7. This development may indicate a perverse "feminization" of the television news anchor insofar as an insistent emphasis on physical appearance to the neglect of professional accomplishment has historically characterized women's experience in the public sphere. An indication of the extent to which this tyranny of "beauty" can now shape mass cultural phenomena is provided in the field of contemporary pop music. Since the advent of music video in the 1980s, the importance of musical acts' eye appeal has increased to such a degree that models have sometimes been hired to lip sync and otherwise "visualize" a song that is actually sung by someone else outside the audience's range of view. The most notorious such case involved the male duo, Milli Vanilli (see "Milli Vanilli," 1990), but the mere fact that men are increasingly subject to the imperative of "sex appeal" by no means implies that they now suffer its oppressive burden to the same extent as do women.

8. The phrase is from Calvin C. Hernton's classic 1965 text, *Sex and Racism in America,* which cites numerous instances of white-perpetrated violence against black men perceived to embody a threat to white femininity. Though such instances may be much less frequent now than at the time of Hernton's writing, a structure of sociosexual relations that confers an inordinately threatening status upon black men remains very firmly in place in the United States. Consider, for instance, the intense response to the April 1989 attack by a group of black youths on a white woman jogger in Central Park. This response, like the incident itself, was highly overdetermined, and too complex to analyze here, but it culminated in a widely publicized call by real estate magnate Donald Trump for application of the death penalty. It was suggested by numerous people that the intensity of the response was a function of the racial and gender identities of the parties involved, and that a different configuration (white attackers or black or male victim) would not have produced the same degree of outrage or media coverage. See Wolff (1989), and Donald Trump's full-page display ad (1989); see also the daily coverage provided by the *New York Times* during the period from 21 April through 1 May 1989.

9. I want to emphasize that I consider this management of black male sexuality to be an operation that is continually under way in U.S. culture, with any black man subject to its direct effects at any moment. The very appearance of a black man on the network newscast may seem to indicate that *he,* at least, has been judged safe for exposure before the bourgeois white audience, and his use of articulate and "objective" journalistic language would then serve merely as a sort of seal of his innocuousness. This could only be true, though, if the recognizably "professional" black male were generally seen as distinct from the mass of black men whose presence on U.S. streets is routinely considered a threat to the well-being of the larger community. As any of us who have been detained and questioned by white urban police for no reason can attest, however, this is not the case. Just as every black man might suddenly manifest an ideological challenge that would certainly have to be kept in check (by a Roone Arledge or a Don Hewitt, for instance, in the broadcast news context), so too does every black man represent an ongoing threat of untamed sexuality that must continually be defused. Thus Max Robinson's expert use of Received Standard English was not merely a mark of his already having been neutralized as a threat to white bourgeois interests; rather, it was itself the neutralization of the threat, continual proof against black male insurgency.

10. Smitherman (1977, p. 83) herself points out that the black rap traditionally testifies to masculine prowess, citing its emphasis on braggadocio and explaining that, "[w]hile some raps convey social and cultural information, others are used for conquering foes and women" (p. 82). Kochman (1969), Abrahams (1962), and Mitchell-Kernan (1972) have also noted the peculiarly male-identified nature of the black rap, which, in its musical manifestations, has increasingly been appropriated and transformed by members of other social groups—and especially by black women—since the mid-1980s; see, for example, the relatively early titles referenced by Berlant (1988). For the definitive account of the social significance of rap music, see Tricia Rose, *Black Noise* (1994).

The invocation of "homosexuality" in this sentence—and in other sections of the book where African Americans' sexual identifications are at issue—is deliberate. My point is not to register what many have protested are the clinical connotations of *homosexual* in contrast to the putatively more expansive resonances of *gay* or *queer,* but to indicate the limited degree to which many men of color feel identified with these latter terms. Indeed, *gay,* especially, conjures up in the minds of many who hear it images of a population that is characteristically white, male, and financially well-off; thus it can actually efface, rather than affirm, the experiences of women and of men of color. (This is why some groups of black men who might have identified as gay have chosen instead to designate themselves by terms they feel reflect a specifically Afrocentric experience. Consider the case of "Adodi," which has been used by black men in both Philadelphia and Boston [see Pincus, 1988].) I use *homosexual,* then, to signal the difficulty of fairly designating any "minority" group, due to the inevitably complex and multifaceted nature of minority identity.

11. Nor was he the last. My own performance in this volume (let alone in the other sites of my intellectual practice) sets me up to be targeted as too white-identified or too effete (or both) to be a "real" black man in certain contexts. That I already identify *myself* as gay may mitigate my vulnerability on that score somewhat. At the same time, the fact that my work takes the form of scholarly writing that circulates primarily within the academy largely insulates me from charges that I am not sufficiently engaged with the day-to-day concerns of the black populace, even as it substantiates the claim. This latter paradox constitutes a dilemma not for black intellectuals alone, certainly; but the embattled position that blacks still occupy in this country—socially, politically, economically—makes the problem especially pressing for us.

12. I address the significance of Black Arts nationalism at length in Chapter 2.

13. There is an evident irony here, in that the intense masculinism of black nationalist discourse was developed as a reaction against the suppression of black manhood and black male sexuality (often taking the form of literal castration, and at any rate consistently rhetorically figured as such) enacted by the dominant white society. Of course, the emphasis on traditional masculinity is not unique to *black* nationalism, either in the United States or elsewhere. For an extensive discussion of the relation between European nationalist ideologies and the promulgation of a masculine ideal, see Mosse (1985).

14. The *Jet* obituary figures a general journalistic ignorance of the appropriate terms to be used in reference to the AIDS epidemic. "AIDS victim," with its connotations of passivity, helplessness, and immutable doom, and its reduction of the person under discussion to a medical condition, was long ago rejected by HIV-affected communities in favor of "person with AIDS" (PWA) or "person living with AIDS" (PLWA). Additionally, AIDS is not a "disease"; it is a "syndrome"—a constellation of symptoms (and in the instance of AIDS many of the characteristic symptoms are themselves diseases) that indicates an

underlying condition—in the case of AIDS, suppressed immunity caused by infection with HIV.

15. For some commentary on this phenomenon, see Beam (1986), particularly the essays by Tinney, Branner, and Max Smith.

16. Among Jackson's misstatements is his reference to the "AIDS virus." There is no virus that "causes AIDS," only HIV, which produces the immunosuppression that allows the conditions that constitute AIDS to flourish. Moreover, neither HIV infection nor AIDS "comes from" either homosexuality or "promiscuity"; HIV is a virus extant in the biosphere that is merely *transmitted* through sexual contact.

It is particularly ironic, by the way, that the homophobia-informed task of legitimizing Robinson's AIDS diagnosis should have been undertaken by Jackson, whose 1988 presidential campaign was characterized by support for lesbian and gay political interests.

17. For an extensive analysis of this characteristic of AIDS-education programs in the United States, see Crimp (1987).

18. See Clifton Brown, "A Career of Impact"; Callahan; Heisler, "Magic Johnson's Career Ended"; Leerhsen et al.; Murphy and Griego.

Needless to say, the perceived momentousness of Johnson's announcement of his HIV-infection and retirement resulted in press and media coverage of overwhelming extensiveness, which is itself a fact worthy of close critical attention. For the sake of coherency, I have based my analysis here primarily on accounts provided in the *Los Angeles Times* and the *New York Times,* owing, in the first case, to the paper's comprehensiveness in covering what was effectively a local story, and, in the second, to the publication's great degree of influence in the realm of journalism and beyond.

19. See Clifton Brown, "A Career of Impact"; McCallum, "Unforgettable"; and Stevenson, "Magic Johnson Ends His Career."

20. See, for instance, Elliott, "Athletes' Endorsements"; and Mulligan (1991).

For a pre-announcement assessment of Johnson's and other NBA players' careers as corporate spokesmen, see Silverstein (1991). For a profile of one of Johnson's own successful business ventures, see Krier (1991). For an overview of Johnson's corporate holdings as of November 1991, see "Magic's Business Interests."

21. On the historicity of the link between male heterosexuality and masculine gender identity, see Chauncey (1994), especially Chapters 3 and 4.

22. In a noteworthy demonstration of the difference a judiciously used auxiliary verb can make, the *Los Angeles Times*'s Heisler opted to maintain Johnson (rather than Johnson's physician) as the authoritative subject of the developments he publicized, but unlike Gina Kolata, who also focused specifically on the prospect of Johnson's addressing the mode of his own infection, Heisler indicated the nearly inevitably speculative quality of such discussion by referring to how Johnson "*might have* contracted the virus" (my emphasis). By contrast, Kolata much more problematically asserted simply that "Johnson did not say how he became infected" ("Studies"). See Heisler, "Magic Johnson's Career Ended," p. A33.

23. The fact that as late as 1991 Kolata, a regular reporter on the *New York Times*'s AIDS beat, was still invoking "risk groups" rather than risky behavior as a primary factor in the spread of HIV indicates just how abominably irresponsible and inaccurate the "mainstream" press has been in covering the epidemic. Unfortunately, signs of improvement in this coverage have not been forthcoming.

24. On Johnson's television appearance, see Bonk and Scott (1991); Shilts (1991); Stevenson, "Johnson's Frankness"; and Charles Stewart (1991).

25. Johnson seems to have been right to worry about how Hearn was doing since, in the same interview, Hearn vowed to "stand in front of an onrushing train and let it run over me" if rumors of Johnson's homosexual activity were true, indicating a homophobic anxiety that could well be life-threatening.

26. See Almond, "Magic's Decision"; Almond and Heisler (1992); Berkow, "All-Stars"; Clifton Brown, "Criticism" and "Set the V.C.R."; Harvey (1992); Heisler, "Controversy" and "One More Time"; "Johnson Accepts Australian Bid"; Kolata, "Experts"; McCallum, "Inside the NBA"; and "Magic Should Stay Out."

27. Clifton Brown, "For One Stirring Afternoon" and "Johnson Makes a Big Point"; Heisler, "From the Beginning"; Howard-Cooper, "Who Else?"; McCallum, "Most Valuable Person"; Murray, "Why Can't?"; and Vecsey, "Magic Makes Highlights."

28. Almond, "Improvement." See also: Clifton Brown, "Johnson, Unbowed," p. B14; Friend, "Part-Time Superstar," p. B14; Heisler, "Magic Johnson to Rejoin Lakers," p. A21; and Vecsey, "Magic Words."

In apparent contrast to his colleagues in the press, Dave Anderson, a perennial skeptic and naysayer throughout the Johnson saga, invoked the athlete's increased muscularity only to wonder, "has he simply created more muscles to be bruised or pulled?" neglecting to indicate how, even if he had, this would distinguish him from any similarly bulked-up HIV-negative athlete. See Anderson's (1992) extremely problematically titled article, "The Lakers Don't Play Angola."

29. Quoted in Larry Stewart, "Player Reaction," p. C6. See also Friend, "Just Like Starting Over."

30. See Araton, "Bashing and Trashing"; Bonk (1992); Heisler, "Magic Johnson Retires."

31. Clifton Brown, "Johnson, Unbowed," p. A1; Downey, "Magic," p. C4; and Heisler, "Happiness," p. C1.

32. See Araton, "Malone Admits Error" and "Malone Is in the Eye of the Storm"; Friend, "Johnson Says" and "No Anger"; Heisler, "Magic Johnson Retires," p. A18; Howard-Cooper, "Peer Pressure," p. C1; Malamud (1992); Murray, "It's Mailman's"; and Larry Stewart, "Player Reaction," p. C6.

33. Nor should it be assumed for one second that gay-identified men—most of whom since 1982 or so have probably given the ramifications of HIV a great deal of thought—necessarily reject or seek to question conventional conceptions of acceptable masculinity, their apparent flouting of those conceptions with respect to sexual orientation notwithstanding.

34. For instance, soon after announcing his HIV seropositivity, Johnson was appointed by President George Bush to the National Commission on AIDS, only to become frustrated, like the panel's other members, with the administration's failure to adopt its recommendations; he resigned from the Commission in disgust in September 1992 (see Cimons, 1992; Heisler, "Magic Has a Lot," p. C1; Hilts, "Bush Asks Johnson" and "Magic Johnson Quits"; and "Magic Johnson Says He Is Likely to Quit"). In the realm of information dissemination, a March 1992 cable-television broadcast featuring Johnson and host Linda Ellerbee addressing children's questions about AIDS (*A Conversation with Magic*) was characterized by the influential, conservative *National Review* as presenting "What Children Shouldn't Know" (McConnell, 1992). And when Johnson's straightforward guide for young people, *What You Can Do to Avoid AIDS,* was published in the spring of 1992, four national retail chains initially refused to carry it, three of them citing its

potential offense to their shoppers (see O'Brien, "AIDS Book . . . 'Self-Censored' " and "AIDS Book . . . Continues to Spark Controversy").

Chapter 2: Nationalism and Social Division in Black Arts Poetry of the 1960s

1. For an overview of the development of black nationalism in the Black Arts movement, see Baker, *The Journey Back,* especially Chapter 4.

2. We might consider this project as one instantiation of the fundamental conservatism that Jennifer Jordan (1986) has suggested characterizes black cultural nationalism, whose negotiation in the Black Arts movement she reviews in her article on "Politics and Poetry."

3. For example, see Joyce A. Joyce's (1987) objection to the use of post-structuralist theory in African-Americanist literary criticism.

4. This is not to deny the power of such black collectivization as was generated, for example, in the context of public readings by Black Arts poets during the late 1960s and early 1970s (see Baker, 1980, pp. 128–29); rather, it is to point up the principle of intraracial division on which such collectivization—always necessarily partial—inevitably depends, which principle is evidenced in the published texts that must by definition outlast the live event itself.

5. It is also possible—to point in a direction that diverges substantially from my primary concerns in this volume—that the intraracial division effected in Black Arts poetry is a function of the African-American people's status as a sort of mutated colonial entity. During the late 1960s, analyses of the colonialized nature of black communities in the United States were forthcoming from both social scientists and black activists. Indeed, in his introduction to *Black Nationalism in America,* John H. Bracey, Jr., posits just such a conception of black America, citing as his justification a number of contemporary studies in sociology and political science (1970, p. lvi; among the authors Bracey cites, Robert Blauner in particular clearly outlines the issues at stake in conceptualizing African-American communities as colonial entities). Given this, it is interesting to note that Abdul R. Jan-Mohamed has identified as one of the cultural manifestations of colonialism a mapping of the social entity along a "manichean" duality that defines a morally "good" constituency—the colonizers, more often than not—against one that is seen as inherently "evil"—the colonized. (See both *Manichean Aesthetics* [1983] and "The Economy of Manichean Allegory" [1985].) While I do not believe that the situation of African Americans can be unproblematically posited as a colonial one, its historical *sine qua non*—the slave trade—can certainly be considered as a manifestation of the colonizing impulse. Consequently, it seems possible that, just as the economics of slavery developed in a particular manner after the initial appropriation of the "resources" from the African continent, there occurred concomitant mutations in the cultural realm in which we can still trace the remnants of an essential colonial logic. Thus, the *I–you* dichotomy that characterizes Black Arts poetry might represent the internalization within the African-American community of the manichean ethic that JanMohamed identifies with the colonial situation proper. Further work in this area, while clearly beyond the scope of my analysis here, might well prove critically useful.

6. Consider, for example, Emily Stoper's wry and telling 1989 reflection that the "[r]adical feminists" who emerged in the wake of the black power movement that she chronicled in her 1968 dissertation on the Student Nonviolent Coordinating Committee "never rested their hopes on political change; perhaps they knew better, since many of

them were veterans of the New Left and even of SNCC itself" (p. xii). On the gender politics of the Black Power movement, see Wallace (1979, 1990).

Chapter 3: What's My Name?? Designation, Identification, and Cultural "Authenticity"

1. It is worth noting, however, that there was clearly continued controversy over designatory terminology even after this landmark event, with writer Kelly Miller, for instance, considering the question, "Negroes or Colored People?" (and generally coming down in favor of the former), as late as 1937.

2. That same understanding informed the relatively early condemnation of "Negro" issued by Richard Moore in his 1960 tract, *The Name "Negro": Its Origin and Evil Use.*

3. It should be noted that Smitherman invokes a specifically *socio*linguistic constructionism partly by way of correcting what she sees as both Whorfian *and* Humboldtian linguists' tendency to overstate the constitutive effects of language per se ("'What Is Africa?'" p. 117). For Humboldt's contribution to linguistic theory, see his *On Language* (1988); for the basis of Whorfian linguistics, see Whorf (1956, pp. 207–70).

4. I am well aware of the degree to which such notions of linguistic "reflection" have been problematized by recent (post-) structuralist interventions in the philosophy of language. Indeed, it seems to me that Smitherman's theory of the "dialectical" quality of linguistic meaning itself partakes of the insights engendered by those interventions. Consequently, my references to such reflection—made here for the sake of convenience and clarity in elaborating that theory—should be understood as already implicating that problematization, and not as indicating my rejection of its importance.

5. We should note, too, that the socially constituted significance of any instance of linguistic terminology is itself conditioned by the various subjective dispositions of those whom it concerns. This undoubtedly accounts, at least in part, for the apparently contradictory findings of Fairchild, on the one hand, and Hecht and Ribeau, on the other. In a study conducted by the former, white subjects were discovered to be more likely to ascribe "negative" traits—loudness, laziness, rudeness—to persons identified as "black" than to those identified as "Negro" or, especially, "Afro-American." Hecht and Ribeau, meanwhile, found that persons identifying themselves as "Black" reported experiencing *less* "negative stereotyping" by whites than did those identifying themselves as "Afro-American." One implication of this difference, as Hecht and Ribeau themselves suggest in the context of their own study, is that individuals differ in their sensitivity to discriminatory treatment, and that those subjective differences might themselves affect individuals' choices of self-designatory terms, the additional social significances of those terms notwithstanding. (See Fairchild, 1985, pp. 51–52; and Hecht and Ribeau, 1987, p. 323.)

6. See, for instance, "African-American or Black"; Bray (1990); John Sibley Butler (1990); Freund (1989); "Jackson and Others"; Martin (1991); Morris (1989); Peretz (1989); Thernstrom (1989); "What's in a Name?"; and Williams (1990).

7. Baugh mistakenly attributes Thernstrom's claim to Charles Paul Freund, in whose February 1989 *Washington Post* column it was quoted.

8. This difficulty accounts, in large part, for my use of the term *African-American*—in addition to *black*—throughout this volume, despite the problems with it to which I allude in this chapter.

9. One commentator who *does* undertake to analyze Jackson's motives for advocating

the adoption of "African-American" is Ben Martin (1991). Unfortunately, by skeptically identifying those motives with a general desire among black leaders to reaffirm African Americans' "victim status"—the possible legitimacy of which he both refuses to entertain and fails systematically to refute—Martin severely undercuts his insights about the largely mythological character of any such nationalist impulse as informs the claims for "African-American." Contrasting slightly with Martin, Stephan Thernstrom (1989) sees those claims as driven specifically by Jesse Jackson's personal ambitions, rather than by a group-oriented political agenda developed by Jackson together with his associates.

10. This is because the copyright holders for the songs in question have withheld permission to quote from the materials.

I should also say here that, by focusing my analysis on the narrative that "People Everyday" presents, I do not mean to suggest that the social significance of the song inheres entirely in its lyrical semantics. Indeed, as Simon Frith (1988) has pointed out, a number of important signifying contexts overlap to constitute the "social mark" made by popular music, whose referential field thus greatly exceeds that of its lyrics themselves (pp. 105–8). Such extended lyrical sampling and rewriting as rap music entails, however, produces a trans-historical verbal text that demands and richly repays specific analysis, however much it is interrelated with other, equally important signifying elements.

11. Indeed, Tricia Rose has gone so far as to suggest that Speech and Arrested Development exemplify a reevaluation of conventional masculinity within the context of black hip-hop culture ("The Big Idea"). While this may appear to be the case based on some of the group's material (Rose herself focuses specifically on 1994's *Zingalamaduni*), whether that reevaluation consistently characterizes Arrested Development's work strikes me as dubious. For Rose's extended consideration of "Sexual Politics in Rap Music," see *Black Noise* (1994), pp. 146–82.

12. I was gratified to learn, after formulating the analysis of "People Everyday" that I present here, that it closely approximates the brief exposition offered by Paul Gilroy (1994) in his extended critique of "revolutionary conservatism" in black popular culture. See his "'After the Love Has Gone,'" pp. 53–54 n. 7.

On the other hand, Todd Boyd (1994) offers a lengthy analysis of both "People Everyday" and "Tennessee"—in their video as well as specifically audio formats—that identifies the works as gender-politically progressive, an assessment with which I obviously disagree. I do not, for example, see either the invocation of the "Black Queen" or the "valorization of women" that it supposedly represents as unimplicated in a highly problematic sexist outlook; nor do I see Speech's sharing of rapping duties with a woman as necessarily disrupting his masculinist orientation (see Boyd, pp. 294–302; see pp. 300 and 299 for the referenced passages).

13. The fullest recent exposition of this problematic character is provided by Anthony Appiah's *In My Father's House* (1992).

Chapter 4: Class Acts: The "Street," Popular Music,
and Black-Cultural Crossover

1. For an account of rap's emergence in the context of a larger hip-hop culture, see Tricia Rose, *Black Noise* (1994), especially pp. 21–61.

2. A number of writers have commented on MTV's narrowcasting policy of the early 1980s and have noted the peculiarities of the target audience that it produced. See Farley

and Vamos (1986); Gehr (1983); Hoberman (1983); Levine (1983); Wolmuth (1983); and Zeichner (1982).

It is worth noting that, as far as narrowcasting is concerned, a lot of the work of delimiting a target audience was rendered practically unnecessary for MTV at the time of its inception since, even as late as the early 1980s, cable television was available primarily in white rural and suburban communities. It was as the clientele for cable expanded during the latter half of the decade that the station's continued targeting of a young, white, male audience—which it translated into the exclusion of most black acts from its telecast roster—precipitated increasing controversy.

3. Indeed, at a number of points since its inception, the AOR radio format has represented a white-rock reaction against the musical cultures of various socially marginalized groups. For instance, as Jon Pareles and Patricia Romanowski (1983) point out, the vehement anti-disco movement of the late 1970s and early 1980s was centered at AOR stations around the country, and as such both fomented and channeled homophobia and racial hostility among the AOR constituency. See the entry on "Radio" in Pareles and Romanowski, pp. 454–55.

4. It should be noted here that the playlist guidelines of AOR stations have also often limited radio access for white artists working in styles considered too esoteric for "classic rock" audiences. Ironically, though, a number of such acts actually gained exposure in the early 1980s on MTV itself, despite its similarly restrictive policy. A case in point is the "rockabilly" band Stray Cats, which, according to *People* magazine's Roger Wolmuth, "thrived in Europe" but "had little luck cracking the rigid playlists on commercial stations" in the United States. After MTV began televising the band's "Stray Cat Strut" video, however, the record "started to sell in Seattle even though we didn't have any radio stations playing the group," as a spokesman for the band's record company put it to Wolmuth in 1983 (pp. 96, 99). Similarly, the album *Rio* by British band Duran Duran recorded high sales in sections of Dallas that were wired for cable and carried MTV, while languishing in record stores in other parts of the city. According to Norman Samnick of Warner Communications, original parent company of MTV, the band "owe[d] its life" to the station (Cocks, "Sing," p. 56).

This apparent paradox is explained largely by the fact that, however much MTV executives hoped to tap a "mainstream" rock audience, the station nonetheless depended on videos by relatively "noncommercial" artists during the early 1980s, since there were at that point comparatively few classic rock videos in existence or available for telecast. Given this situation, MTV did slightly expand the operative conception of commercially viable rock-and-roll (critically acclaimed videos by such artists as Laurie Anderson and Captain Beefheart were still judged as too "avant-garde" for regular airplay; see Levine, 1983, p. 56), while at the same time continuing to exclude from that category black artists *in general,* whose racial identity was apparently seen as immutably determining the musical style in which they worked.

5. Aerosmith's function here approximates that of an industry tool that emerged soon after Run-DMC's crossover had been effected. In February 1987, *Billboard* began publishing an "airplay-only" singles chart under the heading of "Hot 30 Crossovers." It recorded the most frequently played cuts from stations that featured "the top-selling pop hits in their market—but . . . lean toward black and/or dance in their music mix," and from stations that played "the black hits in their market—but . . . lean toward pop crossovers" (Freeman, 1987). On the face of it, this was a curious phenomenon, since the establish-

ment of "crossover" as a discrete category into which a record might be charted would seem to undermine the actual crossover of a song from one market ("Black," for instance) into another (such as "pop," or "top 40"). Insofar as the new chart served as an aid for radio programmers, however, it showed up the function of crossover with respect to the popular music establishment—to offer "pop" stations the appeal of ethnic flavor without the danger of overstated racial difference. As the programming director for WHQT Miami, which reported for the crossover chart, put it, "[i]f I were programming a top 40 [station], I'd certainly be looking at this chart to pick up a competitive edge with some fresher music" (Freeman, 1987, p. 83). Thus the crossover chart, by representing a market other than "rock" or "pop" where black artists could make a showing, was a means of regulating the irruption of black music into the white "tradition" while at the same time enabling radio stations to manipulate that music among the various conventional chart categories to their fiscal advantage.

6. As Henry Louis Gates, Jr., has pointed out, the "talking book" is a key rhetorical figure in black slave narratives from the eighteenth and early nineteenth centuries. It is worth noting that the trope has also been deployed in numerous other contexts where literacy constitutes a highly politicized sign of cultural and social superiority. See, for instance, Lévi-Strauss's (1961) account of its usage among the Nambikwara Indians of Brazil ("A Writing Lesson"), made famous in language and literary studies through Derrida's essay, "The Violence of the Letter" (1976).

7. Here, as throughout this chapter, the "Motown" referred to is that of 1959–1972, before the company moved from Detroit to Hollywood.

8. Indeed, Steve Perry has argued that appeals such as George has made for "authenticity" in black music are actually based in a capitalistic black nationalism that itself elides class as a meaningful category. See "Ain't No Mountain High Enough" (1988).

9. It should be stressed that, for all its invocation in the journalistic media, the distinction between "commercial" and cable television is a false one. Not only is cable TV supported by corporate sponsors who telecast commercials over cable stations, just like conventional TV, but on MTV this goes even further, for, as Richard Gehr noted in 1983 (and as has long been widely recognized), music videos themselves are really nothing more than advertisements for the audio recordings they feature and for the various other "tie-in" products with which they may be associated (p. 40).

10. For a concise, extremely well-informed consideration of breakdancing in the larger contexts of hip-hop and of black social dance in different African-diasporic locales from the nineteenth century on, see Banes (1994), pp. 121–36 and, especially, pp. 143–53.

11. This point is also made by the well-established breakers Mr. Wiggles and Crazy Legs in their interviews for the PBS television show, "Everybody Dance Now."

12. In making this critique of Sir Mix-A-Lot's production, I do not mean to contradict Laura Jamison's assessment of its great good humor; I do, however, mean to indicate that the cost of such unexaminedly sexist humor is too high to be borne by an African-American constituency the mass-popularization of whose culture has greatly outpaced its social and political progress (see Jamison, 1994, p. 53).

13. This effect may actually be less intense in black-produced programming—such as is offered by Black Entertainment Television, for instance—than it is in other videocast contexts. For one thing, BET generally broadcasts a wider variety of African-American–oriented music videos than does, say, MTV; and by interspersing those broadcasts with other types of black-oriented programming, it projects a more expansive con-

ception of African-American culture than is found on more "mainstream" stations. On the other hand, such viewer request–based video stations as The Box, while appearing to respond solely to audience "tastes," actually implicate viewers in the manipulative construction of "authentic" African-American culture by offering package deals that combine separate but similarly "black" videos in single requestable blocks; by underwriting viewer selection of such videos through the presentation of black-coded advertising that extends the motifs those videos manifest, as in the instance I examine in this section; and, not least, by dictating at the outset the selection of black-music videos from which viewers can choose their requests—a selection that, however much it might diverge from that offered by MTV, is not necessarily any less restrictive in the conception of African-American culture that it bespeaks.

14. For Tricia Rose's discussion of "pro-woman" rap by female African-American rappers, see *Black Noise* (1994), Chapter 5.

Chapter 5: Gender Politics and the "Passing" Fancy: Black Masculinity as Societal Problem

1. In her comprehensive study of the fictional mulatto figure, Judith Berzon (1978), too, has affirmed that "[t]he tragic mulatto is usually a woman" (p. 99), though by resting her explanation of this fact solely on the stereotypic sympathy that a racially "tainted" woman supposedly inspires, Berzon largely neglects the phenomenon that *founds* that sympathy, which I want to interrogate here—to wit, the extremely complex sociopolitical significance of mulatto identity.

As for the *locus classicus* of the tragic mulatto's literary-critical exposition, Sterling Brown's (1933) "Negro Character as Seen by White Authors"—while it allows that "'octoroon' has come to be a feminine noun in popular usage"—nonetheless suggests the uniformity of the properly *mulatto* character, "whether shown in male or female" (p. 160). If my assessment here differs from Brown's somewhat, this is partly because I am using the term *mulatto* in a broad sense to refer not only to individuals who are "half" white and "half" black, but also to those with one-quarter and one-eighth Negro "blood" (quadroons and octoroons). Moreover, it seems to me that even if all literary mulattoes are depicted as having the same basic "character," the *significance* of that character will be different for women than it is for men.

2. Eve Raimon (1994) analyzes to greatly illuminating effect Brown's appropriation in *Clotel* of Lydia Maria Child's 1842 story, "The Quadroons." See her Chapter 2.

3. Then, too, since Mary *is* a female child, there is nothing that stops her, as well as Clotel, from constituting a sexual threat to Gertrude's placid domesticity, her filial tie to Horatio presenting no real barrier to his having sexual relations with her, should he so choose. Insofar as homosexual relations were not generally recognized in the context under consideration, and neither white women nor men of African descent enjoyed the degree of social agency that white men did, the male "mulatto" would not have represented the same type of threat to white domesticity as the "mulatto" woman did.

4. Of course, non-Europeans, of whatever gender, have also been constructed by the Western imagination as objects of intense sexual temptation, but the eroticization of the racial Other has never been officialized and culturally legitimated to the degree that the eroticization of woman has. Thus, while the illicitness of sexual relations between Europeans and non-Europeans can actually intensify the latter's appeal (as, indeed, I think it

does in the case of the mulatto woman), to the degree that the nineteenth-century African-American novel still conforms to received gender-political codes, it will most explicitly figure sexual enticement in terms of feminine charm rather than racial exoticism, the potency of which, as I suggest here, is typically sublimated in—and expressed through—the mulatto character's fascinating feminine allure.

5. Michael Awkward (1995), too, has noted the problematical quality of Griffin's undertaking, though he also sees in it "the skeletal foundations of a theory of reading across racial lines." See *Negotiating Difference,* pp. 11–13; see p. 13 for the quoted passage.

6. Griffin's self-affirming experience of black male physicality in this encounter eerily prefigures a white man's later request that the "black" Griffin—who has hitched a ride in the white man's car—"expose" himself while the two are riding along on a Mississippi night. Insisting to Griffin that he is "not a queer or anything," the man justifies his request by explaining that "I don't get a chance to talk to educated Negroes," thus suggesting that he, like Griffin in the hotel bathroom, would have his own sense of himself (as an "educated" man) affirmed through his experience of the "black" male body. See pp. 88–89; p. 89 for the quotations.

7. This is not to say that Griffin and Halsell themselves are not deeply affected, as *individuals,* by their experiences in passing, but rather that the subject positions that they previously occupied remain fundamentally unaltered, however difficult the two of them might now find it to inhabit them. For a further consideration of the politics of white-authored passing narratives such as those by Griffin and Halsell, see Amy Robinson's (1993) doctoral dissertation, "To Pass/ /In Drag," especially Chapter 4.

Chapter 6: The Reassuring Shock of Recognition:
Blackness, Social Order, and Crimes of Identity

1. For an account of this critique from the time of its currency, see Hoverstein and Kanamine (1994).

2. This suggestion is furthered by the trial's incorporation—to apparently great humorous effect—of testimony by the entertainer Al Jolson, famous for his vaudevillian blackface performances. Summoned to respond to Alice Jones's claim, in a letter to Kip Rhinelander, that she had met and spoken with Jolson in the Adirondacks in the early 1920s (which he denied), Jolson punctuated his comments with an assortment of one-liners that evidently provided the court proceedings with much needed comic relief (see "Rhinelander Says He Pursued Girl"). At the same time, however, it would seem that Jolson's very presence in the courtroom, by both inevitably recalling his blackface act and emphatically registering his actual whiteness, contributed to the policing of the boundary between black and white that was at issue in the case. In this way, that presence might be said to have worked in concert with blackface itself, which, as Eric Lott (1993) has suggested, largely functioned to reaffirm the black–white racial distinction (see, for example, pp. 149–53 in *Love and Theft*). It is also worth noting, given my concern in this volume with the significance of a racialized masculinity, that Lott argues, among other things, that what was registered as mere "blackness" constituted specifically a form of desirable *masculinity* for white men who enacted blackface during the nineteenth century. A version of this argument appears on pp. 49–53 of *Love and Theft.*

3. After the 1925 decision in the fraud trial, Kip Rhinelander's apparent removal from New York immediately thereafter ("Alice Rhinelander Seeks Separation"), and his

nearly four years of continued absence from Alice (who claimed, despite her initial indications, to have made "the utmost peaceable efforts . . . to keep her husband" in the time since the first court ruling), the latter filed an alienation-of-affections suit against Kip's father, whom she accused of having worked to undermine the marriage from the beginning ("Philip Rhinelander Sued"). The case was closed in the late summer of 1930 by means of an agreement awarding Alice Rhinelander a $31,500 cash settlement, plus an annuity of $3,600 ("Rhinelander Case Closed").

4. For a useful review of the genetics at issue in racial classification, see Appiah, 1992, pp. 34–39. Regarding the presentation, in Phipps's appeal, of "expert testimony" as to the "scientifically insupportable" character of racial classification, see *Jane Doe v. State of Louisiana*, p. 372; and Trillin (1986, p. 75).

5. At the point when Susie Phipps filed her suit, the most recent case in which the "no doubt at all" requirement had been invoked was one in which the father of a young child sued for the release of his daughter's birth certificate. The state was withholding the document because, its representatives said, there was reason to believe that the child's ancestry was 1/256 black, in which case the recorded designation of "white" would have to be changed. Since in this case it was the state that was seeking to alter the document, the court demanded that it present evidence leaving "no doubt at all" as to the need for the change. Citing its failure to do so, the court decided in the father's favor, and ordered the state to release the birth certificate as it had been filed. Soon after this case was closed, the Louisiana legislature adopted the "one-thirty-second" rule of black identification whose repeal the Phipps case helped bring about. See *State ex rel Schlumbrecht v. Louisiana State Board of Health.*

6. In her work on sexual and racial "passing," Amy Robinson (1994, esp. pp. 719–31) usefully addresses this problematic by suggesting that social identity derives less from a given subject's approximation to universal visibility than from observers' skill at discerning and reading signs of group identification.

7. Obviously, my interest here is specifically in a particular media representation of Simpson, and not in his guilt or innocence in the murders or in his implicitly acknowledged physical abuse of Nicole Brown Simpson (see Mydans, 1994), which warrants its own extended critique. While it is clear, I think, that such guilt or innocence cannot possibly be conceived as separate from issues pertaining to Simpson's media "image," that image itself has significances beyond his guilt or innocence in the case per se, and it is one of these latter that I am examining here.

8. Needless to say, the entire Kerrigan affair, including the significance of Kerrigan's rivalry with fellow skater Tonya Harding, warrants sustained consideration. Cynthia Baughman's 1995 *Women on Ice* compilation promises to be the most wide-ranging examination to date of the Harding–Kerrigan "spectacle."

9. The problematic quality of that binarism—not to mention its anomalousness—is gaining increasing attention throughout mainstream U.S. culture. See, for instance, *Newsweek*'s February 1995 consideration of the matter, "What Color Is Black?" as well as the concluding reflections in Shirlee Taylor Haizlip's memoir (1994, pp. 265–68).

10. For indeed, Stant, along with Derrick Smith, was convicted of conspiring to commit assault. See "Kerrigan Attacker and Accomplice Sent to Jail."

11. Though, as we should be careful to note, he is perfectly able to further this campaign by *procreation*, as is evidenced by the physical appearances of his and Nicole Brown Simpson's children.

Chapter 7: Extra-Special Effects: Televisual Representation and the Undoing of "The Black Experience"

1. This is not to say, of course, that a great deal of work has not already been done on televisual representations of African Americans, much of it focusing on specific individual programs. On *Amos 'n' Andy*, see Cripps (1983). For an extended consideration of the show's broadcast history in both radio and television, see Ely (1991).

2. Consider, for instance, the study on *The Cosby Show* of the 1980s and 1990s, which indicated that white viewers accustomed to the evident affluence of Bill Cosby's television family took it to suggest the decreasing necessity of further activism on behalf of African Americans' equitable social treatment. See Jhally and Lewis (1992), especially pp. 135–38.

3. On the various conflicting contemporary readings of *Julia*'s racial- and gender-political significance, see Bodroghkozy (1992).

4. I am using *simulacral* in the sense developed by Jean Baudrillard, among others, to refer to a representation that usurps the supposed primacy of the objectively "real" entity conventionally imagined to serve as its "original." See *Simulations* (1983).

It may actually be through the theorization of televisual realism as simulacral that we can explain the failure (as putatively exemplified by *The Cosby Show*) of lived reality to approximate the social scenarios that popular series seem to envision. Following Foucault by positing the simulacrum as that which suspends resemblance by "subvert[ing] the hierarchical relation of model to copy," Scott Durham (1993) reads Pierre Klossowski's *Diana at Her Bath* as a narrativization of the simulacrum that—because its temporality reveals the undoing of the narrative subject's self-resemblance—exposes its fundamentally utopian, and hence objectively unrealizable, character. See Durham's "From Magritte to Klossowski," p. 20, for the quoted passage; for Foucault's theorization of the simulacrum, see his *This Is Not a Pipe* (1983).

5. On televisual "relevancy," see Barnouw (1990), pp. 430–40; and Feuer, "MTM Enterprises," especially pp. 1–4.

6. The concept is, of course, Fredric Jameson's. See *The Political Unconscious* (1981).

7. Indeed, it is all the more possible to conceive racial-group politics in *Room 222* as undergoing a type of *repression* when we consider that jokes—such as those Pete Dixon makes in response to racially charged situations—constitute a primary affective indicator of the repressive process in Freud's foundational theorization of it. See Freud's 1915 "Repression" (1963), especially pp. 108 and 110–11.

Further, it is the repression enacted in *Room 222* that actually founds its allegorical character—its status as a text through which another, more or less related, one may be discerned and read, according to the preliminary formulation offered by Craig Owens (see "The Allegorical Impulse," Parts 1 and 2; p. 54 for the current citation). As Owens indicates, the very logic of psychoanalysis—which presupposes that the significance of past (and characteristically repressed) occurrences can be identified through the interpretation of a subject's present symptoms—renders allegory crucial to its project ("The Allegorical Impulse," p. 53).

In Owens's extensive theorization of its function in the postmodern context, allegory is presented as a fundamentally deconstructive (and *self*-deconstructive) phenomenon that, in Paul de Man's formulation, "persists in performing what it has shown to be impossible to do" (*Allegories of Reading*, 1979, p. 275; cited in Owens, "The Allegorical Impulse," p. 79). For instance, Owens suggests that, in order to function as a critique of the museum site as "dumping ground," as Owens claims they do, the "combine paintings" of Robert Rauschenberg "must also declare themselves to be part of the dumping ground they describe. They thus relapse into the 'error' they denounce, and this is what allows us to identify them as allegorical" ("The Allegorical Impulse," p. 78). Regarding *Room 222,* we might identify as the pertinent "error" the insistent racio-political commentary that constitutes the show's discernible burden while at the same time serving as the object of its critique. Notably, it is precisely in such a (self-)deconstructive moment that *Room 222*'s allegorical character merges with its potential simulacral function since, as Scott Durham (1993) indicates, the simulacrum enacts a similar self-subversion, constituting as it does "a figure that suspends and reverses the authority that calls it into being" (p. 21).

Such self-deconstruction as apparently operated in *Room 222* does not, it must be emphasized, *negate* the racio-political commentary manifested therein; it is precisely that commentary that I propose we take seriously and that, after all, constitutes a primary object of my analysis here. Rather, the contradictions that characterize the program are intrinsic to the cultural text per se and, in this case, do no more than indicate the as-yet-underappreciated complexity of representational processes in relation to racial-identity politics.

8. In other words, however much the "workplace families" presented in many comedic television series since the late 1960s resemble the traditional domestic configuration, they do not necessarily perform the same sociocultural work as the latter, in either its televisual or "real-life" manifestations. On some of the significances of the television workplace family, see Feuer, "The MTM Style"; and Bathrick (1984).

9. The eleven episode summaries (of a total 111) in Eisner and Krinsky (1984) that I have in mind are those for "Triple Date," "Fathers and Sons" (p. 712); "The Whole World Can Hear You," "Half Way" (p. 713); "The Long Honeymoon" (p. 714); "I Gave My Love," "The Quitter," "And He's Not Even Lovable" (p. 716); "The Nichols Girl" (p. 717); "I Didn't Raise My Girl to Be a Soldier," and "Mismatch Maker" (p. 718).

Chapter 8: Backing Up, Crossing Over, Breaking Out: Social Significances of Pop-Musical Form

1. Indeed, what Piper (1993) sees as conceptual art's especial aptness for political critique largely explains the extensively conceptual orientation of the *Black Male* exhibition itself.

2. Owens, too, considers Anderson's work as instantiating a relation between feminist critique and postmodernist cultural practice; see "The Discourse of Others," especially pp. 169–70, 184. And Susan McClary (1991) discerns such a feminist critique in the very form of Anderson's musical compositions.

3. In light of these comments, it is worth noting that, by the early 1990s, Anderson's performance work (or at least what she presented in Cambridge, Massachusetts, on 7 February 1992) had become much more politically explicit and didactic than it had been throughout the 1980s.

4. Indeed, Anderson has ironically cited not only her *crossover success,* but the *commercialization* that it implies, which seemed to culminate in 1986 with her appearance in a print ad for the American Express card aimed at college students ("How to buy a performance"). In the 1994 retrospective *Stories from the Nerve Bible,* Anderson reproduces this

ad, with the original headline—"How to buy a performance"—modified to read, "How to buy a performer . . ." (p. 227).

5. Anderson's intertextual engagement with Lou Reed registers as particularly ironic at this point, given their development of a personal and domestic partnership subsequent to their meeting in 1993, seven years after the release of *Home of the Brave*. See Holden (1995), p. 36.

6. The *desperation* with which we often attempt to locate a human subjectivity among the electronic apparatuses with which we are confronted daily was thematized early on by Jean Cocteau (1951, 1979) in *The Human Voice*.

7. In this vein, see my discussion of director Jennie Livingston's interpellation as "film maker" following the critical and commercial success of her feature documentary, *Paris Is Burning* ("'The Subversive Edge'").

8. Bellon and Diggs are identified in John Rockwell's (1986) review of Anderson's New York City concert appearance; my comments on their performance are based on observations made during Anderson's live appearance in Milwaukee in 1986.

9. Given this, it is particularly noteworthy that Anderson apparently did engage the significance of gender difference in her use, during her 1995 "Nerve Bible" tour, of a supporting duo that was not even human, but computer-generated, and to whom she gave the names "Bruce" and "Agnes." See Holden (1995), p. 36.

10. Relatedly, it is worth noting Bernard Gendron's (1986) insightful observation regarding the degree to which backing vocals—like other aspects of pop-musical production—manifest simultaneously as both a "core" and a "peripheral" element in any given production. See especially pp. 28–31.

WORKS CITED

Books and Selections from Books

Abelove, Henry, Michèle Aina Barale, and David M. Halperin, eds. *The Lesbian and Gay Studies Reader*. New York: Routledge, 1993.

Abrahams, Roger D. *Talking Black*. Rowley, MA: Newbury House, 1976.

Anderson, Laurie. *Stories from the Nerve Bible: A Retrospective 1972–1992*. New York: HarperCollins, 1994.

_____. *United States*. New York: Harper & Row, 1984.

Appiah, Kwame Anthony. *In My Father's House: Africa in the Philosophy of Culture*. New York: Oxford UP, 1992.

Awkward, Michael. *Negotiating Difference: Race, Gender, and the Politics of Positionality*. Chicago: U of Chicago P, 1995.

Baker, Houston A., Jr. *Afro-American Poetics: Revisions of Harlem and the Black Aesthetic*. Madison: U of Wisconsin P, 1988.

_____. *The Journey Back: Issues in Black Literature and Criticism*. Chicago: U of Chicago P, 1980.

Banes, Sally. *Writing Dancing in the Age of Postmodernism*. Hanover, NH: Wesleyan UP/UP of New England, 1994.

Baraka, Imamu Amiri [LeRoi Jones]. "American Sexual Reference: Black Male." 1965. *Home: Social Essays*. New York: William Morrow, 1966, pp. 216–33.

_____. "Black Art." 1966. *Selected Poetry*, pp. 106–107. Also in Randall, 1971, pp. 223–24.

_____. *Black Magic: Poetry, 1961–1976*. Indianapolis and New York: Bobbs-Merrill, 1969.

_____. "Black People!" 1967. In Randall, 1971, pp. 226–27.

_____. "CIVIL RIGHTS POEM." 1967. In *Selected Poetry*, 1979, p. 115.

_____. "Poem for Half White College Students." 1965. In Randall, 1971, p. 225.

_____. *Selected Poetry of Amiri Baraka/LeRoi Jones*. New York: William Morrow, 1979.

_____. "SOS." 1966. In Randall, 1971, p. 181.

Barnouw, Erik. *Tube of Plenty: The Evolution of American Television.* 2nd rev. ed. New York: Oxford UP, 1990.

Bathrick, Serafina. "*The Mary Tyler Moore Show:* Women at Home and at Work." In Feuer, Kerr, and Vahimagi, 1984, pp. 99–131.

Baudrillard, Jean. *Simulations.* Trans. Paul Foss, Paul Patton, and Philip Beitchman. Foreign Agents Series. New York: Semiotext(e), 1983.

Baughman, Cynthia, ed. *Women on Ice: Feminist Responses to the Tonya Harding/Nancy Kerrigan Spectacle.* New York: Routledge, 1995.

Beam, Joseph, ed. *In the Life: A Black Gay Anthology.* Boston: Alyson, 1986.

Benveniste, Emile. "Relationships of Person in the Verb." *Problems in General Linguistics.* Trans. Mary Elizabeth Meek. Miami Linguistics Series 8. Coral Gables, FL: U of Miami P, 1971, pp. 195–204.

Berzon, Judith R. *Neither White nor Black: The Mulatto Character in American Fiction.* New York: New York UP, 1978.

Bodroghkozy, Aniko. "'Is This What You Mean by Color TV?': Race, Gender, and Contested Meanings in NBC's *Julia.*" *Private Screenings: Television and the Female Consumer.* Ed. Lynn Spigel and Denise Mann. A *Camera Obscura* book. Minneapolis: U of Minnesota P, 1992, pp. 143–67.

Bracey, John H., Jr., August Meier, and Elliott Rudwick, eds. *Black Nationalism in America.* Indianapolis and New York: Bobbs-Merrill, 1970.

Branner, Bernard. "Blackberri: Singing for Our Lives." In Beam, 1986, pp. 170–84.

Bronson, Fred. *Billboard's Hottest Hot 100 Hits.* New York: Billboard/Watson-Guptill, 1991.

Brooks, Gwendolyn. *Report from Part One.* Detroit: Broadside Press, 1972.

Brown, Elaine. *A Taste of Power: A Black Woman's Story.* New York: Pantheon, 1992.

Brown, Sterling A. "Negro Character as Seen by White Authors." 1933. *Dark Symphony: Negro Literature in America.* Ed. James A. Emanuel and Theodore L. Gross. New York: The Free Press/Macmillan, 1968, pp. 139–71.

Brown, William Wells. *Clotel; or, The President's Daughter: A Narrative of Slave Life in the United States.* 1853. Intro. William Edward Farrison. New York: University Books/Carol, 1969.

Butler, Judith. *Gender Trouble: Feminism and the Subversion of Identity.* Thinking Gender. New York: Routledge, 1990.

———. "Passing, Queering: Nella Larsen's Psychoanalytic Challenge." *Bodies That Matter: On the Discursive Limits of "Sex."* New York: Routledge, 1993, pp. 167–85.

Carmichael, Stokely. Address of 28 July 1966. In Bracey, Meier, and Rudwick, 1970, pp. 470–76.

Carmichael, Stokely, and Charles V. Hamilton. *Black Power: The Politics of Liberation in America.* New York: Random House, 1967.

Carter, Lawrence E. *Crisis of the African-American Male: Dangers and Opportunities.* Silver Spring, MD: Beckham House, 1993.

Centers for Disease Control [CDC]. *HIV/AIDS Surveillance Report* July 1991.

Chauncey, George. *Gay New York: Gender, Urban Culture, and the Making of the Gay Male World, 1890–1940.* New York: Basic Books/HarperCollins, 1994.

Child, Lydia Maria. "The Quadroons." 1842. *The Other Woman: Stories of Two Women and a Man.* Ed. Susan Koppelman. Old Westbury, NY: The Feminist Press, 1984, pp. 1–12.

Cleaver, Eldridge. "The Primeval Mitosis." *Soul on Ice.* 1967. New York: Dell, 1968, pp. 176–90.

Cocteau, Jean. *The Human Voice.* Trans. Carl Wildman. 1951. Printed with *The Eagle Has Two Heads.* Adapt. Ronald Duncan. 1947. London: Vision Press, 1979.

Crimp, Douglas. "Pictures." 1979. *Art after Modernism: Rethinking Representation.* Ed. and intro. Brian Wallis. Documentary Sources in Contemporary Art. New York: The New Museum of Contemporary Art; Boston: Godine, 1984, pp. 175–87.

Cripps, Thomas. "*Amos 'n' Andy* and the Debate over American Racial Integration." *American History/American Television: Interpreting the Video Past.* Ed. John E. O'Connor. New York: Ungar, 1983, pp. 33–54.

Davis, F. James. *Who Is Black? One Nation's Definition.* University Park: The Pennsylvania State UP, 1991.

Davis, Ossie. "Our Shining Black Prince." Eulogy delivered at the funeral of Malcolm X, Faith Temple Church of God, 27 February 1965. *Malcolm X: The Man and His Times.* Ed. and intro. John Henrik Clarke. 1969. Trenton, NJ: Africa World Press, 1990, pp. xi–xii.

de Man, Paul. *Allegories of Reading.* New Haven: Yale UP, 1979.

Derrida, Jacques. "The Violence of the Letter: From Lévi-Strauss to Rousseau." *Of Grammatology.* Trans. Gayatri Chakravorty Spivak. Baltimore: The Johns Hopkins UP, 1976, pp. 101–40.

Douglass, Frederick. *Narrative of the Life of Frederick Douglass, an American Slave.* 1845. Ed. and intro. Baker. Harmondsworth: Penguin, 1982.

Du Bois, W. E. B. *The Souls of Black Folk.* 1903. New York: Signet/NAL Penguin, 1982.

Easthope, Antony. *Poetry as Discourse.* London and New York: Methuen, 1983.

Eisner, Joel, and David Krinsky. *Television Comedy Series: An Episode Guide to 153 TV Sitcoms in Syndication.* Jefferson, NC: McFarland and Co., 1984.

Ely, Melvin Patrick. *The Adventures of Amos 'n' Andy: A Social History of an American Phenomenon.* New York: The Free Press, 1991.

Emanuel, James A. "Blackness Can: A Quest for Aesthetics." In Gayle, 1971, pp. 192–223.

Fauset, Jessie Redmon. *Plum Bun: A Novel without a Moral.* 1928. Intro. Deborah E. McDowell. Black Women Writers Series. Boston: Beacon, 1990.

Feuer, Jane. "MTM Enterprises: An Overview." In Feuer, Kerr, and Vahimagi, 1984, pp. 1–31.

———. "The MTM Style." In Feuer, Kerr, and Vahimagi, 1984, pp. 32–60.

Feuer, Jane, Paul Kerr, and Tise Vahimagi, eds. *MTM: "Quality Television".* London: British Film Institute, 1984.

Foster, Hal. "(Post)Modern Polemics." *Recodings: Art, Spectacle, Cultural Politics.* Port Townsend, WA: Bay Press, 1985, pp. 121–6.

Foucault, Michel. *This Is Not a Pipe.* Trans. and ed. James Harkness. Berkeley: U of California P, 1983.

Freud, Sigmund. "Identification." *Group Psychology and the Analysis of the Ego.* Trans. and ed. James Strachey. 1922. Intro. Peter Gay. New York: Norton, 1989, pp. 46–53.

———. "Repression." 1915. Trans. Cecil M. Baines. *General Psychological Theory: Papers on Metapsychology.* Ed. and intro. Philip Rieff. New York: Collier/Macmillan, 1963, pp. 104–15.

Frith, Simon. "Why Do Songs Have Words?" *Music for Pleasure: Essays in the Sociology of Pop.* New York: Routledge, 1988, pp. 105–28.

Gates, Henry Louis, Jr. "The Trope of the Talking Book." *The Signifying Monkey: A Theory of African-American Literary Criticism.* New York: Oxford, 1988, pp. 127–69.

Gayle, Addison, Jr., ed. *The Black Aesthetic*. Garden City, NY: Doubleday, 1971.

Gendron, Bernard. "Theodor Adorno Meets the Cadillacs." *Studies in Entertainment: Critical Approaches to Mass Culture*. Ed. Tania Modleski. Theories of Contemporary Culture 7. Bloomington: Indiana UP, 1986, pp. 18–36.

George, J. Carroll. *The Black Male Crisis*. Cincinnati: Zulema Enterprises, 1993.

George, Nelson. *Where Did Our Love Go? The Rise and Fall of the Motown Sound*. New York: St. Martin's, 1985.

Gianakos, Larry James. *Television Drama Series Programming: A Comprehensive Chronicle, 1959–1975*. Metuchen, NJ: The Scarecrow Press, 1978.

Giovanni, Nikki. "For Saundra." 1969. In Randall, 1971, pp. 321–22.

_____. "My Poem." 1969. In Randall, 1971, pp. 319–20.

_____. "The True Import of Present Dialogue: Black vs. Negro." 1968. In Randall, 1971, pp. 318–19.

Goldberg, RoseLee. "Performance: The Golden Years." *The Art of Performance: A Critical Anthology*. Ed. Gregory Battcock and Robert Nickas. New York: Dutton, 1984, pp. 71–94.

Gordy, Berry, Jr. *To Be Loved: The Music, The Magic, The Memories of Motown*. New York: Warner Books, 1994.

Gramsci, Antonio. "The Intellectuals." *Selections from the Prison Notebooks*. Ed. and trans. Quintin Hoare and Geoffrey Nowell Smith. New York: International Publishers, 1971, pp. 3–23.

Griffin, John Howard. *Black Like Me*. 1961. New York: Signet/NAL, 1962.

Haizlip, Shirlee Taylor. *The Sweeter the Juice: A Family Memoir in Black and White*. New York: Simon & Schuster, 1994.

Halsell, Grace. *Soul Sister*. New York: World, 1969.

Harper, Frances Ellen Watkins. *Iola Leroy*. 1892. Intro. Hazel V. Carby. Black Women Writers Series. Boston: Beacon, 1987.

Harrison, Linda. "On Cultural Nationalism." *The Black Panthers Speak*. Ed. Philip S. Foner. Philadelphia and New York: Lippincott, 1970, pp. 151–54.

Henderson, Stephen. *Understanding the New Black Poetry: Black Speech and Black Music as Poetic References*. New York: William Morrow, 1973.

Hernton, Calvin C. *Sex and Racism in America*. 1965. New York: Grove, 1966.

Hewitt, Don. *Minute by Minute*. New York: Random House, 1985.

Hilliard, David, and Lewis Cole. *This Side of Glory: The Autobiography of David Hilliard and the Story of the Black Panther Party*. Boston: Little, Brown, 1993.

Humboldt, Wilhelm von. *On Language: The Diversity of Human Language-Structure and Its Influence on the Mental Development of Mankind*. Trans. Peter Heath. Intro. Hans Aarsleff. Texts in German Philosophy. Cambridge: Cambridge UP, 1988.

Hutchinson, Earl O. *The Assassination of the Black Male Image*. Los Angeles: Middle Passage, 1994.

Jameson, Fredric. *The Political Unconscious: Narrative as a Socially Symbolic Act*. Ithaca, NY: Cornell UP, 1981.

JanMohamed, Abdul R. *Manichean Aesthetics: The Politics of Literature in Colonial Africa*. Amherst: U of Massachusetts P, 1983.

Jhally, Sut, and Justin Lewis. *Enlightened Racism: The Cosby Show, Audiences, and the Myth of the American Dream*. Boulder, CO: Westview Press, 1992.

Johnson, Earvin "Magic." *What You Can Do to Avoid AIDS.* New York: Times Books/Random House, 1992.

Johnson, James Weldon. *The Autobiography of an Ex-Colored Man.* 1912. Ed. and intro. William L. Andrews. Twentieth-Century Classics. New York: Penguin, 1990.

Jordan, Jennifer. "Cultural Nationalism in the 1960s: Politics and Poetry." *Race, Politics, and Culture: Critical Essays on the Radicalism of the 1960s.* Ed. Adolph Reed, Jr. Contributions in Afro-American and African Studies 95. New York: Greenwood Press, 1986, pp. 29–60.

Jordan, June. "Okay 'Negroes.'" 1966. In Randall, 1971, p. 243.

Jordan, Winthrop D. *White over Black: American Attitudes toward the Negro, 1550–1812.* The Institute of Early American History and Culture. Chapel Hill: U of North Carolina P, 1968.

Kardon, Janet. *Laurie Anderson: Works from 1969 to 1983.* Philadelphia: Institute of Contemporary Art, University of Pennsylvania, 1983.

Larsen, Nella. *Passing.* 1929. *Quicksand and Passing.* Ed. and intro. Deborah E. McDowell. American Women Writers Series. New Brunswick, NJ: Rutgers UP, 1986, pp. 137–242.

Lee, Don L. *See* Madhubuti, Haki R.

Lévi-Strauss, Claude. "A Writing Lesson." *Tristes Tropiques.* Trans. John Russell. 1961. New York: Atheneum, 1967, pp. 286–97.

Lifson, Ben. "Talking Pictures." In Kardon, 1983, pp. 32–47.

Locke, Alain. "Negro Youth Speaks." 1925. In Gayle, 1971, pp. 17–23.

Lott, Eric. *Love and Theft: Blackface Minstrelsy and the American Working Class.* Race and American Culture. New York: Oxford UP, 1993.

McClary, Susan. "This Is Not a Story My People Tell: Musical Time and Space According to Laurie Anderson." *Feminine Endings: Music, Gender, and Sexuality.* Minneapolis: U of Minnesota P, 1991, pp. 132–47.

Madhubuti, Haki R. [Don L. Lee]. *Black Men: Obsolete, Single, Dangerous? Afrikan American Families in Transition: Essays in Discovery, Solution and Hope.* Chicago: Third World Press, 1990.

_____. "Don't Cry, Scream." *Don't Cry, Scream.* Detroit: Broadside Press, 1969, pp. 27–31.

_____. "Move Un-Noticed to Be Noticed: A Nationhood Poem." In Henderson, 1973, pp. 340–43.

Marincola, Paula. "Chronology" of works by Laurie Anderson, 1969–1983. In Kardon, 1983, pp. 63–83.

Mill, John Stuart. "What Is Poetry?" 1833. *The Norton Anthology of English Literature,* 4th ed. Gen. ed. M. H. Abrams. Vol. 2. New York: Norton, 1979, 1051–59. 2 vols.

Mitchell-Kernan, Claudia. "Signifying, Loud-Talking and Marking." *Rappin' and Stylin' Out: Communication in Urban Black America.* Ed. Kochman. Urbana: U of Illinois P, 1972, pp. 315–35.

Moore, Richard B. *The Name "Negro": Its Origin and Evil Use.* New York: Afroamerican Publishers, 1960.

Morse, David. *Motown and the Arrival of Black Music.* 1971. New York: Collier/Macmillan, 1972.

Mosse, George L. *Nationalism and Sexuality: Respectability and Abnormal Sexuality in Modern Europe.* 1985. Madison: U of Wisconsin P, 1988.

Moynihan, Daniel Patrick. *The Negro Family: The Case for National Action*. Washington, DC: Office of Policy Planning and Research, U.S. Department of Labor, 1965.

Mr. Fresh and the Supreme Rockers. *Breakdancing*. New York: Avon, 1984.

Murphy, Timothy F., and Suzanne Poirier, eds. *Writing AIDS: Gay Literature, Language, and Analysis*. Between Men—Between Women. New York: Columbia UP, 1993.

National Center for Health Statistics [NCHS]. *Health, United States, 1989*. Hyattsville, MD: Public Health Service, 1990.

Neal, Larry. "The Black Arts Movement." 1968. In Gayle, 1971, pp. 272–90.

Norback, Craig T. and Peter G., and the Editors of *TV Guide* Magazine. *TV Guide Almanac*. New York: Ballantine, 1980.

O'Hara, Frank. "The Day Lady Died." *The Selected Poems*. Ed. Donald Allen. New York: Vintage, 1974, p. 146.

Owens, Craig. "The Allegorical Impulse: Toward a Theory of Postmodernism," Parts 1 and 2. 1980. In *Beyond Recognition*, pp. 52–69, 70–87.

_____. *Beyond Recognition: Representation, Power, and Culture*. Ed. Scott Bryson, Barbara Kruger, Lynne Tillman, and Jane Weinstock. Intro. Simon Watney. Berkeley: U of California P, 1992.

_____. "The Discourse of Others: Feminists and Postmodernism." 1983. In *Beyond Recognition*, pp. 166–90.

_____. "Sex and Language: In Between." In Kardon, 1983, pp. 48–55.

Pareles, Jon, and Patricia Romanowski, eds. *The* Rolling Stone *Encyclopedia of Rock & Roll*. New York: Rolling Stone Press/Summit Books, 1983.

Pearson, Hugh. *The Shadow of the Panther: Huey Newton and the Price of Black Power in America*. Reading, MA: Addison-Wesley, 1994.

Perry, Steve. "Ain't No Mountain High Enough: The Politics of Crossover." *Facing the Music*. Ed. Frith. New York: Pantheon, 1988, pp. 51–87.

Pronger, Brian. *The Arena of Masculinity: Sports, Homosexuality, and the Meaning of Sex*. New York: St. Martin's, 1990.

Raimon, Eve Allegra. "(S)tra(te)gic Mulattoes: Nationalism, Interraciality, and the Figure of the 'Tragic Mulatto' in Nineteenth-Century American Reform Fiction." Diss. Brandeis U, 1994.

Rampersad, Arnold. *I, Too, Sing America*. New York: Oxford UP, 1986. Vol. 1 of *The Life of Langston Hughes*. 2 vols. 1986–1988.

Randall, Dudley, ed. *The Black Poets*. New York: Bantam, 1971.

Robinson, Amy. "To Pass/ /In Drag: Strategies of Entrance into the Visible." Diss. U of Pennsylvania, 1993.

Rose, Tricia. *Black Noise: Rap Music and Black Culture in Contemporary America*. Hanover, NH: Wesleyan UP/UP of New England, 1994.

Ross, Andrew. "Hip, and the Long Front of Color." *No Respect: Intellectuals and Popular Culture*. New York: Routledge, 1989, pp. 65–101.

RuPaul. *Lettin It All Hang Out: An Autobiography*. New York: Hyperion, 1995.

Sanchez, Sonia. "a chant for young / brothas & sistuhs." In Randall, 1971, pp. 240–42.

Shaw, Arnold. *Black Popular Music in America: From the Spirituals, Minstrels, and Ragtime to Soul, Disco, and Hip-Hop*. New York: Schirmer/Macmillan, 1986.

Shepherd, John. "Music and Male Hegemony." *Music as Social Text*. Cambridge: Polity, 1991, pp. 152–73.

Smith, Max C. "By the Year 2000." In Beam, 1986, pp. 224–29.

Smitherman, Geneva. *Talkin and Testifyin: The Language of Black America.* Boston: Houghton Mifflin, 1977.

Sollors, Werner, and Maria Diedrich, eds. *The Black Columbiad: Defining Moments in African American Literature and Culture.* Harvard English Studies 19. Cambridge, MA: Harvard UP, 1994.

Southern, Eileen. *The Music of Black Americans: A History,* 2nd ed. New York: Norton, 1983.

Stein, Gertrude. *Everybody's Autobiography.* New York: Random House, 1937.

Stoper, Emily. *The Student Nonviolent Coordinating Committee: The Growth of Radicalism in a Civil Rights Organization.* Martin Luther King, Jr., and the Civil Rights Movement 17. Brooklyn: Carlson, 1989.

Terrace, Vincent. *The Encyclopedia of Television: Series, Pilots and Specials 1937–1973,* Vol. 1. New York: Zoetrope, 1986. 3 vols.

Tinney, James S. "Why a Black Gay Church?" In Beam, 1986, pp. 70–86.

Torres, Sasha, ed. *Living Color: Race, Feminism, and Television.* Console-ing Passions. Durham, NC: Duke UP, 1996.

Twain, Mark [Samuel Langhorne Clemens]. *Pudd'nhead Wilson.* 1894. *Pudd'nhead Wilson and Those Extraordinary Twins.* Ed. Sidney E. Berger. Norton Critical Editions. New York: Norton, 1980, pp. 1–115.

Van Vechten, Carl. "My Friend: James Weldon Johnson." 1927–1959. *"Keep A-Inchin' Along": Selected Writings about Black Art and Letters.* Ed. Bruce Kellner. Contributions in Afro-American and African Studies 45. Westport, CT: Greenwood Press, 1979, pp. 113–19.

Wallace, Michele. *Black Macho and the Myth of the Superwoman.* 1979. The Haymarket Series. London and New York: Verso, 1990.

Waller, Don. *The Motown Story.* New York: Scribner's, 1985.

Warner, Michael, ed., for the *Social Text* Collective. *Fear of a Queer Planet: Queer Politics and Social Theory.* Cultural Politics 6. Minneapolis: U of Minnesota P, 1993.

Whitburn, Joel. *The* Billboard *Book of Top 40 Hits.* New York: Billboard, 1985.

White, Walter. *Flight.* 1926. New York: Negro Universities Press, 1969.

Whorf, Benjamin Lee. *Language, Thought, and Reality: Selected Writings.* Ed. and intro. John B. Carroll. Cambridge, MA: MIT P, 1956.

Wilson, Harriet E. *Our Nig; or, Sketches from the Life of a Free Black, in a Two-Story White House, North. Showing That Slavery's Shadows Fall Even There.* 1859. Intro. Gates. New York: Vintage, 1983.

Wilson, Mary. *Dreamgirl: My Life as a Supreme.* 1986. New York: St. Martin's Paperbacks, 1987.

Newspaper, Magazine, and Journal Articles

Abrahams, Roger D. "Playing the Dozens." *Journal of American Folklore* 75 (July–September 1962): 209–20.

Adams, Jane Meredith, and Michael Grunwald. "A Trio of Quirky Backgrounds." *Boston Globe,* 15 January 1994: 1, 6.

Adler, Bill. "The South Bronx Was Getting a Bad Rap until a Club Called Disco Fever Came Along." *People Weekly,* 16 May 1983: 42–44, 49.

"African-American or Black: What's in a Name?" *Ebony,* July 1989: 76–80.

"Alice Rhinelander Seeks Separation." *New York Times,* 30 December 1927: 9.

All about Michael. Spec. "Extra" issue of *People Weekly,* November–December 1984.

Almond, Elliott. "Improvement in Magic's Condition Paves the Way Back." *Los Angeles Times,* 30 September 1992: C4.

_____. "Johnson's Wife Tests Negative for HIV." *Los Angeles Times,* 19 December 1991: C8.

_____. "Magic's Decision to Play Continues to Spur Controversy." *Los Angeles Times,* 29 January 1992: C4.

Almond, Elliott, and Mark Heisler. "Opponents Weigh the Risk of Playing against Magic." *Los Angeles Times,* 24 January 1992: C1, C9.

Altman, Lawrence K. "Decision Disappoints AIDS Experts." *New York Times,* 3 November 1992: B11.

Amory, Cleveland. Review of *Room 222. TV Guide,* 25 October 1969: 52.

Anderson, Dave. "The Lakers Don't Play Angola." *New York Times,* 1 October 1992: B9.

Araton, Harvey. "Bashing and Trashing Becoming the Word." *New York Times,* 28 October 1992: B13.

_____. "Johnson's Return to League Isn't Welcomed by Some." *New York Times,* 1 November 1992: S1, S11.

_____. "Malone Admits Error of Omission." *New York Times,* 18 November 1992: B12.

_____. "Malone Is in the Eye of the Storm." *New York Times,* 8 November 1992: S5.

_____. "Players, Temptation, and AIDS." *New York Times,* 10 November 1991: S1, S11.

_____. "With Gold in Hand, Johnson and Bird Chart Their Futures." *New York Times,* 10 August 1992: C3.

Baraka, Imamu Amiri [LeRoi Jones]. "The Black Aesthetic." *Negro Digest,* September 1969: 5–6.

Barron, James. "Dueling Magazine Covers: A Police Photo vs. a 'Photo-Illustration.'" *New York Times,* 21 June 1994: B8.

Baugh, John. "The Politicization of Changing Terms of Self-Reference among American Slave Descendants." *American Speech* 66.2 (Summer 1991): 133–46.

Bennett, Lerone, Jr. "What's in a Name?" *Ebony,* November 1967: 46–54.

Benza, A. J., and Michael Lewittes. "Hot Copy: The Face of RuPaul." *New York Daily News,* 15 February 1995: 18.

Berkow, Ira. "All-Stars to Give Magic a Nervous Embrace." *New York Times,* 7 February 1992: B9, B11.

_____. "Magic Johnson's Legacy." *New York Times,* 8 November 1991: B11.

_____. "Unspoken Concerns about Magic." *New York Times,* 3 October 1992: 31.

Berlant, Lauren. "The Female Complaint." *Social Text* 19/20 (Fall 1988): 237–59.

"Black, Blind and on Top of Pop." *Time,* 8 April 1974: 51–52.

Blauner, Robert. "Internal Colonialism and Ghetto Revolt." *Social Problems* XVI (Spring 1969): 393–408.

Bonk, Thomas. "Magic Answers the Rumors Again." *Los Angeles Times,* 24 October 1992: C1, C8.

Bonk, Thomas, and Janny Scott. "'Don't Feel Sorry for Me,' Magic Says." *Los Angeles Times,* 9 November 1991: A1, A25.

Boyd, Todd. "Check Yo Self, Before You Wreck Yo Self: Variations on a Political Theme in Rap Music and Popular Culture." *The Black Public Sphere.* Spec. issue of *Public Culture* 7.1 (Fall 1994): 289–312.

Boyer, Peter J. "The Light Goes Out." *Vanity Fair,* June 1989: 68–84.

Bragg, Rick. "An Agonizing Search for Two Boys." *New York Times,* 28 October 1994: A22.

———. "Mother of 'Carjacked' Boys Held in Their Deaths." *New York Times,* 4 November 1994: A1, A30.

Bray, Rosemary. "Reclaiming Our Culture." *Essence,* December 1990: 84, 86, 116, 119.

Brown, Clifton. "A Career of Impact, A Player with Heart." *New York Times,* 8 November 1991: B11, B13.

———. "Criticism Won't Stop Johnson's All-Star Bid." *New York Times,* 5 February 1992: B11.

———. "For One Stirring Afternoon, Magic Johnson Dazzles Again." *New York Times,* 10 February 1992: A1, C4.

———. "Johnson Makes a Big Point in Style." *New York Times,* 11 February 1992: B16.

———. "Johnson, Unbowed by H. I. V., Will Return to Pro Basketball." *New York Times,* 30 September 1992: A1, B14.

———. "Set the V.C.R.: Johnson Says This May Be His Last Game." *New York Times,* 8 February 1992: 32.

Brustein, Robert. "The Premature Death of Modernism." *The New Republic,* 28 May 1984: 25–27.

Burkett, Kathy. "To See, or Not to See: Is Anderson to the '80s What Warhol Was to the '60s?" *Ms.,* July 1986: 14, 17.

Butler, John Sibley. "Multiple Identities." *Society* 27.4 (May–June 1990): 8–13.

Callahan, Tom. "Stunned by Magic." *U.S. News & World Report,* 18 November 1991: 82–84.

Cimons, Marlene. "Magic Johnson, in Rebuke to Bush, Quits AIDS Panel." *Los Angeles Times,* 26 September 1992: A1, A19.

Cocks, Jay. "Sing a Song of Seeing." *Time,* 26 December 1983: 54–56, 61–64.

———. "Why He's a Thriller." *Time,* 19 March 1984: 54–60.

Coe, Robert. "Four Performance Artists." *Theater* [Yale School of Drama/Yale Repertory Theater], Spring 1982: 76–85.

Cohen, Rhonda S. "Dancevideo: A Cheerleading Winner." *Dancemagazine,* April 1988: 86–87.

Coleman, Mark. Review of Run-DMC, *Raising Hell. Rolling Stone* 481 (28 August 1986): 78.

Crimp, Douglas. "How to Have Promiscuity in an Epidemic." *AIDS: Cultural Analysis/Cultural Activism.* Ed. Crimp. Spec. issue of *October* 43 (Winter 1987): 237–71.

DeCurtis, Anthony. "Pittman Leaving MTV." *Rolling Stone* 483 (25 September 1986): 17.

de Roos, Robert. "The Spy Who Came in for the Gold." *TV Guide,* 23 October 1965: 14–17.

Dowd, Maureen. "Testimony Conflicts at Military Hearing on Abuse by Fliers." *New York Times,* 18 August 1993: A1, A20.

Downey, Mike. "Magic: 'That Court Is Where I Belong.'" *Los Angeles Times,* 30 September 1992: C1, C4.

———. "This House Won't Be the Same." *Los Angeles Times,* 11 November 1991: C1, C15.

Du Bois, W. E. B. "Postscript: The Name 'Negro.'" *The Crisis: A Record of the Darker Races* 35.3 (March 1928): 96–97.

Durham, Scott. "From Magritte to Klossowski: The Simulacrum, between Painting and Narrative." *October* 64 (Spring 1993): 17–33.

Dyer, Richard. "White." *The Last "Special Issue" on Race?* Intro. Isaac Julien and Kobena Mercer. Spec. issue of *Screen* 29.4 (Autumn 1988): 44–64.

Elliott, Stuart. "Athletes' Endorsements May Now Be in Doubt." *New York Times,* 8 November 1991: B13.

_____. "Magic Johnson's Ad Career Is Still in a Wait-and-See Phase." *New York Times,* 7 February 1992: D18.

Estrich, Susan. "The Last Victim." *New York Times Magazine,* 18 December 1994: 54–55.

Fairchild, Halford H. "Black, Negro, or Afro-American?: The Differences Are Crucial!" *Journal of Black Studies* 16.1 (September 1985): 47–55.

Farley, Ellen, and Mark N. Vamos, with Christine Dugas. "How Many Teenagers Still Want Their MTV?" *Business Week,* 4 August 1986: 73.

Finch, Susan. "Phipps Loses Appeal to Alter Racial Status." *Times-Picayune* [New Orleans], 19 October 1985: A21, A29.

Finn, Robin. "Arthur Ashe, Tennis Champion, Dies of AIDS." *New York Times,* 7 February 1993, Sec. 1: 1, 43.

Flood, Richard. Review of Laurie Anderson, "O Superman." *Artforum,* September 1981: 80–81.

Freeman, Kim. "Hot 30 Crossover Chart Tracks New Breed of Radio." *Billboard* 99.9 (28 February 1987): 1, 83.

Freund, Charles Paul. "The Power of, and Behind, a Name." *Washington Post,* 7 February 1989: A23.

Frey, Jennifer. "A Boy of Summer's Long, Chilly Winter." *New York Times,* 18 October 1994: B15, B19.

Fried, Debra. "Repetition, Refrain, and Epitaph." *ELH* 53.3 (Fall 1986): 615–32.

Friedman, Jack. "Video's Dandiest Dance-Maker Is Ex-Cheerleader Paula Abdul." *People Weekly,* 23 March 1987: 101–5.

Friend, Tom. "Johnson Finally Says the Magic Words: 'It's On.'" *New York Times,* 30 January 1996: B11, B13.

_____. "Johnson Says Malone Comments Hurt." *New York Times,* 7 November 1992: 31.

_____. "Just Like Starting Over for Lakers." *New York Times,* 3 November 1992: B11.

_____. "No Anger by Johnson on Malone's Remarks." *New York Times,* 4 November 1992: B22.

_____. "Part-Time Superstar Welcomed by Lakers." *New York Times,* 30 September 1992: B9, B14.

Garabedian, John. "Unseasonable." *Newsweek,* 6 October 1969: 113–14.

Gehr, Richard. "The MTV Aesthetic." *Film Comment,* July–August 1983: 37–40.

Gerard, Jeremy. "Max Robinson, 49, First Black to Anchor Network News, Dies." *New York Times,* 21 December 1988: D19.

Gibbs, Nancy. "End of the Run." Cover story. *Time,* 27 June 1994: 28–35.

Gilroy, Paul. "'After the Love Has Gone': Bio-Politics and Etho-Poetics in the Black Public Sphere." *The Black Public Sphere.* Spec. issue of *Public Culture* 7.1 (Fall 1994): 49–76.

Giordano, Al. "No Rush to 'African-American.'" *Washington Journalism Review* 11.3 (April 1989): 13.

"Glenn Burke, 42, a Major League Baseball Player." *New York Times,* 2 June 1995: A26.

Goldman, Albert. "Analyzing the Magic." *All about Michael,* pp. 73–77.

Harper, Phillip Brian. "Private Affairs: Race, Sex, Property, and Persons." *GLQ: A Journal of Lesbian and Gay Studies* 1.2 (May 1994): 111–33.

_____. "'The Subversive Edge': *Paris Is Burning,* Social Critique, and the Limits of Subjective Agency." *Critical Crossings.* Ed. Judith Butler and Biddy Martin. Spec. issue of *Diacritics* 24.2–3 (Summer–Fall 1994): 90–103.

Harvey, Randy. "IOC Board Approves Magic for Barcelona." *Los Angeles Times*, 4 February 1992: C3.

Hays, Constance L. "Husband of Slain Boston Woman Becomes a Suspect, Then a Suicide." *New York Times*, 5 January 1990: A1, A21.

Hecht, Michael L., and Sidney Ribeau. "Research Note: Afro-American Identity Labels and Communication Effectiveness." *Language and Ethnic Identity*. Ed. William B. Gudykunst. Spec. issue of *Journal of Language and Social Psychology* 6.3–4 (1987): 319–26.

Heisler, Mark. "Controversy Won't Change Magic's Mind." *Los Angeles Times*, 30 January 1992: C1, C6.

_____. "From the Beginning to the End, It's Magic." *Los Angeles Times*, 10 February 1992: C1, C13.

_____. "Happiness Is First, Then Questions." *Los Angeles Times*, 30 September 1992: C1, C5.

_____. "Magic Has a Lot Up in the Air." *Los Angeles Times*, 23 July 1992: C1, C6.

_____. "Magic Johnson Retires, Cites Controversies." *Los Angeles Times*, 3 November 1992: A1, A18.

_____. "Magic Johnson's Career Ended by HIV-Positive Test." *Los Angeles Times*, 8 November 1991: A1, A33–34.

_____. "Magic Johnson to Rejoin Lakers Despite HIV." *Los Angeles Times*, 30 September 1992: A1, A21.

_____. "Magic's Return Tied to Exam by His Doctor." *Los Angeles Times*, 10 August 1992: C1, C11.

_____. "One More Time for Goodby." *Los Angeles Times*, 8 February 1992: C1, C12.

_____. "Scott Had Feared the News." *Los Angeles Times*, 9 November 1991: C10.

Herbert, Bob, moderator. "Who Will Help the Black Man?" A symposium. Cover story. *New York Times Magazine*, 4 December 1994: 72–77+.

Hilts, Philip J. "Bush Asks Johnson to Join AIDS Panel." *New York Times*, 12 November 1991: B13.

_____. "Magic Johnson Quits Panel on AIDS." *New York Times*, 26 September 1992: 5.

Hirschorn, Michael. "Why MTV Matters." *Esquire*, October 1990: 90.

Hoberman, J. "Video Radio." *Film Comment*, July–August 1983: 35–36.

Holden, Stephen. "To the Mountaintop and Back." *New York Times*, 5 February 1995, Sec. 2: 30, 36.

Hoverstein, Paul, and Linda Kanamine. "'Time' Criticized over O. J. Cover." *USA Today*, 22 June 1994: D1.

"How to buy a performance." Advertisement for the American Express Card. *Cornell Daily Sun* [Ithaca, NY], 28 February 1986: 13.

Howard-Cooper, Scott. "Peer Pressure Might Have Had Effect." *Los Angeles Times*, 3 November 1992: C1, C5.

_____. "Who Else Could Have Been MVP?" *Los Angeles Times*, 10 February 1992: C13.

"Identity Crisis." *Newsweek*, 30 June 1969: 62.

"I Spy: Comedian Bill Cosby Is First Negro Co-star in TV Network Series." *Ebony*, September 1965: 65–71.

"Jackson and Others Say 'Blacks' Is Passé." *New York Times*, 21 December 1988: A16.

Jamison, Laura. "Crib: Sir Mix-A-Lot: Baby Got Gat." *Vibe* 2.6 (August 1994): 52–53.

JanMohamed, Abdul R. "The Economy of Manichean Allegory: The Function of Racial Difference in Colonialist Literature." *"Race," Writing, and Difference*. Ed. Gates. Spec. issue of *Critical Inquiry* 12.1 (Autumn 1985): 59–87.

Janofsky, Michael. "Third Suspect Arrested by F. B. I. in the Attack on Olympic Skater." *New York Times*, 15 January 1994: 1, 36.

Jet, 9 January 1989, obituary spread: 14–15, 18.

Jewell, K. Sue. "Will the Real Black, Afro-American, Mixed, Colored, Negro Please Stand Up?: Impact of the Black Social Movement, Twenty Years Later." *Journal of Black Studies* 16.1 (September 1985): 57–75.

Johnson, [Earvin] Magic, with Roy S. Johnson. "I'll Deal with It." *Sports Illustrated*, 18 November 1991 (released on 12 November): 16–26.

Johnson, Robert E. "Michael Jackson: The World's Greatest Entertainer." *Ebony*, May 1984: 163–65+.

"Johnson Accepts Australian Bid." *New York Times*, 30 January 1992: B16.

Joyce, Joyce A. "The Black Canon: Reconstructing Black American Literary Criticism." *NLH* 18.2 (Winter 1987): 335–44.

Kahn, Joseph P. "Max Robinson: Tormented Pioneer." *Boston Globe*, 21 December 1988: 65, 67.

Kaminer, Ariel. "The Super-Duper Model." *New York*, 13 March 1995: 16.

Karnow, Stanley. "Bill Cosby: Variety Is the Life of Spies." *Saturday Evening Post*, 25 September 1965: 86–88.

"Kerrigan Attacker and Accomplice Sent to Jail." *New York Times*, 17 May 1994: B13.

Killens, John Oliver. "'Our Struggle Is Not to Be White Men in Black Skin.'" *TV Guide*, 25 July 1970: 6–9.

Kindred, Dave. "Magic Should Face Reality." *Sporting News*, 12 October 1992: 7.

Klein, Joe. "Off to the Culture War." *Newsweek*, 12 June 1995: 28–29.

Kochman, Thomas. "'Rapping' in the Black Ghetto." *Trans-action*, 6 (February 1969): 26–34.

Kolata, Gina. "Experts Try to Dispel Unease on Johnson." *New York Times*, 2 February 1992: S7.

_____. "Studies Cite 10.5 Years from Infection to Illness." *New York Times*, 8 November 1991: B12.

Krier, Beth Ann. "The Magic Touch." *Los Angeles Times*, 2 August 1991: E1, E7.

Lacayo, Richard, with Sylvester Monroe. "In Search of a Good Name." *Time*, 6 March 1989: 32.

Larson, Kay. "Something Future, Something Past." *New York*, 23 July 1984: 48–49.

Leerhsen, Charles, et al. "Magic's Message." *Newsweek*, 18 November 1991: 58–62.

Levine, Ed. "TV Rocks with Music." *New York Times Magazine*, 8 May 1983: 42, 55–61.

Lewis, Neil A. "Officer Cleared in Main Tailhook Case." *New York Times*, 22 October 1993: A12.

Longman, Jere. "Attacked Figure Skater Is Unable to Compete." *New York Times*, 8 January 1994: 1, 35.

_____. "F.B.I. Begins Own Search for Kerrigan's Assailant." *New York Times*, 12 January 1994: B13.

_____. "Kerrigan Attacked after Practice; Assailant Flees." *New York Times*, 7 January 1994: B7, B9.

_____. "Kerrigan May Be Back on Skates within Days." *New York Times,* 11 January 1994: B10.

Lyles, Barbara. "My Turn: What to Call People of Color." *Newsweek,* 27 February 1989: 8–9.

McCallum, Jack. "Inside the NBA: Orlando, Sí, Barcelona . . . ?" *Sports Illustrated,* 20 January 1992: 56–57.

_____. "Most Valuable Person." *Sports Illustrated,* 17 February 1992: 18–21.

_____. "Unforgettable." *Sports Illustrated,* 18 November 1991: 28–37.

McConnell, Margaret Liu. "What Children Shouldn't Know." *National Review,* 14 December 1992: 45–46.

McGuigan, Cathleen, et al. "Breaking Out: America Goes Dancing." Cover story. *Newsweek,* 2 July 1984: 46–52.

Madigan, Mark J. "Miscegenation and 'The Dicta of Race and Class': The Rhinelander Case and Nella Larsen's *Passing.*" *Modern Fiction Studies* 36.4 (Winter 1990): 523–29.

"Magic's Business Interests." *Los Angeles Times,* 8 November 1991: D1.

"Magic Johnson Says He Is Likely to Quit Bush's AIDS Panel." *New York Times,* 14 July 1992: A18.

"Magic Should Stay Out of All-Star Game, Barkley Says." *Los Angeles Times,* 4 February 1992: C3.

Malamud, Allan. "Notes on a Scorecard." *Los Angeles Times,* 3 November 1992: C3.

Martin, Ben L. "From Negro to Black to African American: The Power of Names and Naming." *Political Science Quarterly* 106.1 (Spring 1991): 83–107.

Martinez, Michael. "Citing 'Controversies,' Johnson Retires Again." *New York Times,* 3 November 1992: B9, B11.

"Max Robinson: Fighting the Demons." *Newsweek,* 2 January 1989: 65.

"Max Robinson, 49, first black anchor for networks; of AIDS complications." *Boston Globe,* 21 December 1988: 51.

Miller, Kelly. "Negroes or Colored People?" *Opportunity: Journal of Negro Life* 15.5 (May 1937): 142–46.

"Milli Vanilli Didn't Sing Its Pop Hits." *New York Times,* 16 November 1990: C20.

Morris, Edmund. "Just 'Americans.'" *Washington Post,* 12 February 1989: C7.

"MTV Turns Ten." *Rolling Stone,* 12–26 December 1991: 71, 74.

Mulligan, Thomas S. "The Magic Touch: What Now?" *Los Angeles Times,* 8 November 1991: D1, D6.

Murphy, Dean E., and Tina Griego. "An Icon Falls and His Public Suffers the Pain." *Los Angeles Times,* 8 November 1991: A1, A35–37.

Murray, Jim. "It's Mailman's Biggest Delivery." *Los Angeles Times,* 3 November 1992: C1, C5.

_____. "Why Can't the Magic Continue?" *Los Angeles Times,* 11 February 1992: C1, C5.

Mydans, Seth. "Fearful Mrs. Simpson Is Heard On Tapes of Emergency Calls." *New York Times,* 23 June 1994: A20.

"Navratilova's View on Magic." *New York Times,* 21 November 1991: B16.

New York Times, 21 April–1 May 1989. Daily coverage of Central Park rape case.

Njeri, Itabari. "What's in a Name?" *Los Angeles Times,* 29 January 1989, Sec. 4: 1, 4.

"No. 32 Is Lifted to the Rafters as Magic Johnson Is Honored." *New York Times,* 17 February 1992: C8.

Novak, Ralph. Review of Laurie Anderson, *Home of the Brave. People Weekly,* 2 June 1986: 10.

O'Brien, Maureen. "AIDS Book by Magic Johnson Continues to Spark Controversy; No Orders Placed by Walmart." *Publishers Weekly,* 29 June 1992: 13.

———. "AIDS Book by Magic Johnson 'Self-Censored' by Three Retail Chains." *Publishers Weekly,* 8 June 1992: 17, 20.

Ono, Yumiko. "Earth Tones and Attitude Make a Tiny Cosmetics Company Hot." *Wall Street Journal,* 23 February 1995: B1, B8.

Orth, Maureen. "Stevie, the Wonder Man." *Newsweek,* 28 October 1974: 59–65.

Owens, Craig. "Amplifications: Laurie Anderson." *Art in America,* March 1981: 120–23.

Palmer, Robert. "Rap Music, Despite Adult Fire, Broadens Its Teen-Age Base." *New York Times,* 21 September 1986, Sec. 2: 23–24.

"Paperback Best Sellers." *New York Times Book Review,* 1 July 1984: 28.

Pareles, Jon. "As MTV Turns 10, Pop Goes the World." *New York Times,* 7 July 1991, Sec. 2: 1, 19.

Passantino, Rosemary. "User Friendly." *High Fidelity,* June 1986: 74–75, 88.

Peretz, Martin. "Cambridge Digest: Identity, History, Nostalgia." *New Republic,* 6 February 1989: 43.

"Philip Rhinelander Sued by Son's Wife." *New York Times,* 14 July 1929: 10.

Pincus, Elizabeth. "Black gay men in Boston organize." *Gay Community News* 15.46 (12–18 June 1988): 3, 9.

Piper, Adrian [M. S.]. "Passing for White, Passing for Black." *Transition* 58 (1992): 4–32.

———. "Two Kinds of Discrimination." *The Yale Journal of Criticism* 6.1 (Spring 1993): 25–74.

"Premières: Old Wrinkles." *Time,* 3 October 1969: 84–86.

Randolph, Laura B. "Magic and Cookie Johnson Speak Out for First Time on Love, AIDS, and Marriage." *Ebony,* April 1992: 100–109.

Reibstein, Larry, with Thomas Rosenstiel. "The Right Takes a Media Giant to Political Task." *Newsweek,* 12 June 1995: 30.

"Rhinelander Case Closed." *New York Times,* 6 September 1930: 17.

"Rhinelander Loses; No Fraud Is Found; Wife Will Sue Now." *New York Times,* 6 December 1925: 1, 27.

"Rhinelander Says He Pursued Girl." *New York Times,* 18 November 1925: 4.

"Rhinelander Sues to Annul Marriage; Alleges Race Deceit." *New York Times,* 27 November 1924: 1, 16.

Rhoden, William C. "An Emotional Ashe Says That He Has AIDS." *New York Times,* 9 April 1992: B9, B15.

Robinson, Amy. "It Takes One to Know One: Passing and Communities of Common Interest." *Critical Inquiry* 20.4 (Summer 1994): 715–36.

Rockwell, John. "Music: Laurie Anderson at the Beacon." *New York Times,* 4 March 1986: C13.

Rose, Frank. "Multimedia Techno-Waif." *The Nation,* 8 September 1984: 185–86.

Rose, Tricia. "The Big Idea: So-Called Hardcore." *Vibe* 2.9 (November 1994): 144.

Sanchez, Sonia. "blk/rhetoric." *Negro Digest,* September 1969: 64.

Schwartz, Tony. "Are TV Anchormen Merely Performers?" *New York Times,* 27 July 1980, Sec. 2: 1, 27.

_____. "Robinson of ABC News Quoted As Saying Network Discriminates." *New York Times*, 11 February 1981: C21.

See, Carolyn. "'I'm a Black Woman with a White Image': Diahann Carroll Explains Some of the Reasons behind Her Success." *TV Guide*, 14 March 1970: 26–30.

Shayon, Robert Lewis. "Can TV Overcome?" *Saturday Review*, 29 October 1966: 24.

_____. "Changes." *Saturday Review*, 18 April 1970: 46.

_____. "Living Color on Television." *Saturday Review*, 24 November 1962: 25.

_____. "Living Color on Television—2." *Saturday Review*, 9 February 1963: 57.

Shilts, Randy. "Speak for All, Magic." *Sports Illustrated*, 18 November 1991: 130.

Silverstein, Stuart. "Sponsors Ready for Magic Matchup." *Los Angeles Times*, 1 June 1991: D1, D4.

Slater, Jack. "A Sense of Wonder." *New York Times Magazine*, 23 February 1975: 18–32.

Small, Michael. "Laurie Anderson's Whizbang Techno-Vaudeville Mirrors Life in These United States." *People Weekly*, 21 March 1983: 107–8.

Smith, Danyel. "Still Thirsty." *Vibe* 2.6 (August 1994): 54–59.

Smitherman, Geneva. "'What Is Africa to Me?': Language, Ideology, and *African American*." *American Speech* 66.2 (Summer 1991): 115–32.

Snider, Roxanne. "Mother of Invention." *Maclean's*, 25 August 1986: 42.

Specter, Michael. "Magic's Loud Message for Young Black Men." *New York Times*, 8 November 1991: B12.

Springer, Steve. "An Off-the-Wall Retirement?" *Los Angeles Times*, 17 February 1992: C1, C10.

Stevens, Mark. "Three for the '80s." *Newsweek*, 26 March 1979: 92.

Stevenson, Richard W. "Johnson's Frankness Continues." *New York Times*, 9 November 1991: 33.

_____. "Magic Johnson Ends His Career, Saying He Has AIDS Infection." *New York Times*, 8 November 1991: A1, B12.

Stewart, Charles. "Double Jeopardy." *The New Republic*, 2 December 1991: 13–15.

Stewart, Larry. "Player Reaction to Cut Has Effect on Magic." *Los Angeles Times*, 5 November 1992: C1, C6.

_____. "Up-Close, Personal Approach Works in Big Way for Hill." *Los Angeles Times*, 15 November 1991: C3.

Stewart, Patricia. "Laurie Anderson: With a Song in My Art." *Art in America*, March–April 1979: 110–13.

"Tape Shows Face of Attacker." *New York Times*, 10 January 1994: C4.

Thernstrom, Stephan. "Just Say Afro." *The New Republic*, 23 January 1989: 10–12.

Thomas, Evan, et al. "Special Report: Day & Night." Cover story. *Newsweek*, 29 August 1994: 42–49.

Thomas, Robert McG., Jr. "Day Later, It Remains a Shock Felt around the World." *New York Times*, 9 November 1991: 33.

Trillin, Calvin. "American Chronicles: Black or White." *The New Yorker*, 14 April 1986: 62–78.

Trump, Donald. Privately funded full-page advertisement. *New York Times*, 1 May 1989: A13.

Turque, Bill, et al. "He Could Run . . . But He Couldn't Hide." Cover story. *Newsweek*, 27 June 1994: 16–24, 26–27.

Vecsey, George. "Magic Makes Highlights for His Tape." *New York Times,* 10 February 1992: C1, C4.

———. "Magic Words for Earvin: 'Go for It.'" *New York Times,* 30 September 1992: B9.

———. "The Plague Finally Reaches the Box Scores." *New York Times,* 10 November 1991: S11.

Walters, Barry. "The King of Rap." *Village Voice,* 4 November 1986: 19–25.

Wasserman, John L. "The Girl in 'Room 222.'" *TV Guide,* 20 September 1969: 24–27.

"What Color Is Black?" Cover feature. *Newsweek,* 13 February 1995. Comprising: Brian A. Courtney, "My Turn: Freedom from Choice," p. 16; Tom Morganthau, "What Color Is Black," pp. 63–65; Sharon Begley, "Three Is Not Enough," pp. 67–69; Ellis Cose, "One Drop of Bloody History," pp. 70–72; and Connie Leslie et al., "The Loving Generation," p. 72.

"What's in a Name?" *The Economist,* 7 January 1989: 28.

Wilkerson, Isabel. "'African-American' Favored by Many of America's Blacks." *New York Times,* 31 January 1989: A1, A14.

———. "Police Charge Man Who Said Blacks Stabbed Wife." *New York Times,* 29 April 1992: A14.

Williams, Walter E. "Myth Making and Reality Testing." *Society* 27.4 (May–June 1990): 4–7.

Willis, Ellen. "The Importance of Stevie Wonder." *The New Yorker,* 30 December 1974: 56.

Wolff, Craig. "Youths Rape and Beat Central Park Jogger." *New York Times,* 21 April 1989: B1, B3.

Wolmuth, Roger. "Rock 'n' Roll 'n' Video: MTV's Music Revolution." *People Weekly,* 17 October 1983: 96–99.

"Wonderbucks." *Time,* 18 August 1975: 41.

"Wonderful World of Color." *Time,* 13 December 1968: 70.

Wood, Elizabeth. "Laurie Anderson Bends Light, Inverts Sound, and Plays an 'Audacious Violin.'" *Ms.,* February 1983: 100–102.

Young, Tracy. "O, Superwoman." *Vogue,* April 1986: 60, 64.

Zeichner, Arlene. "Rock 'n Video." *Film Comment,* May–June 1982: 39–41.

Zoglin, Richard. "MTV Faces a Mid-Life Crisis." *Time,* 29 June 1987: 67.

Zook, Kristal Brent. "Blackout." *The Village Voice,* 28 June 1994: 51–54.

———. "Warner Bruthas." *The Village Voice,* 17 January 1995: 36–37.

Court Cases

Jane Doe v. State of Louisiana. 479 So.2d 369–74. La. App. 4 Cir. 1985.

Plessy v. Ferguson. 16 S.Ct. 1138–1148. 163 U.S. 537. 1896.

State ex rel Schlumbrecht v. Louisiana State Board of Health. 231 So.2d 730–33. La. App. 4 Cir. 1970.

Audio and Video Recordings

Aerosmith. "Walk This Way." Columbia, 10449, 1976. First released on *Toys in the Attic.* Columbia, 33479, 1975.

Anderson, Laurie. *Big Science.* Warner Bros., 3674-2, 1982.

———. "Language Is a Virus." *Home of the Brave* soundtrack. Warner Bros., 9 25400-2, 1986. Track 5.

_____. "O Superman." 1981. *Big Science*, track 6.

_____. *United States*. Warner Bros., 1-25192, 1984.

Arrested Development. "People Everyday." *3 Years, 5 Months and 2 Days in the Life of . . .* , track 3.

_____. "Tennessee." *3 Years, 5 Months and 2 Days in the Life of . . .* , track 14.

_____. *3 Years, 5 Months and 2 Days in the Life of . . . .* Chrysalis, CDP-21929, 1992.

_____. *Zingalamaduni*. Chrysalis, F2 29274, 1994.

Blondie. "Rapture." Chrysalis, 2485, 1981.

Bloodstone. "Natural High." *Natural High*. London, XPS 620, 1972.

Diana Ross and the Supremes. "In and Out of Love." Motown, 1116, 1967.

Duran Duran. *Rio*. Harvest, 12211, 1982.

Four Tops, The. "Without the One You Love." Motown, 1069, 1964.

Franklin, Aretha. "Do Right Woman—Do Right Man." Atlantic, 2386, 1967.

_____. "(You Make Me Feel Like) A Natural Woman." Atlantic, 2441, 1967.

Grandmaster Flash and the Furious Five. "The Message." Sugar Hill, 584, 1982.

Jackson, Janet. *Control*. A & M, 5106, 1986.

_____. "The Pleasure Principle" video. Dir. Dominic Sena. A & M Video, 1987.

_____. "Rhythm Nation" video. Dir. Dominic Sena. Propaganda Films, 1989.

Jackson, Michael. "Beat It" video. Dir. Bob Giraldi. MJJ Productions, 1983.

_____. "Smooth Criminal" video. Dir. Jerry Kramer and Colin Chilvers. Ultimate Productions, 1988.

_____. *Thriller*. Epic, 38112, 1982.

_____. "Thriller." Epic, 04364, 1984. Also on *Thriller*, track 4.

_____. "Thriller" video. Dir. John Landis. Optimum Productions, 1983.

Jackson 5, The. "Never Can Say Goodbye." Motown, 1179, 1971.

John, Elton, and RuPaul. "Don't Go Breaking My Heart." 1993. MCA, 54796, 1994.

Rawls, Lou. "A Natural Man." MGM, 14262, 1971.

Reddy, Helen. "I Am Woman." Capitol, 3350, 1972.

Reed, Lou. "Walk on the Wild Side." RCA, 0887, 1973.

Reynolds, Debbie. "Tammy." Coral, 61851, 1957.

Run-DMC. *Raising Hell*. Profile, PCD-1217, 1986.

_____. "Walk This Way." *Raising Hell*, track 4.

_____. "Walk This Way" video. Dir. Jon Small. Picture Vision, 1986.

RuPaul. "Back to My Roots." *Supermodel of the World*, track 7.

_____. "Supermodel (You Better Work)." *Supermodel of the World*, track 1.

_____. *Supermodel of the World*. Tommy Boy, TBCD 1058, 1993.

Sir Mix-A-Lot. "Baby Got Back" video. Dir. Adam Bernstein. Def-American Visuals/Rhyme Cartel, 1992.

Sly and the Family Stone. "Everyday People." Epic, 10407, 1969.

Smokey Robinson and the Miracles. "The Love I Saw in You Was Just a Mirage." Tamla, 54145, 1967.

Sting. *The Dream of the Blue Turtles*. A & M, CD 3750, 1985.

Stray Cats. "Stray Cat Strut." EMI America, 8122, 1982.

_____. "Stray Cat Strut" video. Dir. Julien Temple. Gowers, Fields, Flattery, 1992.

Stylistics, The. "You Make Me Feel Brand New." Avco, AV-4634, 1973.

Sugar Hill Gang. "Rapper's Delight." Sugar Hill, 542, 1980.

Supremes, The. *A Bit of Liverpool*. Motown, 623, 1964.

_____. *The Supremes Sing Country and Western and Pop.* Motown, 625, 1965.

_____. *The Supremes Sing Rodgers & Hart.* Motown, 659, 1967.

Talking Heads. *The Name of This Band Is Talking Heads.* Sire, 2SR 3590, 1982.

Temptations, The. "Please Return Your Love to Me." Gordy, 7074, 1968.

Wonder, Stevie. "Fingertips, Pt. 2." Tamla, 54080, 1963.

_____. "Superstition." Tamla, 54226, 1972. Also on *Talking Book,* side 2, track 1.

_____. *Talking Book.* Tamla, 319L, 1972.

_____. "You Are the Sunshine of My Life." Tamla, 54232, 1973. Also on *Talking Book,* side 1, track 1.

Films, Television Programs, and Radio Broadcasts

"AIDS & Blacks: Breaking the Silence." Special series on *Morning Edition* [*ME*] and *All Things Considered* [*ATC*]. National Public Radio. WBUR, Boston. 3–9 April 1989.

All in the Family. Exec. prod. Norman Lear et al. CBS-TV. Broadcast 12 January 1971–16 September 1979.

All Things Considered [*ATC*]. National Public Radio. WBUR, Boston. 20 December 1988.

Arsenio Hall Show, The. Paramount Pictures Corporation. Syndicated television program. WWOR, New York. 8 November 1991.

Boyz N The Hood. Dir. John Singleton. Columbia TriStar, 1991.

Brady Bunch, The. Prod. Sherwood Schwartz. Paramount Pictures TV. Broadcast on ABC-TV. 26 September 1969–30 August 1974.

Brady Bunch Movie, The. Dir. Betty Thomas. Paramount, 1995.

Broadcast News. Dir. James L. Brooks. UKFD/Fox/Gracie Films, 1987.

"Bull Neck." Television advertisement for Schlitz malt liquor. Dir. Marcus Raboy. The End Productions, 1994.

Conversation with Ed Gordon. Black Entertainment Television. 6 April 1993.

Conversation with Magic, A. Writ. and host. Linda Ellerbee. Dir. Robert Hersh. Prod. Bob Brienza. Nickelodeon. 25 March 1992.

Cosby Show, The. Exec. prod. Marcy Carsey and Tom Werner. NBC-TV. Broadcast 20 September 1984–30 April 1992.

"Everybody Dance Now." Writ. Jennifer Dunning. Prod. and dir. Margaret Selby. *Dance in America.* Great Performances. PBS. WNET, New York. 2 October 1991.

Frank's Place. Prod. Hugh Wilson and Tim Reid. CBS-TV. Broadcast 14 September 1987–17 March 1988; 16 July–1 October 1988.

Fresh Prince of Bel-Air, The. Exec. prod. Quincy Jones, Kevin Wendle, Susan Borowitz, Andy Borowitz. NBC-TV. Premiered 10 September 1990.

Home of the Brave. Dir. Laurie Anderson. Cinecom, 1986.

Hoop Dreams. Dir. Steve James. Fine Line/Kartemquin/KCTA-TV, 1994.

Hour Magazine. Syndicated television program. WNYW, New York. 13 November 1986.

"How about That Cherry Tree." Writ. Albert Rubin. Dir. Hy Averback. *Room 222.* WABC, New York. 13 January 1971.

I Spy. Prod. David Friedkin and Mort Fine. NBC-TV. Broadcast 15 September 1965–9 September 1968.

Julia. Creat. and prod. Hal Kanter. NBC-TV. Broadcast 17 September 1968–25 May 1971.

Leslie Uggams Show, The. CBS-TV. WCBS, New York. 28 September 1969.

Martin. Exec. prod. Samm-Art Williams and Martin Lawrence. Fox-TV. Premiered 27 August 1992.

MTV Video Music Awards. MTV. 6 September 1990.

National Public Radio [NPR] News. Report on *All Things Considered.* WBUR, Boston. 9 January 1994.

Oprah Winfrey. Special live television interview with Michael Jackson. ABC-TV. WABC, New York. 10 February 1993.

"Pete's Protégé." Writ. Martin Donovan. Dir. Herman Hoffman. Prod. Jon Kubichan. *Room 222.* WABC, New York. 2 November 1973.

Prime-Time Live. ABC-TV. WCVB, Boston. 5 November 1992.

"Richie's Story" [or "The Problem Is Richie"]. Writ. James L. Brooks. Dir. Gene Reynolds. *Room 222.* WABC, New York. 17 September 1969.

Room 222. Creat. James L. Brooks. Prod. Gene Reynolds and William D'Angelo. ABC-TV. Broadcast 17 September 1969–11 January 1974.

To Sir, with Love. Dir. James Clavell. Columbia, 1967.

"What Is a Man?" Writ. Don Balluck. Dir. Seymour Robbie. *Room 222.* WABC, New York. 3 December 1971.

"You Don't Know Me, He Said." Writ. Douglas Day Stewart. Dir. Seymour Robbie. *Room 222.* WABC, New York. 3 November 1972.

Performances, Art Works, and Exhibitions

Anderson, Laurie. "Natural History." Performance tour. 1986.

_____. "Nerve Bible." Performance tour. 1995.

_____. Performance at Sanders Theater, Harvard University, Cambridge, MA. 7 February 1992.

_____. *United States.* Multimedia performance. Brooklyn Academy of Music, Brooklyn, NY. 7–10 February 1983.

Black Male: Representations of Masculinity in Contemporary American Art. Exhibition at the Whitney Museum of American Art, New York. 10 November 1994–5 March 1995. Cur. Thelma Golden.

Piper, Adrian [M. S.]. *Vanilla Nightmares #20.* Charcoal drawing. 1989. John Weber Gallery, New York.

Wilson, Fred. *Guarded View.* Art installation. 1991. Private collection.

INDEX

Page numbers in *italics* indicate illustrations